D1683633

PROBLEMS IN MIGRATION ANALYSIS

To my mother and father, Renée and William

Problems in Migration Analysis

KENNETH G. WILLIS

Department of the Environment

SAXON HOUSE | LEXINGTON BOOKS

© Copyright Kenneth G. Willis, 1974
All rights reserved. No part of this publication may be reproduced, stored in a retrieval system, or transmitted in any form or by any means, electronic, mechanical, photocopying, recording, or otherwise without the prior permission of D.C. Heath Ltd.

Published by
SAXON HOUSE, D.C. Heath Ltd.
Westmead, Farnborough, Hants, England

Jointly with
LEXINGTON BOOKS, D.C. Heath & Co.
Lexington Mass. U.S.A.

ISBN 0 347 01044 X
Library of Congress Catalog Card Number 74-319

Printed in Great Britain by
Kingprint Limited, Richmond, Surrey

Contents

Preface ix

1 INTRODUCTION

    The nature and importance of migration 1
    Defining migration in time and space 3
    Pattern of migration study 7

2 ECONOMIC PROBLEMS IN MIGRATION

    Introduction 11
    Revenue and costs of migration 13
    Economic controversies of interregional migration 16
    Migration and occupation 19
    Industrial change 28
    Institutional aspects of mobility 30

3 MIGRATION AND GOVERNMENT POLICY

    Government objectives 33
    Implementation of migration policies 37
    Assistance to migrants 40
    Regional policy 45
    Costs and benefits to migration 47
    General characteristics and implications of policies concerned with migration 54

4 MIGRATION AND MOTIVATION

    Introduction 59
    Life cycle 60
    Residential environment 60
    Social mobility 62
    Social and locality participation 63
    Information, motivation and resources 64
    Migration decisions 66
    Conclusion 69

5 DURATION OF RESIDENCE AND FREQUENCY OF MOVEMENT

Introduction	71
Cohort migration	73
Occupational mobility	75
Migration sequences	76
Frequency of movement	77
Conclusion	80

6 MIGRATION MODELS

Current migration models in planning	83
Gravity models	86
Policy models of migration	90
Conclusion	100

7 MIGRATION DATA

Sources	103
Survey design	108
Questionnaire and response problems	111
Quality of data	116
Enumerative and analytical studies	118
Conclusion	120

8 REGRESSION TECHNIQUES IN MIGRATION

Introduction	121
General model	121
Assumptions of regression models	123
Problem of joint influences	125
A priori specification	126
Lagged responses	127
Simultaneous equation bias	129
Indentification problem	132
Interpreting an estimated regression	135
Residuals	136
Canonical correlation	137
Conclusion	140

9 STOCHASTIC PROCESSES IN MIGRATION

Introduction	143
The basic model	144
Applications of Markov chains	145
Properties of Markov chains	146
Homogeneity in time and space	147
Dynamic stochastic models and duration of residence	152
Higher order Markov chains	154
The equilibrium distribution	155
Prediction and goodness-of-fit	159
Mean migration times	160
Conclusion	164

10 SPATIAL AND OTHER MULTIVARIATE TECHNIQUES

Vector and standard distance analysis	167
Eigenvalues and eigenvectors	174
Clustering analysis	176
Factor analysis	178
The measurement of mobility	180

11 ESTIMATING AND PROJECTING MIGRATION

Methods of migration estimation	185
Interregional cohort-survival models	190
Matrix estimation	192
Projecting migration	199
Cross-section models	204

12 CONCLUSION 207

References 219

Index 239

List of figures

2.1	Difference in wage rate or earnings between Northern region and national average	14
8.1	The migration function and scatter of points around it	131
9.1	Alternative initial vectors and time paths	158
10.1	Spherical triangulation method used in computing the distance and angle between each pair of Standard Economic Areas	170
10.2	Rectangular co-ordinate system for computing distance and direction	171
10.3	The summing of angles to obtain migration direction	172

List of tables

1	Duration of residence by age (males and females in England and Wales, 1961)	74
2	1971-based regional projections: net migration estimates and assumptions	85
3	Migration passage times	163

Preface

Governments, central and local, in many countries accept responsibility for influencing the progress of their economies and communities. The form that this influence takes varies considerably between countries and areas, but all decisions to exercise such influence depend upon an assessment of the situation that may be expected in its absence, and the size and direction of changes it will induce.

The book is meant to serve as an introduction to migration analysis for the student who wishes to acquire some working knowledge of the subject as an aid in applied economics, planning and geography. The purpose of the book is to discuss the main attributes of migration — its causation, form and consequences; and the problems associated with analysing migration in theory and practice — the available data, the problem of which techniques to use, and the inference of results from methods of analysis. Practical applications are considered, and implications for planning and government policy drawn.

The book is designed for readers who have only a basic knowledge of statistics and economics, but who, nevertheless, wish to know something about the methods by which planners and policy makers can assess migration, analyse the causes and consequences of it, and so decide upon appropriate policies. Wherever possible methods are illustrated by means of simple numerical examples, so that readers will become familiar with the problems involved, and also partly to enable them to go beyond the scope of this book in formulating and solving problems in their own particular sphere of interest. The text is primarily directed to those non-specialists who wish to use simple econometric techniques in undertaking migration analysis.

I hope that this book will convey the ideas and principles that lie behind the quantitative analysis of migration phenomena. The close and intimate connection that exists, or should exist, between migration theory on the one hand and the organisation and evaluation of statistical material on the other, is one of the themes of this book.

Acknowledgements are due to Professor J.W. House, who provided the author with so much help and encouragement while a graduate student, and to Mr M.C. Whitby and Mr K.J. Thomson of the Agricultural Economics Department, University of Newcastle upon Tyne, who sorted out some of the author's half-formed ideas. But of course I must claim responsibility for obscurities and errors that remain in the text. I owe a special thank-you to my mother, Mrs Renée Willis, who so speedily and cheerfully typed the manuscript despite many other demands on her time. The final word of thanks must be to my wife, Denise, who accepted this piece of work as part of the domestic scene and thus allowed the idea to become a reality.

K.G. Willis,
Leeds 1973

The views expressed in this book are those of the author and do not necessarily reflect those of the Department of the Environment.

1 Introduction

The nature and importance of migration

The genesis of migration lies in dissatisfaction with the contemporary environment. Disparity of opportunity provides the main motive force behind migration, whether this is to enjoy levels of living in terms of income or the physical or social environment. The importance of migration lies in its capacity to adjust resources and help to equate supply and demand.

Technological and economic progress in the economy have important implications concerning the need for mobility of manpower. The response of manpower in adjusting to changes in skills and to areas where these are required may affect economic growth and income distribution among the population. This has been recognised in agriculture, where it is known that industrial development is accompanied by a transfer of labour from farm to non-farm employment. If farm labour is immobile, industrial development may be impeded unless immigrant workers can be obtained. Migration from farms is also seen by the OECD (1965) as a method of improving the structure of agriculture and of increasing labour earnings of those who remain on the farms. Migration and mobility arise through differences in the relative rates of increase or decrease in marginal costs and returns to factors with economic change. This affects industries and regions. Some industries have inelastic demand curves for products and with technical innovation it is necessary for workers to transfer to industries, occupations and regions where marginal costs are lower and marginal returns higher.

Migration and mobility of a population is not an end in itself. The need for migration and mobility emanates from differences in relative changes in employment capacity between industries and occupations and from geographic differences in changes of relative opportunities between areas. Even if there were no economic growth, selective migration is a necressary phenomenon of all modern highly-specialised societies. Persons with unique skills, qualifications or training need to be located where their skills can be used. A person's birthplace or place of existing residence or education does not automatically locate each member of the population at the point at which his particular specialities can be most effectively employed, (i.e. achieve the highest marginal revenue product for his labour). Bogue and Hagood (1953) and Goodrich (1936) both point to differences between the levels of human fertility in areas as an important stimulus to demographic migration. Without migration it would require only a few years for differential fertility between areas to upset the distribution of the labour force.

Through the depletion of resources, changes in technology and changing patterns of consumption, the economic balance between various economic groups is constantly shifting in many parts of Britain. A location which provided the maximum return for a given skill a few decades ago, is seen in many occupations and areas in Britain to provide much less than the maximum return today. In the life time of a single person the necessity for migration and mobility (job, occupation, spatial) may occur repeatedly. Most migration is likely to be selective, affecting various groups differentially. Subsequent discussion of the 'problems' of migration will, primarily, be those concerned with employer, occupation, residence and area change. This is because the employment of similar occupations in different industries makes inter-industry movement relatively easy in most cases, and employer change as the relevant factor in mobility; and when changes in occupation do occur upon industry change, then it is the occupational variable itself that must be studied.

Clearly, equilibrium and maximum return to resources requires mobility of labour resources away from declining industries, occupations and areas, to those with growth and high income. Where redistribution does not occur, and there are instances of severe local unemployment and occupational immobility in regions of Britain, a failure of the allocative mechanism is evident and it is necessary to consider the impediments to mobility among workers. Thirlwall (1966) argued the case for establishing greater control of migration, in the interests of reducing regional unemployment rates and other regional differences and also to achieve national objectives such as an effective incomes policy and fuller utilisation of the nation's manpower. Migration is, therefore, an instrument in the solution of many social and economic 'problems'. As a socio-economic act, migration may not be of interest in itself, other than in the results of its effects; but it does also give rise to 'problems' as well as providing solutions. Migration, in recent decades, has led to pressure on land resources, and in-migration to towns has given rise to many services being operated at increasing costs to scale beyond optimum capacity. Migration, by being selective, and concentrating population and affluence has also given rise to pollution, from the environment being unable to cope with large quantities of waste discharged in specific areas, especially from industry and certain residential areas. This is a notable problem around Los Angeles. Prothero (1965) has also cited migration as instrumental in the spread of diseases and it exposes indigenous populations to health hazards. For all these reasons migration is of increasing importance in the world: as a factor in population growth and change as an instrument in the solution of economic and social 'problems', and as a factor giving rise to 'problems' in some areas.

Defining migration in time and space

A large number of investigations have been carried out into migration, but these studies are often directed at different aspects of the phenomenon, which means that the term 'migration' has been used in widely different senses. Consequently, there rests upon the investigator a responsibility for precise statement and definition. Any specific migration inquiry should adequately define the subject of the migration; the identifiable entity whose migration is under scrutiny, and the nature of the migration — what the minimum move must be before a migration is considered to have occurred. This is necessary because there is no unanimity over the meaning of the term 'migration'. Barclay (1958), in defining a migrant as a person who travels, says 'this is the only unambiguous element in the entire subject'. It is obviously desirable to exclude from the term migration such categories of travellers as tourists and those classified under journey to work. The difficulty arises when general criteria are applied so that such undesirable elements will be excluded. Various criteria proposed would restrict migrants to those travellers whose journey has some minimum duration, or to those whose travel is connected with a change in occupation. The disadvantage of a minimum duration of residence as a criterion in migration is that it emphasises the more permanent parts of the community: the shorter the duration of residence criterion in time the higher will be the migration rate.

All demographic statistics refer to some sort of territorial schema. Traditional analysis in the study of population has used the administrative unit, but for a more meaningful sociological analysis sociologists have always emphasised the 'community' or 'locality' in migration research. The concept of community tends to define locality as the economic and social centre of the people's life, while locality aims at segregating all kinds of settlement according to their geographic location and affinity. Thomas (1938) said, 'The accepted definition of internal migration is a change of residence from one community, or other clearly defined geographical unit, to another within national boundaries'. It is obvious that this definition presupposes the establishment of rules for determining residence, and that in so far as such rules can be determined, migrants — that is, persons who give up one residence to assume another — can be distinguished from persons who have no fixed residence, as well as those who move around without giving up a fixed residence (travelling salesmen etc.). It is improbable, however, that the lines between these classes can be drawn so sharply as to avoid overlapping and there will undoubtedly be many borderline cases.

Sociologists would like to restrict the term 'migration' to a change in residence coupled with a break in community ties. Unfortunately, even among sociologists, there is no general agreement on what a community is,[1] let alone its areal extent. Yet, while the concept has lacked precise field definition and delimitation, its essence has been recognised: the territorial association exhibited by homo sapiens is based more upon relations with other men (group organisation), than upon relations to topographical and other physical environmental features. MacIver (1932) defined community as, 'Any circle of people who live together, who belong together so that they share, not this or that particular interest, but a whole series of interests wide enough and complete enough to include their lives, is a community. Thus, we designate as a community a tribe, a village, a pioneer settlement, a city or a nation. The mark of a community is that one's life may be lived wholly within it'. This definition of a community raises a number of problems for the student of migration. To define the economic and social affinity of clusters of scattered houses is not an easy task, as the term can be applied to different hierarchies of human aggregates. The community may have different meanings for different people, so that the nature and extent of an individual's community is largely a matter of his own definition, within the broader control of the cultural environment, which can have an appreciable influence on standard definition and procedure. Despite the drawbacks in the community concept, the 1961 Yugoslav census programme used the 'locality' concept as a basis for statistics, including migration statistics. With the relative cheapness and ease of modern transport, contacts are more diffuse and the community covers a larger spatial area. The larger the community, however, the greater the probability of significant environmental change within the community; that is, a change in environment through moving within a community may be just as great as a change of place, especially if this were between similar types of communities and areas. Goldstein and Mayer (1963) noted that in the United States there was more variation in mobility patterns between tracts within particular communities, than there was between towns themselves. Such local neighbourhoods varied sharply in their attractiveness to migrants in general, and to different types of migrants in particular.

In analysing statistics of internal migration, the choice of the territorial unit is equivalent to selecting the kinds of migrants to be studied and the definition of migration to be used. Administrative boundaries in Britain and the USA and parish boundaries in Sweden are allowed to play such an important role in the definition of migration because they are the easiest available source of material movements, since only those which cross the boundaries are recorded. In such a case, the greater the area and the larger the community, the greater will be the number of movers classified as non-migratory. There is no fundamental reason for accepting the boundary definition of migration, and the definition and statistical material would be closer to reality if we recorded all changes of residence.

Goux (1962) stressed two important aspects of migration which are often confused: (i) the phenomena of migration so described and (ii) the structure of space in which the migration occurs. The number and proportion of moves within, and migration across, a boundary can differ between communities and areas through variations in the size and form of the spatial units. To take a rather extreme case, the migration rate for the whole of the Northern region of England and Wales in 1961—66 was 35 in-migrants per 1,000 population and 50 out-migrants per 1,000 population. However, both in- and out-migration rates for local authorities in the Northern region, seldom fell below 100 per 1,000. Thomas (1941) concluded mobility was inversely proportional to size of community, and Ahlberg (1953), Hagerstrand (1947) and Lövgren (1956) have all noted this in analysing Swedish data. Theoretical treatment of this phenomenon has been undertaken by Goux (1962), Luu-Mau-Thanh (1962) and Thomlinson (1961). Kulldorf (1955) developed a mathematical model to assess the probability of a movement starting inside an area, crossing the border and ending outside the area; this was based on assumptions of the main features of the migration field — the shape of the community, distribution of starting points (random uniform over the area), and the length and direction of movement. Lee (1957) noted 'a concentration of population. along a boundary results in greater inter-state migration than an even distribution'.

In Britain the most commonly available source of information on migration is now the Census of Population. This data is tied to administrative boundaries,[2] an in- or out-migrant being defined as a person who crosses the boundary of the administrative unit under study. Gross migration rates and numbers are assessed on the basis of these political units, and net migration is similarly related to areas, which vary in size and shape. It seems inevitable that the effect of the administrative structure will be reflected in the numbers of migrants counted and, therefore, in any conclusions drawn on aspects of migration. In an analysis of the influence of spatial structure and socio-economic factors associated with in- and out-migration rates for local authorities on Tyneside in 1961–66, Willis (1972c) concluded that within the same type of units or areas (local authorities, counties, regions) the shape and size of areas did not have a significant effect on composite total gross in- and out-migration rates. When migration flows from a specific local authority area to other specific neighbouring areas were considered, the structure of space was found to be important. The number of migrants between two areas was found to be a function of the shape of the two areas, measured by the degree of compaction around respective centres of gravity, and also the size and length of boundaries of the areas.

Such criteria as distance, duration of stay, the size and shape of the area studied in data collection, and the importance of purpose and change in community affiliations, do not clarify the concept of migration entirely. The community approach has shortcomings in large urban areas where community boundaries are difficult to define and where interest can lie in two or three different centres for different activities. Since there exists no objective, natural criterion on the basis of which migrants distinguish themselves from travellers, one should not expect to arrive at a unique criterion or definition of migration. Nevertheless, it is essential in any study that both the unit for which migration is being described and the exact nature of the move that is classified as a migration should be defined. A spatial and migration typology can best be built up if all residential moves are considered as migration. Shryock (1964) has criticised this definition of migration as 'it would probably be stretching common usage too much', yet he admits that 'there seems to be no obvious cutting point on the basis of demographic theory for determining what part of internal movement shall be called internal migration'. Bogue (1957) also recognised the arbitrary nature of migration definition, but argued that the study of total mobility (all types of movement) would probably be more fruitful as it would be possible to 'then determine the part which each type of spatial mobility plays in effecting population change and redistribution'. In trying to develop a general scheme into which a variety of spatial movements can be placed and a number of conclusions drawn on the volume and characteristics of migrants, Lee (1966) defined migration 'broadly as a permanent or semi-permanent change of residence', and placed 'no restriction ... upon the distance of the move'. Even with such a broad definition as this, there still remains the problem of area. It is essential to define an area of sufficient size to include enough migrants to justify analysis of their characteristics, and a compromise must be made between small areas desirable for homogeneity and large areas desirable for the inclusion of an adequate number of migrants.

Pattern of migration study

The early 1960s marked a significant point in the study of migration, a dearth of studies prior to 1960 being followed by a rapid accumulation of studies since. This change has been discussed by Welch (1970) and seems to have resulted from the crystallisation of various branches in the newly-emerging social science field, and as a response to demands from planners, especially the new breed of regional planners, whose work increasingly required a demographic basis. In academic circles, especially sociology, increased attention was devoted to migration in studies of social structure, mobility, social and economic change and also as a dynamic element in the housing market. The migration studies undertaken tended to raise as many problems as they answered, which created additional demands for deeper analysis of motivations and mechanisms and more refined information on spatial aspects and characteristics of migrants.

The most striking feature of all migration studies is their diversity, not only in terms of scale, coverage and data collection, but also in the use of the data, aims and methods of research. In terms of approach, no single discipline is predominant in the field; economists, sociologists, geographers and planners have all, with their various orientations and inclinations, participated. The orientation of migration studies, in contrast, has been very much guided by the respective academic discipline. Economists have typically examined migration at a macro scale and as an adjustment to the labour market mechanism; sociologists have focused on the study of motivation, the relation of migration to social mobility, and assimilation of migrants; while geographers have described the spatial patterns of mobility and tried to relate these to broad social, economic and environmental changes.

Often migration findings have been a by-product of other studies and as such of only tangential interest in themselves. Studies concerned solely with migration as the prime centre of interest are rarer. Where migration has been the central issue of inquiry, the stimulus has usually been a desire to assess the effects of adverse situations, such as economic depression; or the migration of groups subject to special influences, as in the cases of coalminers facing redundancy, redundant car workers, and the rural–urban movement of agricultural labour; or specific migrant groups attracting particular interest — for example, managers or professional workers. Detailed study of ordinary blue-collar workers or low grade white-collar workers who are not subject to special influences has not usually been undertaken, even though these groups form the largest part of the labour force. There has been a lack of general studies covering all types and aspects of migration and there have been more specific studies in which a particular section of the population, a particular type of movement or a particular aspect of the migration process has been studied in detail.

Individual studies of migration have all been more or less exclusively concerned with their own empirical results. This has been partly due to a dichotomy, at the outset of looking at migration, of whether to take a particular group of subjects to be followed for the duration of the study or to choose a particular area for observation. The first alternative requires indentification of individual units and continuous observation. Individual indentification may or may not be present for worthwhile studies based on areas, and continuous observation is more easily dispensed with in area studies. Results using either source alone are really incomplete and ideally a combination of the two is desirable though rarely used. There is thus a general division of migration information into that based on the observation of individuals and that based on area and ecological correlations.

The varying bases for surveys and their differing aims has led to the under-exploitation of comparison between results. There is a general lack of comparability between surveys in different areas and at different dates for reasons of research design. Quite contradictory conclusions have often emerged as a result. Again, this has meant a widespread failure to make any significant advance beyond a strictly empirical level of analysis. Accounts of migration too, have usually failed to consider simultaneously the effects of geographic, employer, occupational, industrial and social influences on family mobility, carefully disentangling the independent and interacting effects of each.

In 1885 Ravenstein postulated a number of 'laws' of migration which formed the first theoretical analysis of migration and gave the subject the beginning of its theory. This century has seen no comparable excursion into migration theory, despite the attempts by Lee (1966) to formulate more theory in similar 'laws' to Ravenstein's. Many migration studies have been undertaken but few additional generalisations advanced. Theory developed so little that the only generalisation that could be made in regard to differentials in internal migration was that migrants tended to be young adults or persons in their late teens. Demographers have remained largely content with empirical findings and unwilling to generalise. This prompted Vance (1952) to ask, 'Is theory for demographers?'. He contended that demography, for lack of theory, remained unstructured. The following chapters of this book are intended to show that migration does have a considerable amount of socio-economic theory behind it. This is explored at both a micro and macro level and it is applicable in terms of any spatial unit considered. Migrants, individually and collectively are hypothesised as seeking to maximise their utility or real income. This occurs whether they move to a neighbouring house, with no change in money income but with increased utility from closer adaptation between family structure and housing structure, or an inter-area move is involved, with a change of job. This proposed theoretical framework can be used by economists, geographers, planners and sociologists as a basis of approach to migration. Utility for economists is a truism, but its determination can be deduced from socio-psychological theory, which expresses the social position of migrants and the forces that give rise to their aspirations and sets of values. The evolution of and underlying characteristics of individual utility are also explored using a sociological approach. This theoretical framework with empirical examples is integrated with the theory of planning and government objectives as expressing society's wishes as a whole. These are the objectives to which planners should be striving: the satisfaction of society's preferences over and above the individual migrant's preferences.

The second half of this book is devoted to techniques which have been used and can be used to analyse, estimate and evaluate migration and migration theory. Examples of their practical application are given. They are drawn from a variety of disciplines. Unavoidably, some cross-referencing takes place between chapters in discussing various aspects of migration, particularly on methods and ideas, since migration cannot be compartmentalised. This is indicated where it occurs, so that the reader can refer back to a previous chapter or jump to a section of a succeeding one on a specific point.

Notes

[1] Hillery (1955) was able to collect 94 definitions of a community.
[2] 1971 data is also available on a grid square basis.

2 Economic Problems in Migration

Introduction

The economic function of migration is to redistribute labour geographically in accordance with changes in demand for specific types of skill. Migration of both economically and non-economically active persons takes place to maximise individual utility. The importance of monetary economic motives is diminished in the case of the economically non-active, and the social and physical environment assumes greater importance, as with migration on retirement. In a dynamic economy, the pattern of demand for productive resources and for consumption undergoes continual change and for the systems as a whole to be flexible, resources should be able to transfer readily between alternative uses and locations.

Migration takes place according to the ability of the 'market' to adjust both relative factor prices and the relative prices of labour, housing, environment and so on, so as to clear the market. This is the basis of traditional competitive theory, which predicts, for the economically active, that adjustments to the general wage level will call forth just enough supplies to meet the existing effective demand for labour, assuring full employment by migration. A shortage of labour in one sector or area will cause a rise in its price relative to that of labour elsewhere; labour will move in response until demand and supply are equalised and equilibria restored in migration and wage structure. Similarly, in the case of migration for non-employment reasons, migration will take place until house and land prices in the area of destination have risen (say sufficiently to offset advantages of better climate and so on) and those in sending areas have fallen to a point where the marginal utility gained from moving does not equal the cost. According to the classical competitive model, migration (of labour) from area i to area j will occur as long as the average wage in j is greather than in i, with the volume of migration increasing as the wage differential increases, assuming that persons desire to maximise earned income, knowledge is perfect, there are many workers with homogenous skills and tastes and there are no barriers to mobility, social or economic.

In a multi-regional system equilibrium and maximisation of utility (income, employment etc.) occur when the marginal revenue product for all resources is equal in all regions. However, resources are not perfectly mobile and this can give rise to differences in production functions, growth rates, income levels and distributions. For example, the rate of return on capital is determined by the marginal productivity of capital.[1] Areas which have a lower rate of return (lower marginal productivity) would cause capital, if it were mobile, to transfer to areas with higher rates of return. Similarly with labour (in relation to other factors of production), an increase in one region perhaps through a higher birth rate or depletion of natural resources could depress wages and cause labour to move to areas with higher wage rates. Movement of factors of production should take place until marginal value products are equal. The fact that labour and to a lesser extent capital are not completely mobile results in a misallocation of resources.[2] The more immobile a factor of production, the greater the differences between areas in growth, income level, income distribution and employment. The greater the inter-area mobility of a factor of production, the lower the difference in marginal revenue product; that is, the more optimal the allocation of that resource.

Variations in marginal costs, marginal revenue and growth between areas exist only if differing factor mobilities prevail. A permanent differential in, say, growth presupposes some immobility of at least one factor (possibly natural resources). The differences between areas depends on the marginal rates of substitution between factors in each area and the rate of mobility of resources between areas.

If it is assumed that marginal productivities differ between areas (which may reflect different technologies or different organisational levels), marginal revenue products to labour, capital and enterprise will also differ. If area A has a higher rate of return on capital than B and a lower rate of return to labour, area A will grow at a faster rate than B if capital is more mobile than labour (which is likely). Also, if a factor is increasing in supply in an area, the greater the weight of that factor in the production function of the area, the higher will be the rate of growth. If an increase occurs in a factor of minor importance in the production function and the factor is immobile, then misallocation of resources will occur and lower attainment of income be achieved, depending on the marginal rate of substitution of that factor in the production function.

Once factor movement has occurred the incentives for further movement are reduced, since diminishing returns exist, and a convergence in marginal revenue products between areas occurs. If external economies are immobile interregionally, factor movement will persist, but if external economies are mobile, small differences in factor movement between areas will occur. Technological external economies tend to decrease with distance and are, therefore, likely to be immobile interregionally. Pecuniary external economies (market linkages between firms) are also more likely to occur within a region.

As far as the migration of manpower is concerned, there are two important qualifications to the competitive theory. The theory recognises that money-wage differentials between jobs are not a sufficient condition for movement. There are differences which are equalising: differences in job characteristics are compensated for by differing rates of payment. An occupation or area may be attractive because of its non-pecuniary conditions of work — physical conditions, the social status conveyed and the amount and cost of training required (either in direct money costs or in indirect short term losses of earning power). Wage rates and earnings represent money wages not real wages. Competitive theory also recognises that individuals are not always free to move between occupations and this can lead to wage differences which simply do not reflect the 'equalising' conditions mentioned. Cost differences of movement between geographical areas can give rise to wage differences: a sufficient wage difference must exist to make cost of moving worthwhile.[3] Inter-area wage differences can also result from the tastes (preference) of individuals for living in one area rather than another: this is a kind of consumers' surplus. In many rural and mining regions attachment to the area is strong and substantially low wage rates would be required to induce people to migrate, Fig. 2.1. With earnings 10 per cent below national average, Q thousand workers are still prepared to stay in N. region. The consumer surplus of these workers is PRD. Sjaastad (1961) calculated that during the 1940s, the earnings level in a particular state in the United States would have needed to be roughly half the national average in order for migration from that state to offset completely the natural increase and leave a static population.

Revenue and costs of migration

Sjaastad (1962) assessed migration in terms of profit and loss accounting. Migration is treated as an investment from which one expects to receive returns sufficient to offset the costs to the individual of moving. Sjaastad broke private costs down into money and non-money costs. Money costs to migration are the increase in expenditure for food, housing, transport and removal expenses necessitated by migration. Sjaastad thought the order of magnitude of these costs to be very small in the United States

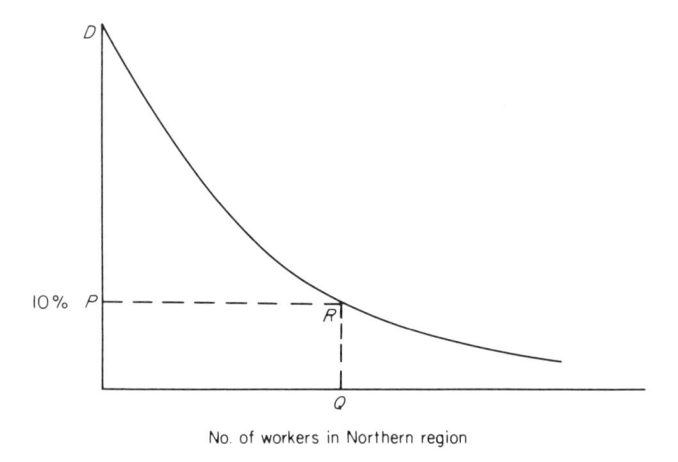

Fig. 2.1 Difference in wage rate or earnings between Northern region and national average

compared with the large state earnings differentials. Non-money costs, on the contrary, were thought to be far more significant than money costs. Non-money costs include earnings foregone while travelling, searching for or learning a new job, and also 'psychic' costs — the 'cost' to the individual of having to leave familiar surroundings, family and friends. Unlike the former costs, psychic costs are not real resource costs, but rather lost consumer surplus on the part of the migrant. It would be possible to take the full amount of the consumer surplus away and leave resource allocation unaffected (other than through distributive effects); that is, people would not move. Thus psychic costs should not be included as part of the investment in migration because they involve no resources for the economy. Psychic costs do affect resource allocation in the sense that more migration would take place if psychic costs were zero for everyone.

The returns or revenue to migration are monetary — earnings differentials between places and the returns accruing to the migrant as a consumer. Both of these are net gains. Additionally there may be a positive or negative revenue from satisfaction or dissatisfaction with the new location compared with the old and the actual travel. Sjaastad ignores non-money returns arising from locational preferences since they represent consumption which has a zero cost of production. If in Britain some people are indifferent to the lower level of earnings in the South West or Scotland because of scenic attractions, these two areas would then have a locational advantage to industry and industry would move to take advantage of lower labour costs. In perfect competition no earnings differentials would persist in an equilibrium situation. Rents to factors such as land would reflect this discrimination and pure rents so paid are not costs of employment since they are derived from tastes in location rather than differences in productivity. Thus migration locational preferences give rise to rents not be counted as costs of employment. This is a distinction between returns to migration representing higher productivity and returns which are merely consumption of zero cost goods. It is useful in considering returns to migration arising from increased efficiency. In practice the distinction is not quantitatively possible, and it must be assumed that tastes result in migration and a spatial distribution of population such that no rents arise from differences in amount and quality of natural amenities, and that this distribution is the optimal distribution (or not seriously different from it).

Speare (1971) attempted to evaluate the profit and loss to the individual of moving, hypothesising that a person will move when the value of all future monetary benefits from moving is greater than the monetary costs involved. Thus if the only profit is the difference in income between origin and destination and the only loss the cost of transporting the migrant and his belongings between two points, then according to Speare migration should take place when

$$\sum_{j=1}^{N} \frac{(Yd_j - Yo_j)}{(1+r)^j} - T > 0$$

where Yd_j = earnings in the jth year at destination
Yo_j = earnings in the jth year at the origin
T = cost of moving
r = rate of interest used to discount future earnings
N = number of years in which future returns are expected

Speare circumvents the problem of choosing the rate of interest and the number of years over which future earnings are to be discounted. The difference in income between the two areas is assumed to be constant in the future so that the above identity reduces to

$$h(Yd - Yo) - T > 0$$

where

$$h = \sum_{j=1}^{N} \frac{1}{(1+r)^j}$$

where h is a constant to be determined empirically. It seems improbable that migrants formally discount their future earnings, but migrants usually do have some time horizon in mind over which all costs (losses) must be recouped. Speare develops his model by introducing more realistic assumptions and his final model has the form

$$IPCh\,(Yd - Yo) - T + g\,\Sigma\,Vi > 0$$

where I = extent of information on job opportunities
 P = probability of obtaining employment at destination
 C = ratio of cost of living at origin to that at destination.

Thus the original wage difference and transport cost model has been modified to include differences in cost of living between the two areas, the probability of obtaining a job in a new area and extent of information on job opportunities. In addition Vi expresses the difference in annual monetary value of the ith non-monetary factor between the destination and the origin, which is taken in this case to be the increase in earnings foregone to be able to live near parents. Non-monetary factors could additionally include type of environment, proximity to friends, psychological costs of moving and so on. These factors alone are assumed to explain migration, and variables such as age and education (which are associated with migration) are assumed to act entirely through the variables in the model.

The model was evaluated empirically by mutiple regression to determine the coefficients for the various costs and benefits.

$$\text{Migration} = \hat{\alpha} + \hat{\beta}_1\,Y + \hat{\beta}_2\,U + \hat{\beta}_3\,I + \hat{\beta}_4\,T + \hat{\beta}_5\,H + \hat{\beta}_6\,Lp + \hat{\beta}_7\,Lwp$$

where U = unemployed (1 or 0)
 H = home ownership
 Lp = location of parents
 Lwp = location of wife's parents.

The private costs and returns to migration were not actually calculated by Speare, but 76 per cent of migrants and 84 per cent of non-migrants were correctly indentified by the model. This work is essentially a profit and loss model of migration and not a cost-benefit model.

Economic controversies of interregional migration

Migration as an equilibrium seeking process poses adjustment problems for such areas as Scotland, the North East and Wales. From the economic theory of labour migration two hypotheses are relevant here. Classical theory assumes that out-migration, by diminishing the number of employable people without affecting a location's natural advantage, would eventually cause wages to increase and therefore halt or even reverse the tendency for net out-movement. This would arise from employers in, say, Wales finding initially too many workers available for changed economic circumstances and lowering the wage to equate supply and demand. This would cause out-migration to the point where marginal physical product was raised to a level where MPP x price of the product (=marginal revenue product) in areas of out-migration was equal to MRP in areas of destination of migrants. In receiving areas, migrants would depress MPP and this would reduce MRP. Equilibrium would be restored when regional marginal revenue products were equal and there would be no motive for further out-movement. Keynesian theory, in contrast, states emigration from an area makes business there less profitable, thus lowering employment and/or wages, and therefore out-migration continues at an even greater rate. Heavy localised unemployment would lead to out-movement, total regional income would be lowered, reducing the size of the market, leading to further unemployment and out-migration. The general atmosphere of business confidence would be affected and new employment to take advantage of unemployed labour would not be forthcoming. Wages would be sticky downwards — a further disincentive. This second hypothesis was further developed by Mydral (1963) and Hirschman (1958) on the process of cumulative causation and the polarisation effects of migration. There is no dispute that interregional differences in welfare, income and employment induce migration; what is at issue is whether the process of migration causes differences to narrow or widen (Thirlwall, 1966).

Oliver (1964) argued in a study of interregional migration, that migration was a function of the difference between national and regional unemployment rates, rather than regional differences *per se*, and concluded that if regional unemployment rate discrepancies narrow, then migration will become less efficacious in reducing them still further. Thirlwall (1966) thought that short-term changes in labour supply can exert an influence on the long-run demand for labour between regions. Migration of unemployed workers from an underemployed region (Scotland, the North East, Wales) to an overemployed region will only eliminate an unemployment rate difference in the long run if the relative decline in labour supply in the underemployed region does affect the long-run demand for labour favourably. Classical economists regarded demand for labour as independently determined and supply as a dependent variable, whereas there is interdependence between supply and demand. This is partly a recognition of the failure of earlier interregional migration models to account for simultaneous equation bias in a meaningful way.[4] Migration, once started between regions, may continue, because it maintains the differences of which it is a function. National wage bargaining eliminates regional wage drift; in overemployed regions higher costs to firms may be offset by higher prices, congestion costs are not borne entirely by entrepreneurs, and there are technological external economies which tend to decrease with distance and pecuniary external economies (market linkages between firms).

The question of whether migration is cumulative or self-correcting resolves into migration's effect on future employment and wages. Clearly, more research needs to be done in this area before more concrete conclusions can be drawn. But it must be recognised that migration is more complex and such simple economic models may be of little value in determining the effect of migration. Mishan (1971c) considered economic loss from migration of manpower and thought it small if, when considering a large flow of out-migrants, account were taken of any rise in the 'real' earnings of workers associated with a reduction in the remaining stock with that particular skill. Since taxes paid by workers are virtually uniform throughout Britain, their effect can be ignored, but the reduction in imports associated with any reduction in population must be considered. This will vary according to regional trade balances (Steele 1972) and marginal propensities to consume.

Barkin (1963) always appears obsessed with the apparent paradox of the inflow of workers to a depressed area as a 'problem' in interregional migration, in reducing the efficiency of out-movement. This is no more than an aggregation problem, perpetuated by lack of knowledge of the types of workers moving between regions. Clearly workers moving to depressed areas are either skilled labour generally unavailable in the area, persons on some sort of career path, or workers expressing a desire to live in the area from non-economic motives. Out-migration from an area may not be by those already unemployed or affected by a particular structural change, so that substantial interregional migration may not reduce long-term unemployment.

The question of interregional migration has become bound up with possible solutions to unemployment, location of industry and urban sprawl problems. Interregional migration theory has not progressed far: too much effort is devoted to simply describing migration patterns. A more comprehensive theoretical model is required and this would perhaps demonstrate the limitations of present regional development policy.

Migration and occupation

Studies such as those by Greenwood and Gormely (1971), Fabricant (1970) and Rogers (1967a), in relating migration to economic variables — income, unemployment and so on — suffer from the failure to disaggregate the population by age and occupation. It is simply not sufficient to compare labour earnings over space and assume that any observed differences arise from disequilibrium in the labour market. Hanna (1959) showed that occupational composition explains a significant proportion of earnings differentials between states. Age can also affect earnings within an occupation. Thus the inconclusiveness of debates on the alleged failure of migration to achieve a reasonable income distribution over space, and that gross in- and out-migration is inconsistent with income differentials, may be a failure to consider the occupational immobility as well as the geographical immobility of the population. This is an aggregation problem and may well give rise to aggregation bias.[5]

It is well known that the incidence of migration varies by age and occupation (Miller, 1965). Tarver (1964) demonstrated that migration rates varied significantly between the twelve major occupational classes in the United States during 1949–50. Of detailed occupations within these groups, the most migrant were members of the armed forces, airline pilots, athletes, clergymen, and professionals engaged in paramedical, natural science, entertainment and recreational activities. The least migrant labour force members were appointive and elective municipal and county officials (midwives, postmasters, sheriffs and bailiffs, marshals and constables) and various craftsmen — job setters — such as metalworkers, railroad conductors, forgemen and hammermen, stevedores and stone cutters. In terms of interstate migration, professional workers had significantly higher migration rates. Willis (1972a) noted that, of 26 major British occupational categories, professional employees were more migrant than other categories in the Northern region and Tyneside, and that they became proportionally very important among migrants moving 40 miles or more. Farmers and service workers increased their proportion up to 39 miles then declined; clerical, transport, labourers not elsewhere classified, construction and electrical workers showed irregular variations, generally maintaining their proportion in the flow with increased distance; while engineering workers, woodworkers, and food, drink and tobacco workers showed a decline in importance with distance. In this latter category miners were an outstanding example, the number migrating declining from 7.2 per cent of all migrants for distances of less than five miles, to 0.6 per cent of migrants moving 40 miles or more. Socio-economic position[6] also influences migration and all regions show the same overall pattern if socio-economic groups are combined into broad categories. However, there are important variations in detail in the United Kingdom (House and Willis 1967).

Rose (1958) noted that 'upper class' neighbourhoods are disproportionately filled with persons who have migrated a long distance while the opposite is true for the 'poorer' classes. Pihlblad and Gregory (1957–58) tried to drawn conclusions about occupational migration patterns from the distribution of various types of employment and the age–sex distribution of migrants. They noted that the residential and migration pattern of teachers was different from that of other professionals due to the more ubiquitous job opportunities. An analysis of census information on migration for the Northern region of the United Kingdom revealed the importance of various types of movement[7] to different occupations. Furnace and metal workers, and glass and ceramics workers showed a high intra local authority movement (68 per cent) compared with other types, and a low inter-urban migration (13 per cent); whereas electrical workers, although their intra local authority migration rate was not low compared with other workers, showed a higher inter-urban migration rate (23 per cent). Workers in the food, drink, paper and printing industries, together with clerical, sales and service, staff administrators, managers and professional workers had above average urban to rural migration. Leather, textile and service workers had a higher proportion of rural to urban movement than average rural to urban migration (Willis, 1972a).

Leslie and Richardson (1961) sought an explanation for the decision to move in life cycle and career pattern theories. Mobility does appear to operate within 'occupational systems' or particular forms of occupations. Different types of worker have different kinds of constraints on their ability or willingness to move, and hence the probability of a given type of worker undertaking a given type of move will be different. Smith (1966) indentified six systems or classes:

(i) bridging occupations which develop attributes marketable in other forms of employment;
(ii) closing occupations which are based on skills linked to a particularly narrow field of activity and sometimes a narrow geographical area (e.g. mining and fishing);
(iii) preparatory occupations (e.g. apprenticeships);
(iv) career step occupations;
(v) incremental hierarchy occupations (e.g. manual steelworking);
(vi) residual (casual labourers, etc).

North East England, Central Scotland and Wales have suffered from having a large proportion of their active population in a closing occupation — coalmining — based on skills linked to a particularly narrow field of activity and geographic area. When its highly specific skill was no longer in demand in the original area, such labour has had to transfer, under the National Coal Board's Inter-Divisional Transfer Scheme, to alternative work in other profitable coalmining areas. (Taylor, 1969); or transfer to another occupation in which the acquired skills are no longer used (House and Knight, 1967). Vimont and Baudot (1965) reported 75—80 per cent of qualified miners and agricultural workers were still in jobs using their original qualifications. They suggest this stability is largely due to the lack of opportunity to transfer elsewhere, using these kinds of qualification as a stepping stone. Such technical training is highly specific and often leads to promotion within the occupation.

Increasingly refined mobility data have not been systematically interpreted in terms of the most relevant structural factors: occupations, work settings and career patterns. Ladinsky (1967a, 1967b) tried to overcome this problem by confining his attention to occupational determinants of geographical mobility among professional workers. Mobile professions are salaried professions — clergymen, lecturers, engineers; and immobile professions are self-employed workers, such as dentists and lawyers. The latter group are tied down by heavy capital investment and/or clienteles built up over the years; whereas salaried professionals have no capital outlays and are not closely bound to clienteles.[8] Migration is blocked to professions that demand costly equipment purchases by the individual himself with close cultivation of clienteles. Attention was also drawn to the occupational community as a communication network, a feature noted by Katz (1958). Ladinsky looked at the hierarchies and sizes of the organisation and industrial structure in which migration took place and pointed to the number of work establishments open to the worker and the degree to which they were decentralised geographically. Professional migration was seen to be typical of small and medium bureaucratic organisations, which are geographically scattered and have short organisational hierarchies and low ratios of managers to managed. Career advancement usually comes by changing organisations. The extent to which working conditions, income and so on are standardised throughout the country was also seen to be a factor, migration occurring more where work and salary varied from job to job. Availability of career paths with the organisation was recognised, but the relative demand for workers was found to be unimportant.

House et al. (1968) showed that almost two-thirds of in-migrant managers to Northern England moved at the request of the firm or by voluntary decision concerned with employment, and three-quarters of managers in all industry groups in the region gave as their main reason for an intended move the prospective increase in salary. Promotion prospects were important motivators of thoughts of moving, company fringe benefits scarcely at all important. The number of moves made by a manager depended on the industry of employment; chemicals and growth industries generally showed greater mobility of managers territorially, metal industries less so; heavy engineering, shipbuilding and manufacture of other metal goods were by contrast industries with relatively immobile managers.

Considerable variation in the rate of out-migration by school leavers from local areas in Northern England was also noted (House, Thomas and Willis, 1968), from 17 per cent in Stanley, and 28 per cent in Billingham, to 38 per cent in Penrith (1964–67). The outflow of the academically more able is a longstanding feature of rural areas, market towns, mining areas and single-industry towns, where local career opportunities are always less than would satisfy the rising tide of sixth-form leavers from grammar schools. Technical college leavers, with their industry-based curriculum, were the most prone to leave home for jobs; more grammar school leavers left for education. Most disturbing, over two-thirds of the secondary modern leavers stayed at home because they had no special skills which they could exploit elsewhere. The ablest and most highly educated formed the majority of out-migrants and most appear to leave the North for good.

The brain drain from the Northern region universities was very modest and there was a smaller compensating inflow (House and Thomas, 1968). Arts graduates had shown a higher drift to the South. The overall picture is one of high mobility and frequent job change in the early years after graduation. At the early stage in their careers graduates attached greater importance to getting experience and further specialised training rather than prospects of immediate salary increases.

The Newcastle research programme was fragmentary and partial rather than presenting a basis for any general theories of migration. It was sociological in character and tended to consider the relationship of industry to migration in preference to occupational change and economic determinants. But occupation is of primary importance in influencing migration and Parnes (1954) put the point succinctly: 'if industrial attachment is only a reflection of attachment to employer or occupation, and if the direction of movement between industries is merely a function of their occupation composition, then the concept of industrial flexibility in labour supply is superfluous. So long as workers are able and willing to change employers and to make specified occupational shifts, their current industrial affiliation becomes immaterial'.

Thomas (1938) concluded, 'that change of occupation is closely associated with change of geographical location may be assumed without proof'. This hypothesis conflicts with evidence presented and is inconsistent with economic analysis. Of course the amount of occupational mobility is dependent upon the disaggregation of the classification (Parnes, 1954).

Although all occupations have some element of vocation (Goss, 1958) and work careers have been found in obscure and lowly occupations, as well as those that are well known to the public or have social prestige (Dubin, 1958), it is in economic terms that occupational change can be analytically appraised. In purely economic terms, migration and inter-occupational mobility is a reallocation of labour resources among economic activitities and areas in reponse to differential changes in economic opportunity. Various occupations require different types and degrees of skill which are acquired through various courses of education and training. This represents differential investment in the human agent and is reflected in the long run by the income opportunities of the various occupations.

Some very highly specialised types of labour are in very inelastic supply.[9] The earnings that such persons receive are mostly in the nature of an economic rent: they enjoy their occupations and would pursue them for very much less than the high renumeration that they actually receive. Transfer earnings are payments made to a factor to keep it in its present use: a payment necessary to prevent the factor transferring to some alternative employment. Economic rent is any payment to a factor over and above its transfer earnings. How much of a given payment to a factor is an economic rent and how much is a transfer earning depends on what sort of transfer is being considered; whether from firm to firm, industry to industry, occupation to occupation, or area to area.

Mobility is, therefore, best seen in terms of costs involved and expected return to job, occupation, industry and area changes. Bancroft and Garfinkle (1963) found craftsmen and professional workers had the greatest occupational stability. Lipset and Bendix (1952) earlier confirmed this in a study of professional employees. Occupational attachment tends to be higher where there is a relatively long period of training and where the cost of changing occupation groups is high; and these types of occupations are usually those which have a high economic rent. Willis (1972a), in a study of blue-collar workers on Tyneside, pointed to the five-year apprenticeships for the vast majority of electrical, engineering and woodworkers and the experience of higher-grade steelworkers as representing differential investment in the human agent, and this was reflected in the long run by the income opportunity of the various occupations (economic rent over and above transfer earnings). Electrical, engineering and woodworkers who have had a lengthy and costly training in their respective occupations tend to be strongly attached to that occupation. The cost of leaving it will be high (in loss of economic rent transferring to an unskilled job or loss in earnings while retraining for another skilled job offering the same real wages) and returns to an occupational shift would have to be high to cover that cost. Hence persons in these occupations would be expected to remain in their occupation and move geographically; except in the unlikely event of the spatial cost of moving being greater than the loss in economic rent, suitably discounted over a number of years, of transferring to an alternative job.

Electrical and woodworkers conform to the pattern of remaining within their respective occupations and moving geographically. Engineering workers, in contrast, are less geographically and more occupationally mobile, presumably because some general engineering skills are more freely convertible. On the other hand, many steelworkers' jobs are semi- or unskilled. This type of worker can acquire new dexterities quickly and can thus change from one type of work to another without sacrificing much in the way of either current earnings, time, or past investment in a specific skill.

Men in skilled crafts move readily from employer to employer, or industry to industry, but seldom change occupation. Semi- or unskilled workers in the steel industry are more likely to change occupation and industry than electrical, wood or engineering workers. Where district job change (location of work-place) is involved the pattern changes. Skilled men more often change their working district when they change jobs than do semi-skilled men or labourers. Within the steel industry there is evidence of a positive relationship between level of skill and length of service. Length of service and probability of leaving varies with age and nature of job within the steel industry. Those with the least years' service tend to be concentrated in the youngest age groups; those with most in the oldest age group. Rollers tend to be concentrated in the older age groups. Age sets the pattern of job mobility in the steel industry, but occupation-job is influential in establishing which in the age group would probably change jobs: occupation set the level while age set the pattern. Among furnace, forge and rolling mill workers those least (job) mobile are the highest paid (rollermen and blastfurnacemen in integrated steelworks), and the stayers — those with long job duration — are older men.

Blau (1965) noted the closer two occupations are to each other in the status hierarchy, the greater tends to be the flow of labour between them. Lipset and Bendix (1952) confirmed this earlier in a 1950 sample study of Oakland workers: though 'there were many shifts between occupational groups specially in the lower brackets, these [were] on the whole shifts between adjacent occupational groups'. Goldstein (1955), in a study of the general population of Norristown, showed that the greatest amount of movement was into groups closely related to the original occupational group. Goldstein further developed this idea, referring to 'perhaps the most fundamental cleavage in American society': the relatively small interchange between manual and non-manual occupations. Goldstein used this cleavage to explain the relative occupational stability of professional workers and craftsmen. As these occupations are at the top of the hierarchy in manual and non-manual groups respectively, employees in these groups have relatively little opportunity to move upwards and no incentive to move downwards, though craftsmen can jump the barrier to become foremen. A study by Stern and Johnson (1964) suggests there are significant differences between industries in the permeability of this barrier.

Job-changing among semi- and unskilled steelworkers, but not among skilled workers, was a process which, in the main, involved men in changes in the type of work they were doing. It was not a process whereby such men transferred their acquired skills from one industry to another or from one district to another. New types of operation had to be learned and new types of skill acquired. For skilled electrical, engineering and woodworkers, job changing frequently involved a change of working district. The object of district changes for these three skilled occupations is the desire to obtain work in which acquired skills would be of use; but among semi-skilled workers, and to an even greater extent among labourers, willingness or ability to change the industry in which they worked and the type of work on which they were employed was greater than their readiness to change their district of work. No incentive exists to change area of work in the steel industry, since this entails changing steel-works. The seniority rule ensures that even such highly paid workers as rollers and blastfurnacemen start again at the bottom of the ladder as labourers in the new plant. This effectively eliminates geographical mobility among steelworkers, except when new works are opened and seniority at the plant has not become established. Such movement — some from steelworks in the North East — occurred before 1962 to the new Spencer (integrated) Works built on a green-field site at Llanwern, Newport. The small amount of geographical mobility that does occur among steelworkers is, therefore, promoted primarily by non-economic factors such as the influence of marriage or relatives.

In general, among blue-collar workers, the more necessary pre-entry training becomes, the less occupational, and the more inter-area mobility, we can expect. Among professional workers, capital investment, clienteles, and organisational structure help to determine the amount of migration. These are merely factors affecting economic profits and losses to the individual.

Similar costs and returns operate within agriculture. The occupational and geographic mobility of farmers in impeded by the fixed costs which have been incurred in agriculture. The amount of capital invested in agriculture has increased rapidly since 1945. But many farmers now find that the capitalised value of the net earnings from assets is less than the acquisition price but greater than the salvage value. Many farmers are able to cover fixed costs but not fixed and variable costs, while others are living out of fixed costs. Nevertheless, they are reluctant to transfer to non-farm employment at least until their assets have further depreciated. Where substantial out-migration has occurred farmers find difficulty in liquidating agricultural assets, especially land in very remote areas. Also, very little agricultural production technology can be transferred to urban skills, and most farm skills must be written off as having zero value in most nonagricultural occupations. Williams (1956) in studying Gosforth, a parish on the western fringe of the Lakeland fells in Cumberland, thought that the economically induced shortage of farm workers had greatly increased the functional importance of the family as an economic unit, creating cohesiveness and solidarity within it. He also noted that a son may have a choice between early marriage, with a risk of losing his parent's farm, and late marriage (when nuptial prospects are poorer) with a chance of inheriting the farm. Nalson (1968) cites the planning of the pre-nuptial conception in an upland area of Staffordshire as a solution to this problem of inheritance by attempting to force the hands of otherwise reluctant parents to provide a home (and maybe a farm) for a son or son-in-law either by purchase or by parents retiring.

The increase in farm size and capital investment have made it more difficult to transfer among farms (OECD, 1965). Since farming varies between regions, the form of capital required for efficient farm operation varies and this, with the increasing specialisation and amount of knowledge required, means most of the mobility is short-distance mobility of tenants. The migration of farm workers is frequently the only long-distance migration. Perkins (1964) found that in the United States one-fifth of all farm migrants returned to farming one year later; the percentage of farmers returning being greater than the percentage of agricultural workers. Migrants who remained in non-farm employment had substantially higher earnings than those who returned to farming. Most of those who entered farming were previous off-farm migrants. Return migration to agriculture may take place after migrants to urban areas have evaluated their individual costs (real as well as monetary, in terms of distance from friends and relatives; different type of environment) as greater than benefits derived. Seen from the individual's point of view, such migration is not inconsistent with theory.

The incentive to agricultural workers to migrate depends upon the potential earnings after migration and the opportunity to migrate depends upon the economic circumstances affecting the occupations for which migrants can qualify. Cowie and Giles (1957) showed that the incentive provided by higher non-agricultural earnings is much more important for those of less than 25 years of age, and that the relative importance of pay and working hours incentives decreases as the age of the migrant increases. However, up to the age of 18, youths are attracted by the relatively high wages in agriculture compared with other available jobs and apprenticeships, though this relationship soon reverses. Migrants from agriculture tend to enter the unskilled and semi-skilled occupations. Outflow is mainly into the engineering and electrical trades, construction, the distributive trades and miscellaneous services, public administration, and professional and scientific services. Movement to the higher occupational orders may be by farmers rather than agricultural workers. After entry into non-agricultural occupations, the occupational mobility of people from farms remains largely a mystery (Whitby, Robins, Tansey and Willis, 1974).

The degree of attachment to an occupation depends on the occupation itself. Members of professional and skilled occupations are unlikely to make a job shift involving occupational change, since these occupations are at the top of the two occupational (white- and blue-collar) hierarchies, so that employees at the top of their respective occupational class cannot easily make worthwhile occupation shifts unless within the same group. Acquired skill and training in these occupations is important, and a change to a job where skill and training were of little or no value would reduce an individual's earning power to that of an untrained employee. Only by exercising specific skills can a worker be sufficiently recompensed for having acquired them initially. Training periods are usually long or difficult, or involve the foregoing of so much income which might be earned elsewhere, that the rate of return on occupational mobility is lower than would be necessary to induce movement, and this encourages spatial migration. Training generally prevents employees leaving declining occupations in sufficient numbers, and creates manpower bottlenecks in other sectors of the economy. Personal and institutional influences are also important as determinants of occupational migration. These include age, previous migration experience, family status, promotion opportunities, pension schemes, seniority and job security. Some of these aspects are discussed in succeeding chapters.

The comparison of changes in occupational mobility with the level or rate of change of occupational earnings is insufficient, since it ignores non-competing occupational groups. Where this is so separate explanations or models of occupational migration and mobility will generally be required.

Industrial change

The response of labour to changed conditions may take the form of changes of job, employer, industry, area of work and, to a lesser extent, occupation. It has already been pointed out that it is unnecessary to analyse inter-industry mobility from occupational mobility and employer change. The function of inter-industry mobility is to redistribute labour between industries, from declining to expanding industries. The extent to which a worker can change industry depends upon his job attachment to an industry and whether he can easily find comparable employment in another industry. This depends largely on similarities of occupational structure.

The definition of inter-industry mobility is complicated by the problems of classification of industries, but it is generally accepted that there are 'patterns' of inter-industry flows between industries. Only recently has data become available (Department of Employment, 1970), but since this is not cross-classified by occupation the extent to which industry flows are merely a fuction of occupation remains a mystery. Industrial attachment seems particularly strong where an occupation closely follows an industry boundary, as in the case of agriculture and the mining and steel industries. Other industries tend to have occupations which are more ubiquitous. Kahn (1964) found only 13 per cent of a sample of 450 redundant men from the British motor industry obtained their first post-redundant job in that industry.

The amount of mobility between any two industries depends on the nature of their relationship to each other and on the structure and organisation of the sectors. Labour with specific occupational training and experience (such as electrical, wood and engineering workers) is often used in more than one industry. In a survey of these workers (who were skilled) and of steelworkers (the majority of whom were semi- or unskilled) on Tyneside (Willis, 1972a), the semi- and unskilled workers were found to be particularly prone to industrial change, whereas skilled workers were more industry tied. Nevertheless, within the skilled category the probability of changing industry varied between occupations. This reflects the fact that some industries are relatively more 'open' or 'closed' to workers than others. Patterns of job shifts that exist between related industries flow partly from the nature of the occupations pursued in them and hence from the transferability of the skills involved in the industries (Parnes, 1954). In terms of potential non-spatial mobility, the particular industry in which a worker is or was employed is much less important than his occupation. The chief flows of electrical workers associated with Jarrow were between the engineering (marine), shipbuilding, and construction industries. The less migrant electrical workers preferred more stable industries, such as public administration (local government) and the electricity supply industry. The construction industry accounted for the major part of woodworkers' migration, but inter-industry mobility is more restricted than for electrical workers. Some movement occurred between public administration, timber and furniture and shipbuilding, but movement between other industries was negligible, due to the smaller number of opportunities for woodworkers elsewhere. The inter-industry flow of engineering workers was found to be mainly between the engineering goods industry; shipbuilding and marine engineering; gas and electricity industries; transport; metal manufacture; food; and mining (Willis 1972a). Migration among engineering workers did not appear to be associated with any particular industry. Unskilled workers are more frequent industrial changers than skilled men, presumably because general labour is demanded in almost all industries and no loss of rent to a particular skill is involved.

The UK Social Survey (1967) found considerable differences between industries in the proportions of workers staying in the industry on changing their jobs. The proportion changing industry on changing jobs ranged from 44 per cent in construction and 47 per cent in services, to 83 per cent in vehicles and food and 84 per cent in public administration and defence, chemicals and timber. Obviously the rates depend on industrial classification and a fine one was used in this case. The Survey identified pairings of industries between which inter-industry mobility was common. 23 per cent of job changers in the vehicle industry went into the engineering and electrical industries, (this was more than the percentage remaining in the vehicle industry) and 16 per cent in timber and furniture changed to the construction industry. Reynolds (1951) thought that if a worker moved often enough he would eventually work in every industry, but each move may be influenced considerably by the industry of his last employment. This type of relationship can lead to particular mobility characteristics and these are treated more fully in Chapter 9, which deals with stochastic processes. Generally, adequate longitudinal data on inter-industry mobility is not available to test this latter hypothesis.

The difficulty of accumulating satisfactory data and formulating adequate explanatory models means the validity of the economic theories of industrial mobility remain unresolved. Wage differentials and changes between industries have no great effect on labour flows between them, yet most job mobility is to positions where individual real income is increased.

Institutional aspects of mobility

Institutional factors are very important in underpinning and shaping the economic forces that basically determine mobility. Government and political forces are one set of factors that can alter economic market forces or forces determining the greatest net benefit to the community; trade unions in all forms are another set.

Where training is specific to an occupation, — whether for electrical, wood or engineering workers, or for doctors, dentists, lawyers and so on — it gives employees an attachment to these occupations. The fact that employees changing occupations must be retrained constitutes the most important barrier to inter-occupational mobility. This barrier is one of cost; the training period, being long, results in income foregone. But institutional barriers often prevent such movement as might otherwise have taken place.

Barriers take two forms (Kerr, 1954). Where trade unions (ETU, AEF, ASW, BMA,) organise their section of the job market as a system of 'communal ownership' the worker is trained primarily for an occupation, and it is to this that he binds himself: the worker is identified by his craft. Electrical, engineering and woodworkers, and professional workers such as doctors tend to move horizontally, between firms, areas and industries while keeping the same kind of job. There also exists what Kerr calls 'the private property' arrangement, in which a worker's training is for an industry — as in the case of steelworkers (British Iron and Steel Trades Confederation) — within which the worker progresses from one job to another on the basis of seniority and ability. Such a system is entered at the bottom of a promotion ladder at each geographically distinct iron and steel works, and to leave it is to incur penalties in loss of status and earnings which accumulate with seniority. Irrespective of whether the average union member moves more or less often than the non-union member, he certainly moves in a somewhat different direction, following the formal channels set by the institutional rules. Electrical, wood and engineering workers, for instance, move horizontally (geographically and industrially within the same occupation); steelworkers, vertically in the seniority area of the firm. Interoccupational mobility is reduced for the former and employer to employer (steel works to steel works) for the latter. The lower the position in the seniority hierarchy, the less the restriction on employer to employer movement: labourers for instance, change employers outside the steel industry a large number of times, because the cost to the employee of doing so is at a minimum. Patterns of movement are reinforced by such union practices as the 'closed shop', while apprenticeship schemes inhibit virtually all mobility during their operation except under exceptional circumstances.

Notes

[1] In perfect competition the monetary price of a fector of production is given by its marginal value product

$$r^M = p \frac{\partial O}{\partial K}$$

The real rate of return r is determined by the marginal productivity of a factor

$$r = \frac{r^M}{P} = \frac{\partial O}{\partial k}$$

[2] In the sense of earning a higher rate of return elsewhere.
[3] Little difference exists between regions in cost of living in Britain. Housing contributes to the largest difference in costs, followed by travel to work and fuel and light. Apart from the South East, where all costs are high, there is little interregional varation (Brown, 1972).
[4] This is discussed in Chapter 8.
[5] Aggregation problems are discussed in Chapter 10.
[6] Allocation of occupied persons to socio-economic groups is determined by considering their employment status and occupation. See *Classification of Occupations,* HMSO 1960.
[7] Types of movement were (a) migrants within local authority urban areas; (b) migrants within local authority rural areas; (c) urban to urban; (d)

urban to rural; (e) rural to urban; (f) rural to rural.

[8] As far as clergymen are concerned, people go to church largely irrespective of the clergyman himself. Students are transient clienteles.

[9] This may arise through unexpected increase in demand, restriction on numbers entering the occupation, or long training giving five years or more time-lag adjustment.

3 Migration and Government Policy

Government objectives

Although rarely concerned with migration *per se*, governments seek to influence internal migration as a means of effecting some goal or goals of policy. Policies designed to influence migration denote any course of action undertaken by government bodies to adjust streams of internal migrants to assumed social, economic or political goals. The *raison d'être* of migration policies is that they must be consistent with and helpful to the nation's general economic, social and political objectives. Migration and labour mobility can be powerful instruments facilitating the achievement of wider policy goals. The government is concerned with maximising the economic welfare of society, and this differs from the economics of the individual migrant's behaviour discussed previously, being concerned with the extent to which the objectives of society as a whole are fulfilled rather than the private objectives of its members. The consequences of migration affect differently the spheres of interest of the migrants, of employers, of industries, regions, and of the community as a whole; the private and the public interest can and do conflict. The motives of the individual for moving or staying and the related costs are different from those which determine the employers' demand for labour. It is recognised that the individual's concept of benefits to be derived from migration includes more than monetary economic considerations. Housing, cost of living, physical and social environment, and family life are taken into account as well as income and working conditions. Preferences for particular jobs, occupations and geographic locations are often determined by deep-rooted socio-historical influences. A particular migration stream may result in the migrants being privately better off, but the economics of migration alone stops short of indicating whether it is on balance a desirable policy, since migration gives rise to costs and benefits to non-migrants both in the area of origin and the area of destination. The case for government intervention in migration rests on its concern for society as a whole (of which the individual is a member); that is, for the entire community in preference to the aspirations of certain sectional interests.

Welfare economics (Mishan, 1971b) indicates the optimum form of production and distribution of goods and services and it is towards this that the government theoretically strives. The necessary conditions for this are efficiency in production and exchange; the bundle of factors used and goods produced in the economy should be so organised that greater output is impossible without greater cost, and the bundle so distributed that greater satisfaction for one person is impossible without less for another. To ensure that the right bundle of goods and factors is chosen it is necessary that the common marginal rate of transformation between any two goods is equal to the common marginal rate of substitution. Similarly, the marginal rate of technical substitution between any two factors must be equal to the marginal rate of indifferent substitution, and the marginal productivity of a factor in the production of a good must equal the marginal rate of indifferent substitution between them. The fulfilment of these efficiency conditions is necessary to the achievement of an *optimum optimorum,* but it is not sufficient. These conditions are fulfilled at all points on the utility possibility frontier, but at only one point is this frontier tangent to a contour of the welfare function. The satisfaction of this tangency condition indentifies the *optimum optimorum.* This requires efficiency in distribution in the sense that it is not possible to make one person better off at the expense of making someone worse off, in such a manner as to increase welfare. That is, the marginal rate of possible substitution between the utility levels of any two individuals must equal the marginal rate of welfare indifferent substitution.

Thus the necessary marginal conditions for the achievement of a Paretian optimum are a common rate of possible substitution throughout the economy: the rate of indifferent substitution must be common and the rates of possible and indifferent substitution must be equal. This holds whether the variables are commodities or factors. For the *optimum optimorum* it is further necessary that the same statement hold with respect to any two utility levels as the variables, in which case indifferent substitution refers to welfare indifference rather than utility indifference. The same condition is necessary for a dynamic optimum having reference to the same factor or good at different points of time.

This welfare economic theory of Pareto optimality analysed in esoteric realms of utility space, is far removed from issues of everyday economic policy. There the goals are not maximisation of a welfare function in utility space, but full employment, stable prices, a high rate of growth and a viable balance of payments. These may well be the appropriate means of welfare maximisation, however. Commodity space has the advantage that its dimensions are tangible, measureable and cardinal, and as such, problems of resource allocation and exchange are more easily handled. But it should be remembered that what is of concern is a welfare function that originates in utility space.

Governments have usually considered migration and mobility as a means of achieving a full employment policy, either because unemployment is higher than the minimum level for frictional unemployment, necessary for flexibility in the labour market, or because there is a persistent excess demand for labour, or because the two exist simultaneously. Complementing financial assistance, trading estates and tax inducements, in order to attract industry to the pre-war Special Areas to relieve unemployment, was the policy of industrial transference. The measures to promote industrial transference were introduced following the report of the Industrial Transference Board (Cmnd 3156, HMSO 1928), and they continued until the Second World War. It was the first instance in British regional policy of promoting the movement of workers to work. The Board regarded the wholesale movement of population out of the Depressed Areas as the only solution to the problem, expecting little success from the introduction of new plants. They stated their views thus:

> It is a bad thing to tell numbers of men and even whole communities that unless they leave all their familiar surroundings they will not be able to earn a living, but we should be shirking every inference from the fact, if we did not emphasize this as the first and strongest of the lessons that our work has provided.

But the previous chapter noted that migration may start cumulative forces of decline and if so it offers no solution. A century of migration from Ireland has never eliminated unemployment there; and one of the main barriers to the establishment of new industries there now is that the market is too small to provide a base for many types of activity. Regional policy since 1945 concentrated on taking work to the workers. The epitome of this was the Local Employment Act of 1960 which, though it was substantially strengthened and amended later, remained the foundation of regional policy until 1972. The 1960 Act was a policy of taking work to the workers in its most extreme form (McCrone, 1969), since many districts, especially in mining areas, were quite unsuitable for industrialisation. Later policy embodied in White Papers on Central Scotland (Cmnd 2188, 1963) and the North East (Cmnd 2206, 1963) favoured development on a sound economic basis in the most favourable locations within a region. Short-distance migration within a region was more likely to be acceptable, whereas large-scale inter-regional migration was held to be undesirable.

Since the First World War, internal migration has figured in the national policies of most Western European countries. Nowhere has this policy actually been known as a population redistribution policy, as it has always formed part of other government programmes, especially those for physical planning and regional development. For some time the British Government has taken measures aimed at reducing the regional imbalance of population distribution and avoiding excessive concentration of population in the South East. More recently, in the French Fifth Plan for 1966–70 the aim of the regional programmes was to reduce population concentration in the Paris region and remedy the lags in certain other regions (Boudeville, 1966).

Governments are very concerned with the loss of productive power and growth in situations where employment disparities exist between regions. Additionally migration and mobility is also seen as a relevant factor in dealing with inflation. Inflation can arise through bottlenecks in labour supply, resulting in a wage–price spiral or in wage drift (Office of Manpower Economics, 1973). This can occur in occupations and in areas. Strong deflation measures are occasionally used, such as those (including Selective Employment Tax) used by the British Government in the late 1960s, to shake out labour from some uses and into others where it was thought national welfare would be increased. The rate of return on these objectives is usually based on purely economic efficiency criteria or to fulfil some goal such as balance of payments. The question of equity remains, and there is nothing in the literature of economics to support the current prejudice that considerations of equity should defer to those of allocation. Thus there is the feeling that some areas should not be allowed to continue to lose population. Regional development can and has been justified on equity grounds.

The failure of migration to adjust labour supply and demand to an equilibrium situation has resulted in Government concern over resulting unemployment. If workers will not move to work (and in a democratic society they cannot be compelled to do so) the Government has considered it necessary to bring work to the workers. Such a policy has not gone without criticism as the most effective means of reducing unemployment (Richardson and West, 1964), though it has still been recognised that the doctrine of 'regional balance' may be justifiable on social and, possibly, economic grounds.

Welfare is increased and Pareto optimality is achieved through exchange. Anything that facilitates the smooth and efficient functioning of an exchange system tends to foster the achievement of Pareto optimality. Migration is a medium of exchange as are other economic measures to improve the economy of lagging regions. Government measures seek to facilitate the exchange of labour and jobs and it is to these measures that we now turn.

Implementation of migration policies

Economic measures form the primary instrument with which to implement policies affecting migration, and, of all European countries, these are most highly developed in the UK. These measures are also usually concerned with other goals as well, such as reducing unemployment in areas and raising income levels. There are three basic types of action open to governments to pursue. These are:

(i) Measures to induce people to move away from declining areas or to and from specific types of areas.
(ii) Measures to enlarge the economic and social base of less prosperous areas. This set of measures can be subdivided, firstly into those designed to induce the movement into depressed areas of capital and skills, in terms of new firms or branches, and of key workers of requisite occupations. Together with these can be set measures to improve the infrastructure and environment of those areas. Secondly, measures sometimes exist to curtail development in prosperous areas with the hope that the resulting pressure of demand will create a spillover into the less prosperous zones.
(iii) Measures of a general nature to lubricate the labour market and, secondly, the effects on migration of measures from social or other policies in other fields.

Some elements of contradiction exist in the detail of these policies, but this is hardly surprising when no clear idea is laid down of what the objectives of overall regional and migration policy should be.

The British Government has declared general amorphous policies of reducing the 'wrong kind' of geographical mobility. For example, one aim of the Scottish plan[1] was to halve migration from Scotland. Similar declarations of Government policy were also made for the Northern region in the early 1960s. This aim was to be achieved by applying the 'carrot-and-stick' method to industrialists.

Measures affecting secondary and tertiary industrial sectors

'Carrots' in various shapes and sizes are given in all Western European countries to industrialists willing to set up firms or branches in development areas. These take the form of grants or loans towards industrial investment, the provision of industrial estates and standard existing factory buildings, and tax exemptions for depreciation of new plant and machinery, plus *ad hoc* exemption for short periods from some local taxes. Grants tend to be higher in Britain than elsewhere, but in other countries fringe benefits are often greater. Assistance to firms in Britain is given under the 1972 Industry Act. The grants given under this Act for buildings, plant and machinery are higher in the special development areas (Tyneside, West Cumberland, West Central Scotland and South Wales Coalfield) than in general development areas. These grants supersede the Local Employment Act grants and are not limited to employment creation. There has thus been a change in policy: the 1970 Local Employment Act tied its 25 per cent grant for buildings to employment. Government aid to encourage growth in development areas in the 1960s resulted in 1963 in a six-fold increase in the absolute Exchequer cost per annum of regional policy. Between 1954 and 1959 the annual average Exchequer cost of regional policy was about £4 million; this increased to £14 million per annum between 1960 and 1963 and £91 million per annum between 1964 and 1967 (DEA, 1969). The Regional Employment Premium should be mentioned as a specific measure started in 1967. This assumed that in development areas REP should have an employment-creating effect through manufacturers lowering prices either absolutely or relative to what they would have been. The introduction of REP was seen as an imaginative attempt at a regional devaluation in conditions of fixed exchange rates, with the additional benefit that the resulting deterioration in the terms of trade would not be borne by the region but by the UK taxpaying community as a whole (Kaldor, 1970). However, REP need not necessarily be used to stimulate employment in development areas; it could be used to pay higher wages, or go in increased profits, or be divided in some way between reducing prices and increasing wages and profits. It could also be spent on additional sales promotion, research and development, quality improvement and so on. The resulting employment will depend on which alternative firms have chosen. REP was originally about 3 per cent of costs, but now, due to inflation, it has fallen to approximately 1 per cent, devaluing its effect.

Grants to new individual enterprises in under-developed areas are also given by the Irish Government and a customs free zone has been created around Shannon airport. The Netherlands provides investment grants and cheaper land in industrial estates in development areas which include the entire north of the country. The German Federal Government, however, only gives loans towards investment in development areas, and in some towns outside congested areas.

Measures to curtail development in prosperous areas are more limited, geographically, in their application. In Western Europe these measures are largely confined to Britain and France. In Britain enterprises wishing to build in congested areas are deterred from doing so by a system of industrial development certificates (IDCs). Industrial development certificates are required for any new building over a specified size and are refused if the Department of Trade and Industry is not satisfied that the development is in line with the distribution of industry policy. The early 1960s witnessed a sharp tightening of industrial development controls in the Midlands and the South East regions, where practically all the refusals are to be found. IDC policy was applied with sharply-increasing stringency between 1960 and 1962, and remained 'tight' throughout the 1960s, with a minor relaxation after 1968. In France control is less rigorous, but industrial firms wishing to locate in the Paris area have to pay an amount relative to the size of the factory, to obtain a permit to do so. A similar policy applies in Italy to firms wishing to locate or build in the Milan, Genoa, Turin triangle.

Britain, France and the Netherlands try to stimulate office decentralisation directly. A permit is required for office development in the Londen area and in the Birmingham conurbation. Permits are only given if the development is in 'the public interest'. At the same time the Location of Offices Bureau has since 1963 been encouraging the movement of offices away from London, by advertising and offering practical information on office transfer. Permits for office development are needed in the Paris region, and in French development areas loans are available for some services. Since 1968 the Dutch Government has provided grants for important service sector projects in development areas.

The principal measures outlined above as instrument variables in Britain's regional policy have failed to come to grips with the size of the problem. Rhodes and Kan (1971) have shown the insignificance of existing Government financial incentives.

> All firms agreed that the presence of larger and more appropriate incentives would have made them consider the Development Areas as a possible location more seriously than they in fact had done. About one-fifth (19%) of the firms indicated that appropriate government incentives would have persuaded them to actually move into a Development Area. A further 30% of offices considered that appropriate incentives might have been instrumental in persuading them to move into the Development Areas, but only if other vital conditions were

satisfied (e.g. communications and availability of staff and suitable premises).

Under the present system of inducements only selective assistance, mainly loans and training grants, applies to growth in the tertiary sector and this is unlikely to influence any organisation's decision making. Moore and Rhodes (1973) estimated the number of jobs required in the regions to bring unemployment down to the national rate, economic activity rates up to the national rate, net out-migration to zero, and employment growth up to the national average would be 85,000 jobs per year over a ten-year period. Present policy was estimated (1963–72) to have created 30–35,000 jobs per annum.

Government policy in this area has failed to secure Government objectives regarding employment and migration, because it has failed to come to grips with net output per capita in the regions. Northern and Western Britain not only suffer from employment decline but also low net output per head. Productivity in Scotland in the late 1960s and early 1970s was 93 per cent of the national average, yet wages were 97 per cent of the national average. This affects the competitive advantage of Scotland *vis à vis* other areas. Low output per head (causing lower employment, income etc.) is partly due to the industrial structure of development areas (higher proportion of declining or slow growth industries). Output per capita is also a function of average size of plant, internal economies of scale and external economies, but no estimates are available of the importance of these. However, since the primary impact of Government policy has been on the location of branch factories in development areas, size of plant and economies of scale may not be great. Bad industrial relations in development areas (e.g. Merseyside) have also played their part.

Assistance to migrants

Assistance to migrants forms the other main set of measures in migration policy. These are directed personally towards the people involved. Government financial aids are designed to counter one set of deterrents to mobility, namely the economic costs of movement for the individual and his dependents. This was and is the object of government assistance to unemployed workers moving to take jobs outside their place of residence, but in countries such as Great Britain in the 1930s it was also one of the main measures to combat poverty. Since the Second World War, assistance to migrants has come to serve two functions: (i) to alleviate unemployment, which is the leading concern of migration assistance in most instances; and (ii) to serve as an instrument of general manpower policy within fairly tight labour markets. This latter aim is to make better use of scarce manpower resources for the benefit of the whole economy. The more highly skilled a society, the greater the likelihood that supply does not equal demand for specific types of workers in all areas.

The increasing diversification of skills calls for greater mobility of workers within and between regions as well as movement of key personnel from prosperous to development areas. For this reason assistance in migration is, in many countries, no longer restricted to migrants from depressed areas nor to those already unemployed.

In Britain, Government financial aids to migrants are of two sorts. The chief scheme is the Employment Transfer Scheme (formerly the Resettlement Transfer Scheme) to encourage unemployed or redundant workers to move away from home and take jobs in another area. The Key Workers Scheme and Nucleus Labour Force Scheme, in contrast, are concerned with holding potential out-migration and stimulating in-migration, but are more sporadic in their operation. The Key Workers Scheme is designed to help employed workers who transfer, either permanently or temporarily, beyond daily travelling distance of their homes to key posts in establishments which employers are setting up or expanding in development or intermediate areas. The Nucleus Labour Force Scheme is designed to help unemployed workers recruited in areas of high unemployment by firms preparing to set up there. Assistance is given to help them move temporarily to the parent factories of these firms, so that when retrained they can return to work in the new establishment. The largest amount of aid, however, is given under the Employment Transfer Scheme. Eligibility under the Employment Transfer Scheme is founded on the lack of 'early prospects of suitable and regular work in the home area', which leaves ample room for the inclusion of individuals who do not live in a designated 'depressed area', but lack the skills and qualifications in demand in their home area. For apprentices emphasis is placed on 'inability to obtain suitable employment or learn a skilled job' in their home area. Workers in certain industries, such as construction, are not eligible if employers cover expenses, or if not are only eligible for certain benefits. Since construction work is temporary the workers cannot be permanently resettled and, while claiming fares, cannot claim household removal expenses.

In general, assistance is restricted to workers without whom vacancies could not be filled, and to unemployed workers or those expected to become unemployed within six months with 'no early prospects of suitable and regular work in their home area'. Thus many workers in cyclical industries — such as shipbuilding and repairing and heavy engineering — become eligible for assistance at virtually any time, and in depressed areas such as Tyneside such workers regularly leave work for better paid jobs elsewhere in the country. On accepting work away from home, the worker seeking aid must state whether he wishes to settle permanently in the new area, or whether he wishes the transfer to be regarded as temporary. The latter kind of transfer still entitles the worker to all benefits under the scheme, but they are granted on the understanding that he will return home if suitable work becomes available.

The range and value of incentives to job mobility in Britain are given in the Department of Employment *Gazette* for April 1972. Removal grants are paid in many Western and socialist countries, although the eligibility criteria vary between countries on all the incentives given (OECD, 1967). In Germany removal grants are paid on the basis of a means test. In Britain migrants do not qualify for support if a suitable local candidate is available in the receiving area and if income from the new job exceeds a certain figure (£2,650 per year in 1972). Starting allowances are paid in Sweden, France and West Germany and most countries give some allowance towards excess costs of lodging and maintenance. Separation allowance may be paid where migrants cannot find housing for their families. In Britain and Sweden migrant workers who want to sell or buy a house are entitled to government support for obtaining mortgages and to government contribution towards legal costs and fees.

Very little research has been undertaken on the effectiveness of these various schemes, although some analysis has been undertaken on workers leaving the Jarrow—Hebburn employment exchange area (Willis, 1972a). Between March 1966 and May 1969, of the 170 requesting aid in Jarrow and Hebburn 79 stated that they wished to settle permanently in their area; but in only two cases were removal expenses paid. The number wishing to move permanently was thus less than half the number claiming grants under the Resettlement Transfer Scheme. Evidence additionally suggested that very few of those wishing to move permanently actually did so. This was in some cases due to housing difficulties in the new areas — especially the South East. Of the 170 leaving Jarrow—Hebburn between 1 October 1967 and 31 March 1969, three actually returned within days through housing and accommodation difficulties.

There was a significant difference between married and single persons receiving grants and allowances and their distribution in the general population. A significant difference existed in the age distribution of Resettlement Transferees and that of the general population. Few of the 15—19 age group claimed allowances in Jarrow, suggesting a lower interregional mobility rate at this age. In the 20—29 age group, the proportion claiming resettlement allowances was substantially greater than their proportion in the total population. A higher percentage in the 30—39 group claimed, but the 40—49 group showed a reversal, with a lower percentage claiming than their representation in the general population. The fifties marks a critical age in the life cycle for migration; the number claiming was negligible compared to the number in the total population.

The main part of out-migration from Jarrow was from two industrial orders — shipbuilding and marine engineering and construction. These two industries supplied migrant labour out of all proportion to their representation as employers in the total labour force. Despite the industrial concentration, a great variety of skills and occupations were involved. There was a predominance of shipyard electricians and pipe-fitters (most of whom work in shipyards or in the construction industry). Occupations connected with the construction industry (steel erectors, platers, riveters, welders) had a greater number of out-migrants compared to other occupations. Those receiving grants and allowances under the Resettlement Transfer Scheme were found to be predominantly skilled or semi-skilled (90 per cent of all those receiving financial assistance). Unskilled workers accounted for only 7 per cent of the beneficiaries, while 3 per cent were unclassified. Weekly earnings expected by the transferred workers were £30 per week — well above average earnings on Tyneside and even the national average in 1968.

Nationally, evidence indicates that Government schemes are coming into greater use in permanent resettlement. The number receiving assistance to settle permanently (in terms of the number receiving removal assistance) has risen in relation to the total number receiving travelling assistance to work in other regions. The effectiveness of the schemes cannot be judged, since it is not known whether these workers would have moved in any case without Government assistance. Certainly, in the case of Jarrow the scheme seemed to have little impact in inducing permanent migration — as stated earlier, only two household removal expenses were paid for the period of 1 October 1967 to 31 March 1969 under the old Resettlement Transfer Scheme. A number of workers in Jarrow and Hebburn were prepared to use the Employment Transfer Scheme, but few to settle permanently. Its use was mainly to maintain or increase the economic rent to a worker, temporarily or during a prospective period of unemployment or short working, until a suitable financially-rewarding job became available again at home.

The third group of policy measures pursued by the Government comprises general ones designed to improve the operation of the labour-market. A reduction in net out-migration from some areas must be offset by increased occupational and industrial mobility and a change to new and expanding industries in the North, Scotland, Wales and the South West. Government measures to lubricate the labour market in Britain have included (a) the establishment of Industrial Training Boards, the expansion of Government Training Centres and a scheme for financial assistance to firms expanding their own training in development areas; (b) improvement in the organisation of the placing services provided by employment exchanges; (c) an improved industrial relations service to give advice to management on problems of recruitment, turnover and so on; and (d) co-operation with industries — coal, railways, textiles — where a large run-down has created a need to minimise dislocation by careful planning. All of these measures have by no means been successful. For example, retraining in Britain is primarily the responsibility of Industrial Training Boards, but if a worker is declared redundant he falls between two stools, for he is no longer the responsibility of the Industrial Training Board, which only retrains workers for its own specific industry, nor will any other Board accept him unless he has a job in its industry. No adequate and widespread retraining programme exists to retrain workers for another industry. Too many resources are thus channelled into retraining within an industry and not enough between industries and occupations.

Contributory factors affecting migration are unemployment benefits, social security benefits, job related earnings when unemployed, income tax rebates and redundancy payments. The Redundancy Payments Act (December 1965) was designed to provide a guarantee in advance that if a man loses his job because of redundancy, he will receive compensation. The expectation was that in return there would be a ready acceptance of the need for change to promote the more economic use of manpower: in other words, that mobility would become acceptable. The National Insurance Act 1966 introduced earnings-related supplements and was intended to take some of the hardship out of unemployment between jobs. It was hoped to facilitate mobility between one job and another. There is no documentary evidence of the effect on migration and mobility of these measures. The opinion most often expressed seems to be that they discourage migration by lowering the advantages of moving permanently to such an extent that the monetary gain from moving would be only slightly more than from remaining unemployed. In addition, social and psychological costs and housing difficulties in the South may result in a real cost to movement rather than a benefit.

Government policy towards environmental and infrastructure improvement also impinges on the propensity to move, but no quantitative estimates are available.

Regional policy

The focus in regional planning has been either population or employment, but regional policies on migration do differ in emphasis. Policies on migration in respect of the Northern region changed appreciably during the 1960s as more positive declarations of intent were made. The 1963 White Paper on the North East stated that 'continued movement on this scale [in 1951–61a net loss of 80,000] out of a region like the North East has naturally given rise to anxiety'. In 1966 the Northern Economic Planning Council adopted much higher estimates of total population and population growth than the General Register Office projections and stated:

> It may be thought optimistic to postulate a reduction of net outflow by 1971 to about one-half of the average experienced over the period 1959–64 . . . and the achievement of a state of balance by 1981. But these are figures which should and can be achieved, provided that continued support is given through government policies.
>
> The aim must rather be to strive for the kind of economy and environment which will attract enterprising people to the region from elsewhere, and in sufficient numbers to outweigh the normal outward movement.

That is, the NEPC was hopeful of achieving a state of migration balance — of inflows matching outflows — by 1981. A later view, in the Outline Strategy for the North (1969), is more optimistic about the situation after the end of the 1970s:

> We do not accept that the region can do no more than hope to retain its own natural increase by the end of the century. Given a broader base of modern growth industry, there are many parts of the region with the physical potential to expand economically and accommodate a much greater share of the national population.

An increasing commitment to reduce the net outflow of migrants was thus made, and even a net inflow envisaged for the later decades of the century. This tendency to halt emigration from one region at almost any cost delays the creation of an integrated strategy for regional welfare between regions.

The idea that a region should have a population target and should stem out-migration is changing and current ideas include:

> We do not think that the interests of the region or of the country, are best served by adopting overriding population targets representing either the avoidance of migration of people from the region or the building up of a region's population by immigration from outside it. We regard the quality of life as more important than numbers (Yorkshire and Humberside Economic Planning Council, 1970).

There is a need to make regional policy makers aware that population and migration are functions of other economic goals and are not goals in their own right, and to consider the effects of their policies on the economic efficiency and equity of welfare in other regions. The level of population and migration should be viewed as an instrumental variable in achieving some value in marginal revenue products of labour capital and other factors of production, tempered by equity considerations concerned with employment, environment and so on. It is important that these should be viewed spatially — that is, incomes, unemployment and similar objectives should only be allowed to deviate by certain ratios between regions.

It is possible that an inflow of migrants to a congested area would result in the marginal costs to the community as a whole exceeding the private costs seen by in-migrants. This tendency will be accentuated if user charges and taxes fail to reflect incremental costs of any required expansion of capacity in local public works — water, sewage, roads and schools. Failure to equalise private and social costs can lead to excessive in-migration with the burden of costs borne by those residents who may not profit directly from sales of goods and services to the newcomers. The costs, in respect of social welfare, of migrating from economically marginal areas may be similarly understated, especially if services still have to be provided for the remaining population. Nevertheless migration is socially and economically advantageous, unless the combined social net cost of a smaller population in the areas of origin outweighs total benefits.

Little analysis and costing of migration and secondary benefits or diseconomies at an intra- or interregional level has been undertaken. Migration objectives at a regional level are still nebulous from the lack of any specified regional welfare functions, apart from the agreed desire of planners and politicians to stop or stem net out-migration from all areas for political reasons. Yet the hard core of regional policies is about manpower, migration and population redistribution. Manpower and migration have figured in national plans, but within industrialised regions policies designed to influence migration have arisen on an *ad hoc* basis in reaction to the manner in which settlements have grown in these areas.

In Britain, intra-regional population redistribution and migration have been concerned almost exclusively with attempts to improve the environment and relieve overcrowding. Outdated urban fabric and overcrowding has resulted in a policy for New Towns and expanded towns. The purpose of this policy was to redress the social balance by creating a better environment for people in conurbations. The policy has not been successful. New Towns have attracted growth industries of a technological character, employing white-collar rather than blue-collar workers, with the consequence that New Towns have attracted young age groups and white-collar professions, while the older and blue-collar workers have continued to reside in the older urban areas.

Costs and benefits to migration

Migration thus far has largely been treated from the point of view of the individual or region and as an isolated factor completely independent and without effect on other individuals and sectors of the economy. Migration is a function of economic and social forces, but in turn it affects the magnitude of these socio-economic and other factors. So what counts as a benefit or a loss to one part of the economy — to one or more persons or groups — does not necessarily count as a benefit or loss to the economy as a whole. Cost benefit analysis is concerned with the economy as a whole: with the welfare of all society and not any smaller part of it. The individual migrant or migration stream comprises only a small part of the economy. The models of Sjaastad and Speare treat migration from the point of view of the individual as an investment from which returns are expected sufficient to offset the costs of moving. While Speare treats this as a cost-benefit model, it is simply a matter of profit and loss accounting to the individual.

It is pertinent to ask whether society as a whole will be better off by allowing migration to continue from rural and lagging urban areas to expanding areas, or by adopting alternative strategies stemming this type of migration and encouraging industry and tertiary employment to move to these areas. This can be assessed by replacing the concept of revenue by the concept of social benefit. Instead of costs to migration, opportunity costs, or the social value foregone when resources are transferred from migration to other economic activities, need to be assessed. Instead of ascertaining the net gain to the migrant, the cost-benefit method attempts to measure the excess of social benefit over cost.

The largest group of problems in a cost-benefit study of migration is that of designating the relevant magnitudes and evaluating them; that is, the choice of items to be valued at market prices and which are to be valued at shadow prices. There are also problems in deciding the methods used to evaluate the shadow prices; in the range of 'intangibles' to be included in the study, the methods used to evaluate these 'intangibles'; the choice of an investment criterion; and the allowance for future uncertainty (Mishan, 1971a).

The problem of what and how to measure is partly determined by the terms of reference of the problem in question. Needleman (1965) considered, for an unemployed worker, taxes foregone and unemployment and national assistance payments made, and the cost of providing a job in lagging regions under the 1960 Local Employment Act. He estimated the net gain to the Exchequer of reducing unemployment in the peripheral regions would, on this basis, be almost £900 per workless man employed. The Development Commission (1972) calculated the expenditure incurred in financing the 18 occupied Development Commission factories in Mid-Wales was £876 per job. At present levels of taxes, unemployment benefits and supplementary allowances, the annual returns to the Exchequer were estimated to be running at the rate of 23 per cent per annum. A more sophisticated analysis, using discounted cash flow techniques of investment appraisal, produced estimates of the annual returns to the Exchequer ranging from 27·6 per cent to 30·9 per cent, depending on the precise assumptions made. It was pointed out that in comparison with these rates of return, a minimum of 10 per cent per annum is required on the low-risk projects undertaken for commercial reasons in nationalised industries.

The Development Commission factories in Mid-Wales are estimated to have slowed the decline in employment between 1961 and 1968 from the 9·1 per cent which would have taken place in their absence to 7·4 per cent. Altogether the factories are estimated to have retained in Mid-Wales 2,973 people who would otherwise have left the area. This reduced the decline of population in Mid-Wales between 1961 and 1969 from a total of 4·3 per cent to 2·7 per cent. Half of these 2,973 'prevented migrants' were in the child-bearing age group and they have, therefore, had an impact on the natural change of the area's population out of all proportion to their number. Had the Development Commission factories not been provided, the excess of deaths over births in Mid-Wales (78 during 1968) would probably have been 36 per cent greater.

Widen the terms of reference and the regional development objective may relate to increases in regional income, employment, reduction in unemployment, economic stability, income distribution, quality of services, environmental enhancement (including conservation), social well-being, personal income distribution and population distribution. Multiple objective cost-benefit analysis has been used in water resource planning (United States Water Resources Council Special Task Force, 1970) and in regional development (McColl and Throsby, 1972). Regional income benefits accruing to migration which may be measured are:

(a) primary benefits: the value of increased outputs of goods and services accruing to residents of the region;
(b) secondary benefits: (i) benefits resulting from externalities, and (ii) benefits resulting from the employment of resources which would otherwise be unemployed or underemployed; and
(c) multiplier effects: additional net income accruing to the region from the existence of migrants or from other economic activities induced by their presence.

Likewise regional income costs may be classified as losses incurred under each of the above headings: costs of resources supplied from the region, external diseconomies, loss of assistance payments contributed from outside the region to previously unemployed or underemployed labour, and losses of regional net income from other workers displaced by migrants or from the operation of migration from the area of origin.

The other objectives may be evaluated in a similar manner. McGuire and Garn (1969) have devised an explicit formula for consolidation of equity and efficiency criteria in the selection of regional development projects in the United States. This was based on the construction of a marginal utility index — including the trade-offs among the arguments of the function. For income and employment McGuire and Garn specified a function of the form

$$\lambda_i = a \left(\frac{\overline{E}}{E_i}\right) + b \left(\frac{\overline{Y}}{Y_i}\right)^\beta$$

where λ_i = area need indicator
$\overline{E}$ = national average employment rate
E_i = area employment rate
$\overline{Y}$ = national median family income
Y_i = area median family income

The parameters determine the trade-off between the equity consideration of improving family income and the efficiency objective of creating jobs, in a scheme of values along any fixed 'indifference curve' — the gradient being the rate at which the decision maker is willing to trade off efficiency for distributional objectives. a would be set equal to O if the creation of a new job was just as important in areas with low unemployment rates as in areas with high rates. Thus any given set of multiple objectives can be considered in this way.

Migration occurs from areas where the marginal revenue product to labour is low. There are three basic choices open to the Government — to stimulate and attract industry to the lagging area, the policy adopted in practice to counter out-migration; to aid migrants to leave lagging areas; or to do nothing. The Government has used various schemes to aid people who are willing to migrate to alleviate hardship. These cover additional private cost to the migrant of moving but take no account of social costs and benefits. The 'do nothing' solution is usually considered unacceptable on equity grounds. Population must have certain living standards, provision of social services and so on.

Warford (1969) attempted to examine the social costs and benefits of a proposed water supply scheme in South Atcham, a rural area immediately south of Shrewsbury. The net cost of three alternatives were considered:

(i) maintaining the existing settlement pattern with no relocation of population;
(ii) combinations of sub-areas that might be abandoned and population relocated;
(iii) a situation in which everyone leaves the area.

The net cost of providing services, employment and living standards in relation to national income, if existing population distribution is maintained, needs to be calculated together with the number of people affected and any additional net cost of providing for future new facilities and services within the area if relocation does not take place. Similarly, a calculation must be made of the net cost of providing services, employment and amenities if the area were abandoned or partly abandoned and the population moved to other specific areas; the numbers involved in different locations; and the additional cost of providing facilities for future growth outside the area. All of the increase in profits through the relocation of population in another area where the marginal revenue product is higher cannot be counted as benefits — it is simply a transfer of purchasing power from one part of the country to another. The reduction in net costs through increased efficiency by relocation must be assessed. It is, therefore, important not to count the same benefit twice. On the social capital argument, out-migration may increase pressure on, for example, schools in areas of destination. To the extent that many areas of origin, such as Tyneside and West Yorkshire, suffer from overcrowding anyway, a reduction here would count as a benefit. Provision per child is generally smaller in Northern England than Southern England and migration from North to South may spread resources more evenly.

Warford considered the costs and benefits of supplying water to the whole of South Atcham, or only certain parts; the effect on agriculture of any relocation of population; and its effect on sewage disposal, telephones, electricity supply, post office mail costs, schools, travel to work, shops, entertainment and markets, the costs of various health services (ambulances and so on), mobile libraries, road construction and maintenance and housing costs. Within the policy limitations accepted in the context of the study, the results, on the above counts, showed that relocation would be preferable to the water supply scheme so far as the quantified factors were concerned. This alternative allowed for envisaged changes in the type of agriculture (for example from dairy to beef and sheep) taking place in some areas as a result of out-movement and the necessity for inward daily travel.

Clearly, if an area were abandoned altogether or operated at a reduced economic activity level, occupational transfers of labour and house values would need to be considered. This would mean assessing for labour (as well as other factors) shadow or accounting prices. The cost of productive services is not always equal to their market prices. Opportunity cost equals market price only when, in the case of labour, a worker is indifferent between one occupation (and/or area) and another. This rarely occurs in practice. It is, therefore, necessary to assess the true cost of a man's labour as equal to the value it produces in the occupation from which it is transferred, plus any additional sum above his existing wage that is required to induce a worker to transfer his labour into a new occupation or area. Thus, a shadow price is estimated. However, it should again be pointed out that psychic costs involve no resource cost and do not affect resource allocation. Optimal allocation of resources must take tastes as given and will differ if people prefer familiar to strange surroundings. Migration transfer incentives to compensate for psychic costs are inappropriate: to compensate for psychic costs would result in resources being used for migration to obtain earnings with a lower marginal utility value than those received before. Psychic costs partly explain earnings differentials larger than those implied by monetary and opportunity costs of migration. These differentials do not represent resource misallocation. Additionally the industry to which the worker transfers needs to be considered. Agricultural workers, and many from traditional industries, are leaving industries the products of which are not subject to purchase tax or value added tax to work in industries which face purchase tax or value added tax. If this tax added 10 per cent to the price of a competitively produced good, the value associated with the labour of a worker moving to such an industry would be 10 per cent more than his wage there, if the worker was indifferent between the two jobs. If the worker is not indifferent, but prefers his existing occupation, then the premium necessary to induce him to move needs to be added. There is also the problem of assessing the migration of unemployed workers. Most workers need some minimum sum, say £14 to induce them to work. An average worker and family may receive £12 per week in transfer payments and benefits for unemployment. If a worker obtains a job in another area for £14, the £12 transfer payment reverts back to the community and the cost to the community of engaging his labour is only £2. There is a gain, therefore, if his weekly labour adds a value in excess of £2.

One of the most difficult problems in cost-benefit is the pricing of intangibles or spillover effects. The market prices of spillover effects are generally zero. For example, migration from rural to urban areas adds to urban problems, such as smoke, pollution, noise and the like, which are not recorded by the market. Increased road congestion results in major new road construction, but 75 per cent of the cost of 'A' class roads is paid for by the Government and not the local residents. Pressure on housing means local open land is built over. The loss of any good – including free goods like clean air, pleasant scenery and freedom from noise, must be valued at the minimum sum people would be willing to accept as just compensation for their loss. These spillover costs plus resource costs must be less than the value of the total benefits if migration is to be acceptable as economically efficient and socially desirable. Migration from 'depressed' areas may actually reduce congestion cost. This occurs when migration takes place from a more 'congested' area (however defined) to a less congested area; for instance, movement from a large industrial city like Glasgow to a small but growing industrial town in, say, Lincolnshire. Similar movement from many areas in Northern England to East Anglia or the South West, would probably have a similar effect in reducing intangible costs. If there are external economies (benefits) and external diseconomies (costs) on other members of society as a result of migration – and it is evident that there are – it can no longer be taken for granted that the market price of a factor, good or service, is an index of its marginal value to society.

In any cost-benefit study there is also the problem of criteria for investment projects: the method by which time profiles of costs and benefits are to be reduced to a single figure for comparison, either by discounted present value or internal rate of return. In addition some allowance has to be made for uncertainty about future costs and benefits.

Riew (1973) has proposed a cost-benefit model of migration and public policy. The model is naïve and Riew does not discuss aspects of pricing – market or shadow prices – the choice of investment criterion or the allowance for future uncertainty. But given that these can be adequately determined, the model does approximate the present value of the net social gain or cost of human migration in economic terms. The present value of the net social gain or cost of migration is expressed as

$$Vn = \sum_i \sum_t [(E'_{it} - E_{it}) - (L'_{it} - L_{it})] (1+r)^{-t} - \sum_i (\dot{E}_i + M_i) -$$

$$\sum_i A_i (1-\alpha) - [\sum_i A'_{gi} - \beta m \overline{Ag}] -$$

$$\sum_j \sum_t \frac{\gamma S_{jt} - \gamma S_t}{\gamma a_t} da_{jt} (1+r)^{-t} - mAg(1-\theta)$$

$$(i = 1, \ldots, m; j = 1, \ldots, q; t = 1, \ldots, n_i)$$

where the expected earnings rise from E to E' on moving to another area and L and L' denote respectively the living expenses in the new and old locations per period, and the expenses to accommodate an equivalent standard of living.

E	is the income foregone during the transition period,
r	is the rate of discount,
i	are the individuals moving, and
t	is the prospective employment period for individual or household i.
M	is the moving expenses including expenses of adjustment at the new location
A	denotes the cost of replacing in the new location the private residential asset left behind, and
α	is the fraction of the sum value of these assets in the old location that are absorbed by the effective demand of the population remaining in the old location.
Ag	is the value of the average per household/individual share of the public assets in the old location, and
$A'g$	is its replacement cost in the new location, with

53

β denoting the fraction of migrants' share of the public assets (mAg) in the old location, which substitutes for otherwise needed additions to the stock of public assets.

$\gamma S_t/\gamma a_t$ denotes the marginal operating cost of local public services at the old location, and

$\gamma S'_j t/\gamma a_t$ the marginal operating cost of providing equivalent public services in the jth community where relocation occurs

where
$$\sum_{j=1}^{q} da_j = m$$

Ag denotes the household share of privately-owned social overhead capital,
m is the number of migrant households, and
θ is the fraction of the migrants' sum share of these assets that substitutes for otherwise needed additions to the assets.

Only when Vn is positive will the migration be in the social interest. This occurs where the earnings differences between the two areas are greater than the cost of living differences plus moving costs, plus the costs of replacing private and public assets of the old location at the new location together with the difference in the marginal operating costs, all discounted.

Despite many problems, cost benefit methods can be successfully applied to the analysis of migration, bringing together the costs of alternative Government policies and shedding new light on the problems involved. Its use at present is limited in range and by policy constraints. The Government's decision on the movement of civil servants out of London will be assessed in the light of the benefit to the country from the better use of national resources; the effect on Government expenditure; the financial and job benefits to the receiving area; and the damage to communications and cost within the civil service.[2] The first term of reference is very wide and doubtless much argument will ensue on the variables within this to be evaluated. For this reason, the interests of society are better served by making public not merely the findings of a cost-benefit study, but also the methods employed and the sources of data.

General characteristics and implications of policies concerned with migration

Government policies aim to influence migration with a view to changing population distribution. This is the chief characteristic of all policies. In most European countries the policies are aimed at decentralisation of population as between regions. Within regions, however, the aim is usually concentration of population. This is evident in the New Towns of Peterlee, Newton Aycliffe, Corby, Cwmbran and Glenrothes, which were designed to concentrate scattered industrial workers and miners into centres near to their places of work and as a solution to the need for reconstruction of run-down neighbourhoods. In development areas generally the policy is one of concentrating settlement in selected areas while aiming at the stabilisation or increase in numbers in the region as a whole.

A common characteristic of all migration policies is simultaneously to mitigate congestion in urbanised areas, and raise the economic level in development areas. The Barlow Report and subsequent post-war policy in Britain aimed at restricting development in congested regions, thereby increasing the real income in those areas, while developing underdeveloped Northern and Western areas to raise monetary incomes. This socialistic philosophy and redistributive policy has continued. The 3 per cent annual growth rate which continued until the mid-1960s obviated the need for strong regional policies, since it is relatively easier to redistribute growth. The National Plan (1965) was very much concerned with growth. It expressed concern with the growth in population and pressure on land in the Midlands and the South East, and the resulting problems of congestion from the growing demand for cars and homes. The National Plan noted the discrepancies between the Midlands and the South and the less prosperous regions, where unemployment rates have been consistently above the national average. It proposed tackling both of these problems.

Out-migration from less prosperous areas is generally not a characteristic of Government policy and is not favoured as the only solution to the problems of these areas, although migration within a region is approved. Migration from the Northern and Western areas of Britain is stemmed not because absorption costs are high in areas of destination (in fact, migrants tend to go to the expanding outer areas of industrial zones in the Midlands and the South), nor because of a loss in the utilisation of social capital (rates of out-migration are only marginal), but because of the fact that such migration is unacceptable for political reasons. The possible redundancy of social capital in areas of decreasing population is frequently referred to as a cost of migration. Brown (1972) has estimated, assuming a uniform normal life of 70 years for assets, that population would have to fall at somewhat more than 2 per cent a year for excess capacity to appear, because, with rising living standards, per capita requirements of energy, water and other services rise. No regional or even sub-regional population seems to be in danger of declining at such rates: $\frac{1}{2}$ per cent a year in the Greater London Conurbation has recently been the highest sub-regional rate of decline.

Individual migrants are assumed to maximise their individual welfare and producers to maximise their profits. In equilibrium the system 'solves', for the price of various factors and an optimal allocation of resources is derived. There may be a divergence between private and social goals: each individual is concerned with his own welfare but his actions may not be positively priced when they affect others, or the community may decide that its objectives differ from that of certain individuals or that they cannot be met through the market mechanism — some public goods are not priced. For these reasons government policy impinges on migration. Thus Italy attempted to stop city-ward migration before 1961 by prohibiting jobless persons from overcrowded rural areas taking up residence in communities of over 25,000. The influx of rural people into the big cities had been too small effectively to release agriculture from surplus labour, but much too large to be absorbed into the urban economy. Rural—urban migration tended to draw off the land too many capable workers, while still being insufficient to supply industry with needed skills. Such movement, it was argued, did nothing to alleviate rural problems. Migration policies like these have rarely been successful. The policy in Italy created more rather than less difficulties, for instead of checking migration it resulted in large clandestine migration into large cities, with consequential slums and illegal and social exploitation of migrants (Galeotti, 1971). Similarly, in the USSR efforts to control migration, in this case by transferring large masses of people to the eastern and northern parts of the country, rendered little lasting success. The number of workers or settlers who stayed there permanently turned out to be negligible, and in some regions out-migration has exceeded in-migration (Sonin and Zhiltsov, 1967).

Policy in Britain has not been a complete success. The northern areas still lag in terms of income and employment. The solution to the regional problem in Britain and to consequential migration has been seen as soluble only in terms of capital development. Some analysis has been made to determine whether capital development yields benefits at least as great as the cost of providing the capacity. This has generally been undertaken in comparison of the cost of the provision of jobs in lagging regions with the saving in unemployment and state benefits and loss in taxes. Leven (1970) has pointed out that we seldom ever think of transferring capacity from one market to another, or attempting to bribe the excess demanders to withhold their demands, or simply transferring capacity from one location or group of users to another by administrative fiat. Regional policy and migration in Britain have shown that it is difficult to solve excess supply or demand only by additions to capital stock, with no possibility of rationalising its use. In migration it may be just as efficient to raise the price of migration, of residing and working in areas like London and other city areas, as to provide capital development to attract population, labour and firms away from these areas. Industrial development certificates in Britain are the nearest approach to an alternative policy — in this case, attempting to transfer capacity by administrative fiat.

Concentration on capital growth as a solution to the economic causes of migration may represent a misallocation of resources. Brown (1972) argued at a crude level of theoretical abstraction that misallocation is not very important so long as factor proportions are flexible and factors are in fact employed. So long as all available labour is employment, the scope for improving total output by shifting it from one region to another may be very modest if its marginal product in low productivity areas is quite a high proportion of that in high productivity areas. The difference between the two might be extinguished if only a small fraction of the labour force moved from the lower-productivity to the high-productivity region. In practice, however, the scope for improvement is probably much greater, since labour in low-pay regions is paid substantially more than the value of its marginal product. In addition, marginal conditions of the Paretian optimum are not a valid criterion of an increase in welfare in a context where they are not all simultaneously satisfied. There exists plenty of evidence that marginal conditions with regard to land and capital are not satisfied throughout Britain, and if only one condition cannot be fulfilled somewhere in the economy, then a first-best (Paretian optimum) situation cannot be achieved. There may be little reason, therefore, to equate labour with marginal conditions.

Paretian conditions constitute a simple statement of the necessary first-order conditions of a first-best, but there is no corresponding set of rules for the achievement of a second-best position in a world where the first-best is unattainable. Nor does there even exist a rigorous criterion of whether a particular change would constitute an improvement even if not an optimum.

Funck (1970) constructed a model for the optimum solution of welfare systems and regional policy decisions, but looked at only two individuals, goods and production factors. The model included externalities in consumption and production. Within the restricted set of assumptions, the results of the model describe relations between regional welfare, production, markets and regional economic policy in an optimum situation. In reality the problem is more complex, so that the neoclassical approach of Funck would quickly approach its limits and other techniques, such as non-linear programming, need to be applied. Quadratic programmes are, at present, limited in size and cannot handle a large number of regions, welfare functions, goods and factors of production.

In the presence of imperfections, the best policy in any situation cannot be calculated with precision from available data. The rules of first-best optimality, coupled with the caveat of second-best, do however, constitute part of the fund of guidelines from which good, if not perfect, policy might be formulated (Winch, 1971).

Notes

[1] Report of the Committee of Inquiry into the Scottish Economy (Toothill Report), Scottish Council Development and Industry, 1961.
[2] The Hardman Report, 'The Dispersal of Government Work from London'. (HMSO) 1973

4 Migration and Motivation

Introduction

Economic model building has focused chiefly on variables and surrogates, such as distance and ecological characteristics, to the exclusion of the behavioural parameters of the migrants. This approach of the economist to migration has been to infer motives from a study of objective structural determinants and then to impute these motives to the migrants. Ecological correlations have been widely used in geographic, demographic and economic work on migration (see Chapter 8), not because investigators were primarily interested in correlations between the properties of areas as such, but with the obvious purpose of discovering something about the behaviour of individuals. Ecological correlations have been used simply because correlations between the properties of individuals are not available. Socialists maintain that this approach constitutes a denial of differential perception and evaluation and places an excessive emphasis on purposive – rational – behaviour. There has recently been increased attention to the migrant's own 'definition of the situation' and account of his own motives, with consequent problems of the difference between 'real' and 'stated' motives. The difficulties associated with this type of investigation are discussed in Chapter 7. The aim of the present chapter is a fuller understanding of the determinants of migration, in particular the way motives can be combined with the theory of migration and its structural characteristics. Taylor (1969) maintains this is *the* problem in migration: the anarchic and infinite collection of motives to be classified within the framework of objective structural determinants. This is similar to the acceptance or rejection of estimated coefficients of regression equations in Chapter 8: the problem of deciding whether observations and results are consistent with theory.

Sociologists have in general been concerned with four main areas of structural characteristics: (i) the family life cycle; (ii) social – intergenerational and career – mobility; (iii) the residential environment, including the changing characteristics of residence and neighbourhood; and (iv) social and locality participation. Studies on the assimilation of migrants transgress (iii) and (iv), but these four categories provide an introductory framework for the analysis of migration and motivation.

Life cycle

Family formation, growth and dissolution have been found to account for a substantial share of residential mobility in the United States (Glick, 1957). When the family life cycle from formation to dissolution is examined, critical stages or turning points can be identified which have an impact on the propensity to move. These stages normally include: (a) marriage − family formation; (b) pre-child −constant size, (c) child-bearing − increasing size; (d) child-rearing − constant size; (e) child-launching − decreasing size; (f) post-child − constant size; (g) widowhood − family dissolution (Foote et al., 1960). Not all stages apply to all couples or people; nevertheless, for married couples, mobility propensity is greatest during the family formation, child-bearing, and child-launching stages.

Rossi (1955), in determining why households moved, concentrated on household structure as a mobility factor, considering the 'major function of mobility to be the process by which families adjust their housing to the housing needs that are generated by the shifts in family composition that accompany life cycle changes'. It now seems obvious that mobility explanations need to incorporate not only structural, but also social-psychological, views. Structural approaches to mobility have focused on family life cycle, objective descriptions of changes in housing and residential environments and linkages between; without the social-psychological views of mobility to understand the needs, values, aspirations and decisions of the individual's subjective evaluation of the various alternatives which he is considering. In practice, the actuation of mobility by family life cycle changes also depends on the size and adaptability of the housing unit, tenure status, the way in which changes in family structure are evaluated and related to housing needs and the availability of housing within the range of household financial resources. Life cycle changes are never perfectly correlated with mobility and their importance is influenced by social-psychological impressions of norms.

Residential environment

The strong outward movement from city to suburbs has long been recognised (Wattenberg, 1948; Thompson and Bogue, 1949), but less is known of surburb types affecting migration (Kalbach, Myers and Walker, 1963−64), although it is broadly recognised that migration contributes to the increasing socio-economic differentiation of cities from their suburbs (Goldstein and Mayer, 1965; Taeuber and Taeuber, 1964).

Changes in the residential environment of the family increase the propensity to move. Changes in neighbourhood character are, in turn, related to the urban housing cycle, but demographic and social composition changes in neighbourhoods may also generate changes in residence. Van Arsdol, Sabagh and Alexander (1964) and Van Arsdol (1966), for example, have suggested that urban settlement has intensified certain natural hazards around Los Angeles — bush fires, earth slides and floods. The increase in settlement densities has led to changes in the biosphere which have given rise to artificial hazards — air pollution and aircraft noise. Subsequent population change and migration was found to be in the direction of hazard-free areas. It was also noted that non-whites, who tend to be more concentrated in health hazard areas, did not perceive smog and aircraft noise to the same degree as the white population.

Wolpert (1966) discussed migration as an adjustment to environmental stress. Factors such as noise—tranquility, danger—security, green—gray, open—congested are disamenities or amenities and affect the individual in terms of tolerance or flexibility along a slack—strain axis in an individual's personality. Behaviour is a function of the interaction of personality and environment. In this way, individuals behave differently in what appears objectively the same environment. Wolpert also discusses the outline of an ecological system model of the interaction between an individual and the environment. Specifically

$$A_{t+1} = L \cdot A_t + P \cdot S + \ldots$$

Where A_{t+1} is a vector listing the attributes of an individual, the matrix L specifies life cycle coefficients as they modify the attributes in the time interval, vector A_t lists the attributes at a previous time period, and matrix P and vector S are respectively the coefficients of potential susceptibility of the individual to environmental elements at that place and the environmental forces acting on the individual. It is also possible in this sort of system to specify feedback relationships indicating environmental changes as a function of an individual's perception, changes and decisions. Such a model, however, has never been evaluated — important gaps still exist in measurement and in knowledge of the coefficients of susceptibility.

A survey of mobility and environmental attitude among blue-collar workers in Jarrow and Whickham on Tyneside (Willis, 1970) noted that environmental reasons for moving formed a small proportion of the total reasons. The relationship between desire to move and environmental disamenity was low for the total populations in Jarrow and Whickham, but important in individual cases. In the area surrounding a chemical works in Jarrow there was a positive wish to move away because of air pollution. Only in such striking cases as this of a noxious environmental influence does environment seem significant in its positive imprint. Elsewhere the existence of minor disamenities fails to have positive impact translated into any definite idea of a residential move or a general positive desire for one. The chief feature of environmental perception, in each sub-area of Jarrow, was the variance associated with each semantic differential used in the measurement. While almost one-third of all strong attitudes expressed regarded the industrial zone of north Jarrow as dirty, 21 per cent of such attitudes regarded it as very clean. This may not appear unreasonable, when it is recalled that residential mobility tends towards an equilibrium in matching individuals to neighbourhoods and that individuals vary very much in their reaction to the environment. Perception of and reaction to the environment probably varies between occupation groups and between environments, although little is known on this point.

Social mobility

Upward mobility aspirations have been used to account for movement to the suburbs of cities, although Bell (1958) advanced this kind of migration as an attempt to find a location in which to conduct family life that is more suitable than that offered by the centres of cities. Leslie and Richardson (1961) found a close association between social mobility expectations and residential mobility intentions and thought that both the need for more living space as the family increases in size and the need to adjust housing to changes in social status were potent forces inducing families to move.

Jansen (1968) in a study of the social aspects of internal migration, postulated that migration in modern industrial societies is less a function of 'forced' moves than a function of the type of career taken up and the importance attached to the career. While thus recognising the dominance of economic forces in migration, Jansen was more interested in the social consequences. One result of this premise would, he thought, be more upward-status mobility among migrants than among non-migrants; and the majority of migrants would make first friends and probably best friends through their jobs, because of limited attachment to local communities.

In his study of migration centred on Bristol, Jansen found greater inter- and intra-generational mobility among migrants than among non-migrants. Migrants were more likely than residents to come from a high-status background; more migrants than non-migrants tended to be in higher-status jobs than their fathers; and migrants moved up the social ladder considerably more classes from their fathers' status than upwardly-mobile residents. Intergenerational changes in status also affected contact with kin; those changing status tending to visit relatives less often than those who had not changed. Greater upward mobility was noted among migrants in the 35–50 age group, compared with younger and older groups of migrants, and also with non-migrants, despite the fact that migrants came from higher-status backgrounds.

Social mobility was also affected by the community of orientation, more upward social mobility occurring in large cities. But migrants, irrespective of their community of orientation did not appear to be disadvantaged in achieving high status compared to those who had lived most of their lives in a large metropolis.

Social and locality participation

Many researchers into migration have regarded high residential turnover as in some way undesirable to the stability and functioning of society (House and Knight, 1966). In particular Goldstein (1958) discussed the possible impact of repeated migration on social and personal disorganisation. Indeed, Rossi (1955) found a positive relationship between socio-economic status and neighbourhood participation both at an areal and individual level. But Rossi concluded that proximity to friends and relatives had little effect on the desire to move or stay, and the closer location of personal relationships was a consequence of stability rather than a cause. This view, however, seems to ignore the two-way relationship between length of residence and formation of friends, and the existing location of relatives may have a strong effect on subsequent mobility.

Propositions of social and locality participation assume that the persons least likely to move are those who are socially integrated in their neighbourhoods. On the other hand, Litwak (1960) advanced the hypothesis that extended family relations can be maintained in an industrial, bureaucratised society despite differential rates of geographical mobility. Institutional pressures force the extended family to legitimise geographical mobility, because technological improvements in communication systems have minimised the socially disruptive forces of geographical distance, and because an extended family can provide an important aid to nuclear families without interfering with the occupational system.

Hubert (1965) thought proximity (to relatives) did not in itself imply or necessitate intense social relations to any degree. The distance between two individuals has a limiting effect on the amount of contact between them, if only to a minimal degree. Beyond this extreme limiting effect, there is no reason why distance should be a factor of any great importance in the maintenance or frequency of contact with kin, and it may be considerably less important than other factors, such as genealogical distance, personal selectivity and so on. Hubert found many middle-class people to be selective in their choice of friends from among their kin, and this affected contact. In addition, the nature of middle-class relationships with kin is not of a kind that demands close proximity or intense contact with them. This is due to the middle-class upbringing and outlook on life and stands in contrast to that of the working class.

Migrants tend to form few friends among the local population in the community. The majority of migrants' friends are either workmates or persons known at previous addresses. The lack of indentification with the local community causes married migrants to have a closer-knit network of conjugal roles: they help their wives more about the house and make visits more often together than married local residents. Wives of migrants tend to display a greater interest in the husband's work and seldom raise objections to repeated moves.

Kin and friends have played an important role in migration. Closely related to the role played by kin and friends in migration is that of the social integration of the migrant in his new community. If a migrant already has friends and relatives in the area of destination, adaptation may become all the easier, but his integration into the new community may be hindered by the 'protection' afforded by relatives and friends. Stacey (1960), in a study of Banbury, showed that quite a number of in-migrants had been absorbed by the traditional society. Young and Willmott (1957) related the problems of families moving from Bethnal Green to a new housing estate. The effect of moving was to limit contact with family and kin and consequently to cause husbands and wives to focus more of their interest on the home. This was encouraged by the difficulty of making friends on the new estate, and the lack of pubs, social clubs and other places to meet neighbours.

Information, motivation and resources

The fulfilment of plans and aspirations depends in part on information on opportunities being available. This has given rise to much research and is the basis of models such as that by Stouffer (1940) on intervening opportunities. Rossi (1955) maintained that the type and effectiveness of mation sources varied with the level of income and the nature of the housing sought. Effective migration depends on the availability of financial resources and at a local spatial area this is concerned with housing.

Housing is the prime motive for local moves, and many workers are willing to make a job shift to another region but cannot find a house to rent or buy at a price they are willing or able to pay. An OECD seminar (1964) claimed that in Britain 'the principal obstacle to geographical mobility is generally agreed to be the shortage of suitable houses'. Manual workers are inhibited from moving because private housing is too expensive and public housing is rationed. The Toothill Committee (1962) and Donnison (1961) noted the reluctance of a tenant to move where this involved a sharp increase in rent. Allocations of local authority housing (with subsidised rents) discriminate against the incomer to the area, usually by a length of residence qualification (Cramond. 1965), since the major objective of such housing is to rehouse the inhabitants of existing substandard housing. Richardson and West (1964) noted that one-third of a sample of unemployed in the North East would have moved to another area if a council house were provided. Factors hindering permanent out-migration of electrical, steel, engineering and woodworkers from the North East were found to be mainly family ties and housing constraints.

Reasons for movement vary significantly with distance. Within-area or local moves are mainly connected with housing adjustments to family and personal needs; and although inter-local authority motivations for migration are varied, the proportion of moves as a result of housing and marriage drop substantially. Transfer by firm and economic motives (to gain employment, and wage-earnings and redundancy motives) become important. Motivations and reasons for migration also tend to vary with the type of move being undertaken. Economic motives figure prominently in primary and secondary moves – to obtain a job or increase earnings – whereas personal and family motives often induce return migration.

Ecological correlations have been widely used in geographic, economic and demographic research on migration, not because research workers are primarily in correlations between the properties of areas as such, but with the obvious purpose of discovering something about the behaviour of individuals. Ecological correlations have been used simply because correlations between the properties of individuals are not available. Where studies concentrate on the individual, most individuals are seen to operate within certain systems – occupational, etc. – but an analysis of attitudes to moving suggests that some workers belong to certain personality types; that is, they exhibit traits which are specific, fairly widespread, predictable reactions to some identifiable condition in the natural environment.

That is, individuals will behave differently in what appears objectively the same environment. These differences may be attributable to differences in inborn stimulus — response characteristics and (or, interacting with) differences in the nature and organisation of learned processes, which include differences in the way the environment is perceived. Psychologists have not agreed on a way of decomposing the concept of personality into component processes which constitute the structure of personality. At a general level the structure of personality comprises perception, learning, traits, opinions, attitudes, and so on.

Opinions and attitudes vary with occupation. Skilled workers feel a great attachment to an occupation, more so than unskilled or semi-skilled workers. Thus, particular types of job movement are relatively easy for skilled workers who have low company ties and high occupation ones. Skilled workers and those with an economic rent exhibit a high degree of occupational satisfaction, identify themselves with the occupation, and reveal a willingness to move to pursue their occupation. A close correlation also exists between attitude to moving and desire to move. Attitudes to moving themselves partly depend on the number of localities lived in, but what is not known is the extent to which workers may have lived in a number of localities as a result of a favourable attitude to migration, or have acquired the attitude through moving.

An important deficiency in attitude and personality studies here in migration is the superficial level of inquiry in which reasons for mobility have been sought. More work by social psychologists is needed into personality traits in types of migration. It is interesting to note here the findings of Smith (1958) on stable and unstable factory workers. He made a diffident beginning to the analysis of the problem of adjustment, and concluded that, while less adapted to the job situation, unstable workers were more free to adapt to their general life situation. It was apparent that, for many stable workers, a steady job was a substitute for parental authority, while unstable workers seemed to be more independent and did not consider stability as a value in itself. A similar detailed sociopsychological investigation of stable residents and frequent migrants would probably reveal much more about the true nature of migration than would be found by continuing motivation surveys to determine whether people move because of 'work', 'environment' or 'personal' reasons.

Migration decisions

The concepts and terminology of behavioural theorists have not been widely used to explain migration decisions. While modern decision theory provides a means of solving a variety of decision problems, its general neglect in migration has probably stemmed from the difficulties involved in trying to apply a decision model to an aggregate of persons. Data on individual migration histories is scarce. Decision theory ordinarily specifies at least three basic elements relevant to the problem of making a decision to act. A choice must be made from a set of possible acts. The relative desirability of an act depends upon which of several possible events occurs or is believed to occur. Lastly, for each possible combination of acts and events there is a consequence, the value of which will help determine the choice of a specific action.

Wilber (1965) tried to utilise this kind of decision theory — a Bayesian model, for analysing decisions to migrate — to age migration in the United States. In the most elementary sense, a migration decision problem was thought to involve a choice between the acts of moving and not moving. A person may prefer not to move, but given additional information about job prospects — the event — may prefer to move. The possible consequences of moving or not moving include not only receiving a higher income and a lower income, but also such things as a different job, different housing, different schools for children and so on. Given a specific act, such as moving, and a specific event such as higher income, there is a consequence, such as obtaining a better job, which possesses some value — a utility — for the decision maker. Wilber assumes that people choose the act, from among a set of possible acts, which maximises their utility. The actions which persons in a population have taken are used to indicate the utility of not migrating and migrating. Data on the working-age population of the United States show that both the monetary value and non-monetary utility of not moving have the highest expected prior and posterior utility.

In this theory of migration behaviour, as in economics in general, the complex psychological problems concerning what motivates the individual — that is what determines his objectives — are avoided by the device of a utility function. The migrant is said to maximise utility and utility is defined as that which the migrant attempts to maximise. This truism is completely general and cannot be false, but it tells us very little about the motivation of goals of migrants and the process by which a decision to move or stay is reached.

Wolpert (1965) attempted to explore some of the behavioural aspects of the decision to migrate. The discussion centred on the first two aspects of a decision — the act and events — and largely ignored the consequences. The consequences are undoubtedly of great importance in any future decision an individual may make. Prior to making a decision the individual is faced with *a priori* probabilities. Once migration has occurred and been found to result in certain consequences the migrant possesses additional information to reassess his respective probabilities of moving. An up-to-date assessment of the probabilities of moving can be made and the *a priori* probabilities, which were based only on information available before migration, replaced by *a posteriori* probabilities, based on additional information from the migration itself. This is one of the difficulties of using retrospective questionnaire studies of migration: the migrant is not recounting the events leading to the decision to migrate (the *a priori* probabilities), but his evaluation of the event according to *a posteriori* probabilities. Hence, few studies have been made of the study of migration: the overwhelming majority of studies have evaluated the consequences of migration in terms of decisions. Wolpert's study is theoretical and surrounds the life cycle and notion of place utility as the 'act' and search behaviour as the events. Place utility is seen as the net composite of utilities which are derived from the individual's integration at some position in space. The individual's evaluative mechanism of utilities is also a self-adjusting process, because aspirations tend to adjust to the attainable. Satisfaction leads to slack, which may induce a lower level of attainment. Dissatisfaction acts as a stimulus to search behaviour. The individual may theoretically have access to a broad environmental range of local, regional, national and international information coverage, but typically only a limited sector is relevant to an individual's decision.

The action space refers to the mover–stayer framework and to a set of places for which expected utilities have been defined by the individual. Search behaviour gives rise to events in terms of additional information. Wolpert further argues that additional behavioural theories are relevant to migration decisions, especially to the problem of uncertainty avoidance. The order in which the environment is searched determines to a substantial extent the decisions that will be made. Empirical observations suggest that alternatives which minimise uncertainty are preferred and that the decision maker negotiates for an environment of relative certainty. Migration evidence reveals a tendency to postpone decisions and rely on feedback information: decisions are reactive rather than anticipatory. This gives rise to lagged response, discussed in Chapter 8. Uncertainty is also reduced by imitating the successful procedures of others; thus migration from A to B further encourages such movement in future time periods and gives rise to a migration system. Migrants from A to B change the socio-economic attraction of B, encouraging further migration and so on.

Migration decisions are determined by changes in circumstances related to the family life cycle, social mobility, the relative changing characteristics of the residence and the neighbourhood and the degree of social and locality participation. The effectiveness of these stimuli depends on an individual's or group's attitude to moving and on their personalities, which may include a desire to minimise uncertainty. These variables are in turn affected by migration decisions. For example, migration decisions affect locality participation in some areas. Associated with each large industrial area are enclaves of mobile population, middle- and upper-middle-class professional and managerial workers on a career step-ladder. Such groups congregate in certain areas and make little or no attempt to establish social or locality contacts in the knowledge that a future move is imminent. This in itself tends to increase the desire to move. Darras Hall at Ponteland is a classic example in relation to the Newcastle labour market area, but other cases can be found around all regional labour market centres, e.g. Collingham (Leeds), Hale (Liverpool) and Flax Burton (Bristol).

Conclusion

In a review of general theory in the study of migration Mangalam and Schwarzweller (1968) concluded that at present no major synthesising effort exists. Despite a heightened awareness of the importance of migration study, an intensification of research activity, and an expansion of technical competencies in researching this phenomenon, a fragmented approach to migration exists, together with a lack of concern for developing a general, sociological theory of migration and, indeed, a paucity of theoretical activity and interest. The many sociological studies of migration have failed to provide an overall general theoretical viewpoint to assist in making sense out of the ever-increasing number of empirical and quasi-empirical researches dealing with the various aspects of migration. Some of the examples given in this chapter have made detached and isolated conceptual and methodological advances. While all the studies referred to indicate the main determinants, the net result of each study cited is a highly-segmented view of a complex phenomenon, and a rather limited perspective of its various dimensions. Mangalan and Schwarzweller regarded Eisenstadt's (1955) study of the absorption of Jewish immigrants into Israel as coming close to a general sociological theory of migration. This study focused on the immigrant's basic motivations and role-expectation throughout the migration process, and the various demands made upon them and facilities offered in the area of absorption. Eisenstadt's study was of international migration, so it has not been considered here in detail. As far as internal migration is concerned, the enormous mass of findings produced by sociological researchers have not been incorporated into the evolving body of general theory. The consequence is that knowledge about migration and phenomena concomitant with migration tends to be fragmentary, non-cumulative and non-sociological.

5 Duration of Residence and Frequency of Movement

Introduction

Many of the questions posed about internal migration cannot be answered by the analysis of census data: new types of migration data are needed. Comparisons of current residence with residence at a fixed previous time overlook multiple, including circular, migrations by individuals. This approach, like the study of net migration, is directly concerned with population redistribution, and only inferentially with specific moves. Duration of residence and frequency of movement, as measures, document migration, whereas census data is only really apposite to the study of population distribution. Duration of residence and frequency of movement are additionally useful in measuring exposure to the general environment of varying places, and differentiating movers by frequency of residential change over a long time period.

Information collected with the US Current Population Survey in 1958, on residence history and smoking habits, has been utilised in papers concerned with the epidemiology of cancer of the lung, colon and rectum. In epidemiological studies of chronic diseases with long latent periods, or in sociological studies of urban and rural populations, classification by current residence carries with it the implicit assumption that residents have experienced long exposure to the general social and environmental conditions characteristic of that place. Tabulation by duration of residence in places of specific types is helpful in ascertaining whether an individual's current classification adequately portrays past residential experience. Residence histories provide valuable information on migration, and the CPS sample provided representative national estimates of duration of residence, number and distance of moves, and life-cycle timing of moves, cross-classified by a standard set of social and economic characteristics. This makes such data a valuable source for the study of migration, health and social welfare planning, and a baseline control for planning epidemiological studies (Taeuber, Chiazze and Haenszel, 1968).

Information on the duration of residence and frequency of movement of migrants allows cause-and-effect relationships to be ascertained, as against cross-sectional ecological correlates, which are the only feasible measures with data based on change in place of residence between two specific points in time. Additionally, it will be seen in Chapter 9 (on stochastic models) that simple measures of migration of turnover cannot be taken as indicative of stable or unstable areas, since they ignore the strong dependence of propensity to leave on length of residence. Duration of residence and frequency of movement also indicate changes required in the Markov property to derive more realistic migration models.

Data from censuses permit the study of net migration and redistributions of population over fixed time intervals. This type of data does not permit the delineation of specific individual acts of migration or relate the successive moves of individual migrants. Bogue (1959) thought longitudinal data 'an ideal system of census statistics for measuring internal migration'.

> The perfect or ideal system of migration analysis would be achieved if, for each individual, the census enumerated a complete migration history, obtaining dates of arrival and departure from each community in which the person had lived. Such a task is obviously beyond the means of any census, and would produce a greater mass of data than could ever be used.

Residence histories relating to three or more residences and points in time allow the extent of return migration, primary migration and progressive or secondary migration to be determined (Eldridge, 1965). Shryock and Larmon (1965) have pointed out that when longitudinal data on employment status, occupation, marital status and so on are obtained, as parts of life histories, it is possible to measure the association between changes of residence and changes of job, and the mobility propensities for the population at risk in various economic and social groups. Some empirical evaluations of these in the UK are discussed later. Shryock and Larmon also point out the long list of questions which can be answered by the use of longitudinal data. These include: (a) a measure of the distribution of the population by number of moves, and a determination of how this distribution develops with chronological age or key events in the life cycle; (b) the extent to which migration is between specific types of areas; (c) the proportion of the population to have spent their lives in the same type of residence; (d) extent of return migration – to same address, area and so on – and the reasons for different types of movement and; (e) changes in occupation, social, job status and so on, concomitant with migration.

Duration of residence is related to frequency of moves. As early as 1943, Rider and Badger concluded, after a study of the movement of families in Baltimore: 'the probability of moving within a specified time ... decreases as the length of maintaining the same residence increases'. Of the original households selected, Rider and Badger found 84, 75 and 69 per cent were still in the same dwelling at the end of one, two and three years respectively. Data on individual moves permit the determination of the extent to which high mobility rates, suggested by census questions on residence at two specified dates, and electoral rolls, which also give residence at specific dates, are the product of repeated movements of the same persons from place to place, or the single moves of a larger number of persons just from one place to another where they become continuous residents. Residential mobility during a given period of time is not independent of previous mobility experience. Persons who have not moved recently are less likely to move in the future than those who have moved recently. This is a more general statement of Goldstein's proposition (Goldstein, 1964) that a small proportion of frequent migrants accounts for a high proportion of all migration.

Cohort migration

Thomas (1938) said of migration, 'The most satisfactory classification is one which preserves the time sequence of migratory acts during the life span or during part of the life span of the individuals studied'. Conventional migration data, no matter how ingenious, can only scratch the surface of the true cohort approach. However, with residence histories each move recorded can be assigned to a specific cohort and to a specific age period during which it occurred. A variety of inter- and intra-cohort comparisons is thus feasible (Taeuber, 1966).

The 1961 Census published data on duration of residence (dwellings) for individual local authority areas; and age—sex, occupation, industry and socio-economic status groups for England and Wales as a whole. Length of residence is partly dependent upon age (Table 1). Only those over 15 can have a duration of residence of 15 years or more. Just after birth everyone has a duration 'since birth', but once a person moves he cannot subsequently return to that category; hence the percentage with life-time duration will diminish through time. Note from Table 1 the difference between males and females in the 15—24 age group and the sharp drop in the 'since birth' category from the 15—24 to 25—44 age groups due to marriage.

One of the most distinctive features of duration data is the glimpse they give into migration as part of the life history of persons. Yet British census

Table 1

Duration of residence by age
(males and females in England and Wales, 1961)

Age last birthday		Less than 1 yr	1 yr	2–4 yrs	5–14 yrs	Over 15 yrs	Since birth
All ages	M	11·79	6·25	18·44	29·04	19·70	14·78
	F	11·35	6·13	18·25	28·76	22·52	12·96
0 – 4	M	15·71	7·25	9·62			67·41
	F	15·68	7·24	9·73			67·35
5 – 14	M	9·56	6·10	21·82	30·12		32·40
	F	9·67	6·04	21·70	30·04		32·56
15 – 24	M	17·50	6·74	14·81	29·93	9·19	21·81
	F	21·65	9·20	18·49	25·63	6·89	18·14
25 – 44	M	15·75	8·99	27·10	35·56	9·63	2·95
	F	13·16	7·79	26·03	40·02	10·54	2·36
45 – 64	M	6·63	3·76	13·74	32·49	42·02	1·35
	F	6·49	3·75	13·17	29·32	45·74	1·53
65+	M	6·50	3·59	12·28	21·61	55·17	0·85
	F	6·99	3·91	13·31	22·28	52·60	0·90

Results percentaged by row
M = male; F = female

Source: 1961 Census, Migration Tables

data is incomplete in failing to distinguish between duration in dwelling and duration in place of residence. United States data (Taeuber, 1961) suggests that the years of leaving home and establishing new families frequently involve changing place of residence as well as the specific dwelling. Relatively few change their residence between birth and late adolescence, whereas by the mid-twenties two-thirds have left their birth places. Durations for older groups suggest that these persons settled down in their late twenties or early thirties and were unlikely to change their place of residence thereafter. Local moving may be continued, but probably many of the shorter durations for these persons reflect a recent move to the suburbs rather than a long distance migration.

The only data on areal duration in Britain that is so far available is that derived from a study of the variations in geographic mobility between and within electrical, engineering, steel and woodworkers (Willis, 1972a). This revealed the great differences between dwelling and area duration: a high percentage of short-term duration for areas. Few workers in any occupation were classified as in a dwelling 'since birth', but for all occupations by area the highest percentage were in this category. Electrical workers had a higher percentage in short-term area duration than any other occupation group considered. Although this small sample did not permit a detailed analysis by age, there was a tendency in all four occupation groups for a higher percentage of workers in the 18–24 age group to have both short dwelling and area duration, while among workers aged 45 or over the highest percentages for dwelling and area were in the longer duration categories.

Occupational mobility

The duration by area data (for electrical, steel, engineering and woodworkers) revealed, for engineering and steelworkers, a gradual increase in the proportions in each duration category up to 'since birth'. In the case of electrical and woodworkers, while 'since birth' had the highest proportion of the total, the percentage in short-term duration was high, indicating more-repeated movement in these occupations. Residential duration in the less than 1 year, 1 year and 2–4 year groups decreases with age; that is, there was increased duration in dwellings with age, but not to the same extent as with area duration.

For the majority, the first area move comes before the age of 24 or shortly afterwards. Those who have not moved area by the 24–44 age group are likely to remain in their birthplace. Engineering workers portrayed a divergent trend from other occupations.

To permit comparisons, 'since birth' durations are usually arbitrarily defined as residentially stable; durations of less than 1 to 14 years as residentially unstable; and durations of 15 years or more, but not 'since birth', as being intermediate stability. According to this criteria, residential stability was found to be higher among electrical workers in Jarrow, than among engineering and woodworkers in Whickham, despite the greater mobility of electrical workers. This occurred because of the high stability of some electrical workers, while a few moving often accounted for the high short-term residence rates.

The 1961 Census records, for England and Wales, duration of residence – dwelling but not area – and this provides some indication of the relative rates of residential stability and movement by occupation. White-collar workers – especially professional and service workers – have the highest short-term residence rates; while farmers, miners, glass and ceramic makers, furnace, forge, foundry and rolling mill workers and leather workers had very low proportions of short-term residence rates in comparison. Electrical, engineering, paper and printing workers, and transport and communication workers, were blue-collar workers who had high proportions of short-term residence rates.

Migration sequences

Residence histories supply basic data permitting almost any conceivable type of migration study and allow the identification of specific places of residence. Taeuber (1965), using residence history data, was able to identify patterns of redistribution, within the hierarchy of urban places, for successive cohorts. Little change has taken place over time in the amount of redistribution among the size-of-residence groups in the USA. As each cohort ages, increasing numbers leave their birthplace and redistribute both up and down the hierarchy of urban places. At each age upward redistribution prevailed over downward. Downward redistribution was largely accounted for by suburbanisation. In a further analysis of residence histories and duration of residence, Taeuber, Chiazze and Haenszel (1968) found strong empirical support for stage migration and counter currents. The stage migration process is one in which the aggregate shift from rural areas to conurbations or suburbs is accomplished not by direct moves, but by a series of less dramatic moves from farm to village, village to town, town to city. Taeuber isolated from the data the number of population-size residences (places) lived in; and the number of exposure residences, based on a count of only those population-size residences in which the migrant had accumulated at least ten years of residence. The number of exposure residences indicated that most adults obtain only a limited variety of residential experience. 89 per cent of the population of the USA in the 18–24 age group have only one exposure residence. With increasing age, the percentage with no exposure residence or one exposure residence declined, but, even at ages 65 and over, one is the modal category and 84 per cent had only one or two exposure residences. Most persons with two residences in their history had two population-size residences but only one exposure residence, and the accumulation of more than two residences is accompanied by a much slower accumulation of population-size residences and by very little accumulation of exposure residences. For most people in the United States, stays at birthplace and at current place account for all or nearly all of their residence histories and, among those whose birthplace and current residence differed in size, the percentage with only one exposure residence tended to be greater the larger the size of birthplace. From the size distributions of two and three exposure residences Taeuber, Haenszel and Sirken (1961) thought many migrations must occur between places within the same size groupings.

In Britain, the south and east of the country has high short-term dwelling proportions and lower long-term proportions compared with the north and west (House and Willis, 1967). 1961 Census data on duration of residence also indicates that local areas with high in- and out-migration rates have the greatest proportion of short-term dwelling residents – these are usually the 'cocktail' and commuter areas surrounding large towns and employment centres. However, the use of existing census data in the analysis of residential duration fails to answer the question of whether high in- and out-migration rates at a local level indicate a high degree of population instability, or if they represent the same migrant element in the community, while the rest of the community forms a stable element.

Frequency of movement

Migration data may be interpreted as documenting high rates of mobility or as demonstrating the prevalence of residential stability. Mobility is emphasised by considering all changes of residence and overlooking the concentration of migration at particular ages in the life cycle. Stability is emphasised by restricting attention to changes of community, ignoring local moves from one house to another, recognising that a few persons who move frequently account for a large proportion of all moves, and noting the long periods of residential stability typical during childhood and again during middle and old age (Taeuber, Chiazze and Haenszel, 1968).

Census data does not allow direct examination of these patterns, being based on current place of residence and previous place at a specified date. Such data provides little information on the frequency of migration and stability of residence in the life cycle and no information as to whether migration rates are the product of single moves of a large number of people, from one specific place to another where they become continuous residents, or repeated movement of the same persons from place to place. The only data collection technique which allows this analysis to be undertaken is a longitudinal survey of individual case histories. At the local community level, high rates of in- and out-migration raise the question of whether they are indicative of a high degree of population instability;

or if instead they represent movement into and out of the community of the same migrant elements in the population, while a large segment remains which, by its continuous residence in the community, provides continuity and stability to the basic population and to the social organisation.

Goldstein (1954) and (1958), in a study of Norristown, Pennsylvania, found out-movement from Norristown consisted largely of persons who had earlier moved into Norristown. He found the out-migration rate of in-migrants was over twice that of the continuous residents of the town. Thus high in- and out-migration rates, as in Norristown, do not necessarily mean a correspondingly high degree of population change or population instability. Since a high proportion of out-migrants were former in-migrants, there occurred no general turnover of the total population but only of the migrant segment. While migrants came and went, a large segment of the population continued to remain in the community between 1930 and 1950, providing a high degree of stability to the population of the community.

A subsequent analysis of Danish data (Goldstein, 1964) supported the view that stability of residence was characteristic of a large majority of the population. It was most typical of the young and older age groups, and least common among those of 25—44 years of age, both male and female. But even for this middle age group at least 70 per cent were stable as judged by the criteria Goldstein employed. At the same time his findings also emphasised that the pattern of repeated mobility was most characteristic of a limited segment of the population, a group which shows a particularly strong tendency to move in and out of the Danish capital several times, over relatively short time spans. Again, this pattern was particularly characteristic of those in the 25—44 year age range. The Danish data emphasises that a high degree of residential stability for most of the population is not at all contradictory with high annual rates of mobility. Weight is lent to the desirability of distinguishing, in migration analysis, between the mobile and the stable portions of the population, and to the need for evaluating migration within the context of the life cycle of the individual.

The frequency of movement of migrants in Britain is not well documented, because of a lack of residence history data. An early attempt was made by Rowntree (1957) using data from the National Register kept during and immediately after the 1939—45 war. A one in 1,000 sample analysed the area and date of all recorded residence moves between 1 January 1948 and 31 December 1950. Results were scanty, but the Eastern region had the lowest average moves per migrant with 1·50, and the Northern region the most with 1·79, for 1948—50. More important, the data showed that for all migrants moving more than once within the three-year period, 43·3 per cent made their second move less than six months after their first; the percentage dropping to 25·9 per cent within six to 11 months and 8·9 per cent in 24 to 35 months. Rowntree noted the effect of age on frequency of migration and hypothesised some sort of relationship between frequency and search for employment.

In a survey of electrical, engineering, steel and woodworkers, Willis (1972a) found that a change of local authority area was not characteristic of all members of an occupation group, but concentrated within certain parts of it. More than one-third of electrical and steelworkers had lived only in their area of birth (Jarrow). The percentage for engineering workers was also high (32·2 per cent) and that for woodworkers slightly lower (26·9 per cent). A few persons in each occupation were found to contribute a disproportionate number of houses and localities to the total count, and so increased the average number of dwellings and localities per worker. However, little significant difference seems to exist in the average number of dwelling moves between different occupation groups. But there is a significant difference between occupations in the average number of locality moves. Electrical and woodworkers were found to have lived in a significantly greater number of localities than engineering and steelworkers. Only 5·2 per cent of the sample of steelworkers had lived in more than three localities or communities; whereas 11 per cent of engineering, 19 per cent of electrical, and 22 per cent of woodworkers had done so. The frequency for all inter-community moves, whether blue- or white-collar, declines with age.

The high in- and out-migration rates characteristic of some communities and occupations do not necessarily mean a correspondingly high degree of population turnover or instability. Goldstein (1958) noted that, in the case of Norristown, a high proportion of in-migrants into the community, were previous out-migrants. Willis (1972a) noted this of particular occupations, especially electrical and woodworkers, where a high percentage of all moves were made by a small proportion in each occupation. While migrants came and went, a large proportion of electrical workers (one-third) and woodworkers (one-quarter) continued to reside in their respective communities, providing a high degree of stability. Most migration within the electrical and woodworking occupation groups consisted in large measure of persons with some previous contact with Whickham and Jarrow, and there was no general turnover of electrical and woodworkers in these areas. The large volume of inter-local authority movement shown to characterise electrical and woodworkers and other occupations with high migration rates is attributable in large measure to the repeated movements of a small number of persons, rather than to single moves of a large proportion of the population. This is composed in part of return movement. Return movement had accounted for a greater proportion of migration of electrical workers to Jarrow than had primary or secondary migration.[1] A similar migration pattern was noted among woodworkers, although return migration was a less important flow to the stock of engineering and steelworkers in Whickham and Jarrow than primary and secondary migration.

Conclusion

Duration of residence and frequency of movement are closely related. The probability of migrating decreases as length of residence increases. Persons who have moved recently are more likely to move in the future than those who have not moved recently. Migration is not independent of previous mobility experience. Increased residence in an area decreases the probability of moving outside the area. The same axiom does not hold for dwelling moves, where the probability of moving can increase, until 2–3 years' residence have been completed before declining. The probability of moving area varies between occupations and between areas. Nearly all studies of migration in Britain have failed to take this into account when trying to account for migration. Different conclusions on motivations and reasons for moving will be drawn, depending on whether frequent migrants or long-duration residents are studied, even though they belong to the same occupational group and are similar in other respects – for example, age. Conclusions drawn from duration of residence and frequency of movement are also relevant to model building, particularly stochastic models. Many models, through failing to account for duration of residence, have been completely invalidated or have drawn peculiar results. This aspect is more fully discussed in Chapter 9. More longitudinal studies are required in Britain to reveal how past mobility experience affects current migration propensities, in relation to housing history, career patterns, value systems, aspiration levels, social mobility and general 'situational' changes through each individual's life-time. Detailed reconstruction of particular moves shows how the various component decisions and actions relate to each other. The longitudinal history, duration-of-residence and frequency-of-movement frame of reference has the great advantage of emphasising the migrant rather than the area as the unit of study.

Note

[1] Primary migrants are defined as those who left their places of birth and are living in a second place; secondary migrants, those who were living outside their places of birth and in a third, fourth (etc.) locality of residence.

6 Migration Models

Theories and empirical examples of migration have been the main concern of previous chapters. The present chapter attempts to show how theories and empirical findings of migration analysis have been used in practice and as an aid in fields and professions requiring knowledge about migration. In particular, the chapter sets out to examine the role of quantitative models in assisting those — often planners, employed in central and local government agencies — whose major concern is with the formulation and execution of migration policies. Initially some preliminary observations are given on the main existing methods used by planners to forecast migration. This is followed by a discussion of the characteristics of different models that have been used and are available, and an opinion is ventured on what might realistically be expected of them.

Current migration models in planning

Projections of local population have been made for some time by the General Register Office (now the Office of Population Censuses and Surveys) for the Department of the Environment (Housing and Planning), to assist central and local planning authorities with the preparation of, and later their quinquennial review of, statutory development plans. They also form an input into structure plans and *ad hoc* studies such as local transportation and land-use exercises. Of all the factors influencing future population, and taken into account in local projections (Schneider, 1956), migration entirely dominates the net change in the population from year to year. Yet it is the variable which receives the least consideration and most haphazard treatment. Migration is allowed for by the OPCS and DOE (Housing and Planning) in only the most rough and ready fashion: the assessment of future migration is not rigorous in the sense that contributing factors are identified and quantified. Projections of the future distribution of gross and net internal migration are based on estimates of migration, associated with selected area types, from existing samples and data such as the census, figures for some New Towns supplied by their development corporations, and data on new housing estate buildings from returns to the Housing and Planning division of the Department of the Environment. Such intuitive estimates of migration are not consistent, and subjective appraisal of the effects of housing and economic developments on migration vary from area to area and region to region. Moreover, no attempt is made to project migration on the basis of projecting determinants, although these are taken into account in the process of arriving at the conclusions. Future migrants are assumed to have the same age—sex structure as those migrants identified by the census, and births and deaths of migrants are derived by applying age-specific rates to the structure without any attempt to account for a typical birth and for death rates as a result of migration itself (for instance, in areas such as Bradford and Kirklees in West Yorkshire, with Commonwealth immigrants).

The reports of the Regional Economic Planning Councils'[1] and Regional Economic Planning Boards'[2] abound in generalisations about migration. Although regional estimates are prepared independently, the aggregate regional totals are controlled via population projections to the Registrar General's national forecast. That is, regional migration must sum to zero or at least to the effect of international migration. Individual regions can produce very erroneous estimates of migration, principally through over-optimistic dreams of the effect of regional policy on the part of some Regional Economic Planning Councils. The desire to cut estimates of net out-migration to unrealistic levels can be seen from the Northern Region Economic Planning Council (1966), which anticipated a reduction of net outflow by 1971 to about one-half of the average experienced over the period 1959—64, and the achievement of a state of balance by 1981. The Office of Population Censuses and Surveys compromised when it estimated that there would still be some net migration from the Northern Region in 1981, but the compromise figure does not appear to have any reasoned basis and was not determined with reference to any of the causal factors influencing migration (Table 2). The net migration estimates and assumptions used by the OPCS from DOE regional estimates for 1971-based regional projections of population are given in Table 2. The estimated reduction in migration from the Northern region from 1971 onwards appears optimistic compared with that for Yorkshire and Humberside and the North West, bearing in mind the continuing higher net migration and unemployment rates in the North compared with the other regions.

Literature about forecasting migration at local planning authority levels is limited, because projections are often prepared for internal use only. However, what information exists suggests that the methods employed by local planning authorities are unsophisticated and take no account of the effect of planning policy on future totals. Simple extrapolation of past migration trends is common (see for example, Durham County Council,

Table 2

1971-based regional projections:
net migration estimates and assumptions

	Quinquennium				
Region	1961–66	1966–71	1971–76	1976–81	1981–86 and later
Northern	−7	−14	−7	−7	−5
Yorkshire and Humberside	−1	−13	−11	−11	−9
North West	−6	−17	−12	−11	−10
East Midlands	+9	+5	+12	+10	+5
West Midlands	+7	−10	−9	−9	−9
East Anglia	+12	+12	+15	+13	+7
South East	+21	−28	−25	−26	−22
Greater London area	−83	−114	−100	−100	−90
Outer Metropolitan	+55	+33	+30	+29	+28
Rest of South East	+49	+53	+45	+45	+40
South West	+25	+20	+19	+16	+12
Wales	+2	−3	0	0	+1
England and Wales	+61	−47	−18	−25	−30

Annual net migration, per 1,000 per year
Source: Department of the Environment

1969). Some planning authorities have attempted to relate future net migration to future employment (e.g. Tyne-Wear Plan, 1973; Nottingham and Derbyshire County Councils, 1969), but in a purely literary way. No consistent relationship between migration and employment was established in these studies and inadequacy arises through the fact that both employment and population were projected in isolation. As far as predictions for planning are concerned, the cause and effect relationship can only be effectively examined by establishing the relationship between population change and movement and the various stimuli to this. The basic demographic approach of cohort-survival may not be applicable. Grigson (1968) thought the method of relating population values to accommodation type to be of benefit in the complex migration of Greater London. This approach of relating migration to employment, housing, education, family size and structure and household formation continues to be developed by some local authorities at an elementary level. Migration tendency by age has been associated, in relation to employment and other characteristics, by the identification of town type with the main features of migration. So far this relationship has been expressed only at a simple statistical level of describing the volume of migration and the characteristics of the area from which it originates and terminates.

Planners are now gradually beginning to move away from the position of producing migration assumptions and estimates 'out of a hat', to producing models of migration with stated assumptions capable of giving some numerical estimate to migration. Many theories about migration have been formulated in a literary way, and some of these have later been restated in mathematical terms. Logic and mathematics are very closely related, so that there is no fundamental distinction between many literary and mathematical formulations of migration. However, both mathematical and literary accounts of migration are not enough for planning purposes. Numerical estimates are necessary in order to make quantitative predictions of migration in planning. Moreover, the use of existing data by itself is not enough. Existing data on migration can be interpreted and analysed only by the use of theory. Demographic and economic theory, especially mathematical demography and economics, has to provide the framework, and modern statistical analysis has to supply the tools in order to achieve the numerical results that are the goals of regional and economic planners. The use of econometrics in migration represents an intermediate position between the extreme non-theoretical empiricism of those demographers and planners who use descriptive statistics, and the non-empirical theorising of some pure demographers and economists; and it can contribute something by providing planners with numerical estimates of the results of adopting various possible policies. Planning decisions can then be based on the significant characteristics of localities, and a more sensitive and realistic policy evolved by appealing to both theory and data and adopting one hypothesis which is consistent with both the facts and the model.

Gravity models

In recent years increasing attention has been paid by social scientists and planners to the so-called gravity and potential concepts of human interaction. The reasons for this interest are not hard to discover. On the one hand, theorists have been trying to discover relationships to explain socio-economic structure and, on the other hand, practical planners have been faced with the necessity of quantifying theories and of providing specific answers to problems of urban and rural development. Gravity and potential concepts have appealed to planners in both connections and on the grounds of their simplicity.

In studies of large numbers of people – migrants – the striking geographical fact observed has been the relationship between distance and the number of moves, first noted by Ravenstein (1885). Ravenstein was concerned with explaining migration, and he presented empirical evidence suggesting that migratory movement tends to be toward cities of large population and that the volume of movement decreases with the distance between the source of migration and the 'centre of absorption'. This empirical regularity between population size and distance was soon formulated into demographic laws of spatial interaction by Zipf (1946), Stewart (1948) and others. Generally, they hypothesised that gross migration between two areas is created by a direct function of the population size of the two areas, modified by a friction against migration caused by the intervening space over which the migration must take place. The number of migrants from some origin was postulated to be some inverse function of distance. The general form of these models was

$$M_{ij} = \frac{P_i P_j}{D_{ij} \beta}$$

where M_{ij} = the number of migrants between centre i and centre j;
$P_i P_j$ = population of areas i and j, respectively;
D_{ij} = distance between centre i and centre j.

If β equals -2, as was originally thought by Stewart and Zipf, movement between two centres would be proportional to the product of their populations and inversely proportional to the square of the distance separating them.

Attempts have been made to explore this distance factor by Pareto or gravity functions (ter Heide, 1963; Lövgren, 1956), by reducing the number of migrants to a standard population.

$$M = \alpha D^{-\beta}$$

where M = the relative volume of migration between two areas — the gross migration rate being defined as $M = \frac{M_{ij}}{P_i P_j}$
α and β are constants to be estimated by regression

Hägerstrand (1962), noting that low β values indicated a gentle gradient and high values a steep gradient, found the former characteristic of twentieth-century migration, where migrants are spread over great distances, and the latter of the nineteenth-century migration fields, with short-distance migration. Differentiation in the response of out-migrants to distance from communities with or without railway stations has also been noted in this way in Scandinavia (ter Heide, 1963). For communities with stations the function reads

$$M = 4775 D^{-1.4}$$

and for communities without stations

$$M = 13050 D^{-1.8}$$

That is, for those communities not having railway stations, out-migration was more susceptible to the influence of geographical distance.

The number of migrants moving a given distance, M, can alternatively be written

$$M = \frac{\alpha}{D^\beta}$$

where α is the number of migrants leaving a specific area.

All these functions tend seriously to exaggerate and overestimate short-distance migration, and this is a major weakness of this type of model. This is a mathematical flaw that is common to Pareto-type formulas, for when distance approaches zero, migration approaches infinity. The relationship between distance and the number of moves has been found to be better described, in terms of error sums of squares between observed and predicted, by other distributions. Subsequent researchers, such as Morrill (1963), Kulldorf (1955), Somermeijer (1961), Morrill and Pitts (1967), have recognised this and tried various other distributions — log normal, exponential and gamma distributions — to improve goodness of fit. However, it is hard to see that distance as such is really a cause or explanation of how far people move. This type of model begs the question. Distance as such is not a hindrance to migration, but is a function of other factors. These factors are the expense and difficulty of travelling over long distances, the wish to maintain contacts in the area of origin, and the fact that information concerning opportunities is easier to obtain, for most types of workers, over short distances. All three factors operate to varying extents.

Stouffer (1940) emphatically denied any direct relevance of the distance factor and proposed that the number of persons moving a given distance is directly proportional to the number of opportunities at that distance, and inversely proportional to the number of intervening opportunities. That is, the function of distance is not necessarily continuous in the formulation

$$\frac{\Delta y}{\Delta s} = \frac{\alpha . \Delta x}{x . \Delta s}$$

where Δy = number of persons moving from an origin to a circular band of width Δs,
x = cumulated number of opportunities between the origin and destination s,
Δx = number of opportunities within the band of width Δs, and
α = a constant.

Stouffer's hypothesis has several limitations. Stouffer did not define opportunities with variables independent of migration. Opportunities in an area are measured by the total number of migrants who have moved into the area from anywhere. Stouffer, therefore, has assumed a relation between migration and opportunities in defining opportunities, and then measures the relationship between migration and opportunities. If the problem is to predict migration between two places, some measure other than migrants must be used in order to do it. As a descriptive device Stouffer's hypothesis is fine in its present form, but it explains nothing of the causes of migration, nor, to be more rigorous, about the variables associated with migration. Many of the most valuable insights that migration gives is aid in interpreting the changes that are taking place in an area. A study of migration reveals how a change has taken place, what movements were involved and the factors which caused it. The major criticism of Stouffer's formulation is that no allowance is made for this kind of analysis at all. Stouffer presupposes that the act of migration has taken place and further presupposes that this situation of change is already explained or understood. All that this model does is to redistribute a batch of migrants somewhere between the point of origin and point of destination, which is only a trivial part of the whole analysis.

Recent developments in gravity models by planners have been made increasingly in the field of using economic and social variables to account for migration. Interesting departures from classical gravity models have thus occurred. Lowry (1966) formulated the gravity model in log linear form and extended it to include push-and-pull factors, in the form of indices of income and unemployment, in his study of gross intermetropolitan movements in the United States during 1950–60. This was found to be an improvement over the simple gravity model in accounting for variance in migration flows between areas. The Lowry model as a technique is more fully discussed in Chapters 8 and 11. Better fits for the Lowry model were obtained by Rogers (1967a), in his analysis of interregional movement within California during 1955–60, and by Masser (1970), in an analysis of 1961 Census migration data between six English conurbations. An alternative form of the general gravity and interaction model was developed by Somermeijer (ter Heide, 1963), in the Netherlands. This extended the original gravity model to incorporate indices of the relative attraction of the origins and destinations of the movers, but differed from Lowry's model in its use of attraction factors. The constants in the model were fitted iteratively, and urbanisation, recreational resources and quality of dwellings were used, in addition to income and unemployment, as attraction factors.

Many of the inter-area models of migration described so far are not suitable for predictive purposes without considerable modifications. Nevertheless, planners have turned to interaction models of migration, in so far as predictive models are concerned, because of the goodness of fit obtained for total movements in empirical work; and also because some models can be specified in such a way that exogenous estimates of some of the independent variables — for example, distance and estimates of total population — can be fairly easily obtained for future dates. But the problem with most interaction models is that the gravity hypothesis works too well in empirical work and accounts for by far the greater part of the variation explained by extended models of the Lowry type. This is because these models, as specified at present, introduce variance through considering absolute numbers of migrants rather than migration rates, and then explain the differences by total size of population or employment and distance. Migration rates between areas would allow absolute differences to be ignored.

Policy models of migration

The chief drawback of simple gravity models of migration is that they are descriptive. As far as planning is concerned they do not provide a policy model. A plan is a statement of some future end-state (usually occurring at a fixed point in time), which is regarded as a desirable objective, coupled with a statement of policies aimed at its achievement. Goals and targets need to be clearly understood before any modelling begins, since they play a large part in its specification. This is a two-way process, however, for until the planners fully appreciate the capabilities of the forecasting procedures they may use, they will not know what kind of information may be available to them or how far it can be trusted. Planning in the broadest sense has been defined by Hall (1970) as 'an ordered sequence of operations, designed to lead to the achievement of either a single goal or to a balance between several goals'. Migration might, therefore, be thought of, following the theory of economic policy developed by Tinbergen (1955 and 1956), as forming part of a welfare objective of the policy maker, which is a function of target variables (or goals which are to be purposefully, though indirectly, influenced by the policy maker) and instrument variables (the means available to the policy maker). A quantitative model sets up the statistical or empirical relationships essentially between the target variables (goals) and the instrument variables (means available to planner or government to influence certain goals); the set of boundary conditions or constraints on the target; the data (variables not subject to control by the policy maker); and the irrelevant variables (side effects in which the policy maker is not interested). With such a system as this, the policy maker and the planner can alter the value of the instrument variables under their control, and determine the effects on migrations and the rest of the economic system if this is included. The effects of distance and intervening opportunities on migration are really a function of employment, information, income, investment and other variables, and it is these that the planner is interested in and the policy maker has some control over, through government spending, investment, taxes, statutory instruments and administrative directives.

Planners have not developed adequate models of migration in space and time, have confined their attention to aggregates (usually total population) and considered only the characteristics of areas, while no attempt has been made to include policy instruments. Migration is determined by two basic sets of variables: the characteristics of individuals and the characteristics of areas. To date, two types of models have been developed which include some of the above characteristics and which are amenable to further development. Price (1959) constructed a descriptive simulation model to assess the probability of an individual moving from one area to another area. Greenwood (1973) used a simultaneous equations model to study the interaction between urban economic growth and migration. Both these models allow the specification of migration as a function of the employment opportunities, income and characteristics of the areas of origin and destination, and in addition they allow these latter variables to be specified in terms of the effect of migration on them and to change as a result of migration.

The probability of an individual I_i moving from one area A_j to another area A_k was specified, by Price (1959), to be a function of

$$P\{I_i\, A_j\, A_k\} = f(A, B, C, D) + f(X, Y, Z) + f\{(A, B, C, D)(X, Y, Z)\}$$

where $f(A, B, C, D)$ is the individual's proclivity to migrate,
$f(X, Y, Z)$ is the selection of a desirable area in relation to the individual's own place of residence, and
$f\{(A, B, C, D)(X, Y, Z)\}$ symbolises the interactions between an individual's characteristics and the characteristics of his own and other areas for four characteristics of individuals and three areas

Individual characteristics are those such as colour, age, sex, marital status and employment status. The probability that a selected individual will migrate is then modified according to the characteristics of the area in which he lives. The probability of migrating is partitioned into parts for the different possible destinations. Factors used in partitioning the probability are derived from certain characteristics of the places of destination, such as population, contiguity, and type of movement (rural–urban, urban–urban, central city–suburban and so on).

Price developed his model as

$$P(I_i\, A_j\, A_k) = \{e_1(A_i) + e_2(B_i) + e_3(C_i) + e_4(D_i)\} +$$

$$\{f_1(X_j) + f_2(Y_j) + f_3(Z_j)\} +$$

$$\{g_1(X_k) + g_2(Y_k) + g_3(Z_k)\} +$$

$$\{h_1(X_j - X_k) + h_2(Y_j - Y_k) + h_3(Z_j - Z_k)\}$$

where e functions relate to the individual's tendency to migrate,
f functions are those relating to migratory push,
g functions relate to pull, and
h functions relate to the path of migration.

From this it would be possible to select the variables to be used, and set about evaluating the functional relationships. After the relationships of the characteristics of the individual to migration were determined, the effects of the place of residence characteristics on migration could be ascertained, and so on.

Price proposed to evaluate his model by collecting information on the basic probabilities of migration and on the characteristics of each state in the USA. A sample of the population of the USA, having the same characteristics and same distribution of residence as the whole population, was also proposed. The first individual in the sample would be selected and, on the basis of the characteristics of that individual and his place of residence, a probability of migration would be computed. This probability would then be partitioned into probabilities that he would migrate to each of the other states in the USA. On the basis of a random-number table, a person would be assigned to a migration status, then to a particular state and area, again using random numbers. This would be repeated for all in the population, and new population totals and state characteristics would be recomputed for the second trial and subsequent trials, on the basis of any net migration which had occurred in the preceding period. Demographic rates could also be used; for example, the population aged by the length of the trial period, marriages, births and deaths taking place. Projected changes in the characteristics of areas could be introduced into the model in order to ascertain their effects on migration.

Although Price's model never became operational, Beshers (1967) developed a similar model, which was used to aid migration research. The main program of Beshers' operational model included a birth component, a death component, a migration by social mobility component, and two feedback subroutines which allowed the probabilities of migration and social mobility to be updated. One feedback routine took account of past history and the other took account of present overflows. The main program was designed as a nonstationary Markov process incorporating cohort features. The major loops in the program incremented calendar time and a separate loop incremented age (of population). Input options were initial population distributions by area and age; transition probabilities by state and age; birth probabilities by age and state; death probabilities by age and area; rules for updating birth and death probabilities; rules for updating transition probabilities by age and area; and updating transition probabilities in the light of constraints on distribution, including updating constraints. These latter two updating options are the most crucial for migration and have received most attention in Beshers' model. They essentially represent the lagged feedback phenomenon so characteristic of migration. New migration probabilities are calculated as a function of the old probabilities and on the basis of the experience of migrants and the new age distribution of the population by area. In this way learning and differential distribution of information is included in the model. Additionally, constraints can operate and affect the new probabilities; for example, by specifying some maximum level of population in an area, the transition probabilities are altered so that this level is not exceeded. Migration can also be made responsive to labour markets – job supply and career prospects; or housing markets – availability, type and so on.

Such a model has interesting applications for policy. Parameter changes can be made and the response determined in time and/or in related variables. Alternative policies can be tried as well as alternative tactics for implementing them. Initially a regression-type model needs to be developed to yield some of the required probabilities in the model.

Population projections and estimates should take into consideration future economic developments and changes: population should be considered simultaneously with other socio-economic variables and not in isolation. Once planners start thinking in these terms they stand a better chance of producing probabilistic-causal, as opposed to purely predictive, models. Gravity and intervening-opportunity models can be predictive, but express no causal relationships. Demographers too, have concentrated on cohort-survival models to the detriment of relating population and migration to other variables of which they are a function and to which they themselves contribute. A simultaneous equation system has many advantages, from both a theoretical and practical viewpoint, in analysing migration in relation to other socio-economic variables. The advantages of using a simultaneous equations system in population studies in planning work has already been documented (Willis, 1972b). It allows migration or the dependent variable to be influenced by economic, social and demographic factors, and these various factors are in turn allowed to be influenced by the migration that occurs. Such a model is also likely to produce more unbiased estimates of the coefficients of parameters affecting migration, and improve model specification. Greenwood (1973) developed a model of this type to examine the interaction of urban economic growth and migration. Here migration is related to other variables that cause migration — wage levels, unemployment and so on — endogenous variables in which the planner is also interested. Greenwood's model took the form

$$OM = f_1(IM, \Delta INC, \Delta EMP, \Delta UNEMP, INCB, UNRB, CLFB, EDUB, AGEE, e_1);$$

$$IM = f_2(OM, \Delta INC, \Delta EMP, \Delta UNEMP, INCB, UNRB, CLFB, e_2);$$

$$\Delta INC = f_3(OM, IM, \Delta EDU, \Delta GOVT, DEW, DNS, e_3);$$

$$\Delta EMP = f_4(OM, IM, NATINC, INCB, \Delta EDU, \Delta GOVT, DEW, DNS, e_4);$$

$$\Delta UNEMP = f_5(OM, IM, NATINC, DEW, DNS, e_5);$$

$$\Delta CLF \equiv \Delta EMP + \Delta UNEMP;$$

$$NATINC \equiv \Delta CLF + OM - IM;$$

where the endogenous variable

OM is gross out-migration between t and $t + 1$; *IM* is gross immigration between t and $t+1$; ΔINC is income change in the period; ΔEMP is the employment change; $\Delta UNEMP$ is the unemployment change; ΔCLF is the civilian labour force change; and $NATINC$ is the natural increase of the civilian labour force;

and the exogenous variable

$INCB$ is the base-period (t) median income of residents in the area; $UNRB$ is the unemployment rate at time t; $CLFB$ is the civilian labour force at time t; $EDUB$ is the median number of school years completed by persons over 25 years of age at time t; $AGEE$ is the median age of the population at time $t+1$; ΔEDU is the change in education between t and $t+1$ school years completed by the population; $\Delta GOVT$ is the change in local government expenditure between t and $t+1$; DEW and DNS are regional dummy variables; and e_i are random errors.

Out-migration is assumed to be a function of in-migration, income, unemployment rate, employment, education and age and change in income, employment and unemployment. In-migration is hypothesised as a function of out-migration, income, unemployment and employment rates, and the change in income, employment and unemployment. Usually planners only consider net migration, whereas demographers have long recognised the necessity of utilising gross in- and out-migration, since the impact of migration on the receiving and sending communities depends upon the characteristics of the movers. In- and out-migrants to and from any given locality are not likely to be identical and in some instances may not even be similar; and, more important, the variables which explain in-migration may not be relevant in explaining out-migration. The use of gross migration figures allows for differences in the determinants of migration and also allows for differences in the consequences of migration that occurs.

Since the model is a simultaneous equations model, ordinary least squares (OLS) is an inappropriate estimation technique (see Chapter 8). OLS assumes that the independent variables explain or influence migration in the models, but are not in turn themselves influenced by migration. Greenwood uses three-stage least squares to estimate his migration system, since some of the equations are over-identified. Both two-stage least squares (2SLS) and three-stage least squares (3SLS) (see Chapter 8) are appropriate for systems estimation. Simultaneously estimating a system, in simplest terms, involves using 2SLS to estimate each equation in the system — one at a time. 2SLS can be interpreted as a transformation using all exogenous variables in the system as instruments followed by the application of Generalised Least Squares (Wonnacott and Wonnacott, 1970). 3SLS involves applying exactly this same procedure to estimate simultaneously all equations in the systems, rather than just one. But the whole point of using 3SLS is to take account of the observed correlation in errors between equations. When there is no such correlation, it can be shown that 3SLS reduces to a set of 2SLS estimates. Since Greenwood did not bother to inquire into the equation disturbances on this point, his declared preference for 3SLS over 2SLS may merely have meant using a more complex method to obtain the same results as 2SLS.

However, the results are worthy of note. The study shows that in-migration of civilian labour force members causes not only a greater employment growth in urban areas (a 1 per cent increase in in-migration induces a 0·232 per cent increase in employment change in metropolitan areas of the United States), but also induces greater income growth in these areas. In-migration is concomitant with urban growth but, in addition, migration of the civilian labour force is influenced by the growth of employment opportunities. A 1 per cent increase in change of employment results in a 2·843 per cent increase in in-migration. The process of economic growth in urban areas is, therefore, self-reinforcing through economic multiplier effects. Greenwood also found that out-migration did not encourage greater income growth such that regional incomes were narrowed through interregional migration. This is clearly contrary to the hypothesis of neo-classical economists (discussed in Chapter 2), that interregional out-migration would eventually restore regional equilibrium and obviate the need for further out-migration. To the extent that out-migration does influence income growth, it appears to depress such growth, as well as depressing employment growth. A 1 per cent increase in out-migration induces a $-0·224$ per cent change in employment and a $-0·23$ per cent change in income. However, out-migration does tend to relieve unemployment in sending localities in the United States – a 1 per cent increase in out-migration inducing a $-0·399$ per cent change in the unemployment rate. Greenwood's study clearly indicates that while migration is a function of the unemployment rate, education, age and so on, at the beginning of the period over which migration is measured,[3] migration influences income, employment and unemployment levels at the end of the period.

Greenwood's model is a cross-section model, which is unfortunate since, for purposes of planning, concerning itself with future events, a time series model would have been more appropriate. A cross-section model contains at least one equation supposed to be valid for each of several different individuals or geographical regions or the like, and is intended to be used in connection with data describing socio-economic features of these individuals or regions. A time-series model regards all of a certain set of time intervals (e.g. years) as describable by a single general set of equations. The equations are supposed to be valid without changes in form or parameters during each of several different (in practice, usually consecutive) time periods, and intended to be used in connection with data describing socio-economic events in these time periods. If data had been made available for several time periods from $t = 1$ to $t = T$, T distinct pure cross-section models, each one applying to a single period, could have been determined. But this would have advanced the application very little as far as planning is concerned. Since planners are interested in future events, a time-series model or a mixed time-series–cross-sectional model is required, in which the required parameters (coefficients of regression), are assumed to be constant over all periods considered.

The variables in cross-section and time models fall into the following types:
(a)   those that vary from one individual or region to another, but do not change or change very slowly with time – demographic variables such as social class, occupation, and educational level of population over 25 years of age;
(b)   those that vary with time but are the same for all individuals or regions at any one time, such as prices, costs of moving, and macro variables such as total income, investment and taxation;
(c)   those that vary with time and from one area or individual to another, such as income and employment.
Variables of type (a) are pure cross-sectional variables and those of type (b) pure time-series variables. Pure cross-section variables are usually exogenous and mixed variables of type (c) are endogenous. The decision whether to use cross-section or time-series models or both (mixed models) depends in practice partly on the nature of the data available under the above types, and partly on the objectives of the study in question. For planning purposes a time-series or mixed model would appear most applicable, especially for predictive uses. The most fortunate situation is one in which data are available individually for a number of areas over a span of time, so that changes in the behaviour of each area and of the group can be traced over time, and differences among units can be studied at any one time.

With the quinquennial census on change of residence, quinquennial surveys of income (Inland Revenue, 1972), and other time-series–cross-sectional data on unemployment and so on, it should be possible in Britain to build a mixed model (cross-section–time-series) of migration or more exactly, residential redistribution for 1961–66, 1966–71, 1971–76 and subsequent periods. Alternatively, other migration data sources which form a continuous time series could be used — electoral rolls, for example. In this type of model lagged variables, x_{it-1}, could be introduced, making the model dynamic in a temporal sense.

Chapter 2 has shown that migration operates within occupations systems so that any model of migration would best be formulated in these terms. It should be capable of explaining occupational migration between areas over time and levels of occupation transfer on migration to other competing occupations and for industries. A simple model might be of the agricultural labour market:

$$\Delta Sa_{it-1, t} = f(Wa_{it-1}, \Delta Wa_{it-1, t}, Wc_{it-1}, \Delta Wc_{it-1, t}, Uc_{it-1}, \Delta Uc_{it-1}, Aa_{it-1}, EDa_{it-1}, \sum_i P_{jt-1, t}, \sum_j P_{jt-1, t}, R_{it-1}, e_i)$$

$$Da_{it} = f(Wa_{it}, Pa_{it-1}, Pm_{it}, T_{it}, e_i)$$

$$P_{ijt-1, t} = f(DUa_{ijt-1}, \Delta DUa_{ijt-1, t}, Wa_{it-1}, Wa_{jt-1}, \Delta DWa_{ijt-1, t}, Wc_{jt-1}, CLF_{it-1}, EDa_{it-1}, Aa_{it-1}, \Delta Wc_{jt-1, t}, e_i)$$

$$P_{jit-1, t} = f(DU_{jit-1}, \Delta DU_{jit-1}, Wa_{jt-1}, Wa_{it-1}, \Delta DW_{ajit-1, t}, CLF_{it-1}, e_i)$$

$$Wa_{it} = f(Da_{it} - Sa_{it}), \Delta RPI_t, PROFa_{it}, UNa_{it}, NWPa_t$$

where

P_{ij} is the number of people moving (out) from area i to area j, corrected for size and shape of areas in time period $t-1$ to t

P_{ji} is in-migration into area i from areas j, corrected for size and shape in time $t-1$ to t

Wa_i is the wage rate in agriculture in area i

Wc is the wage rate in the construction industry — a high proportion of the inter-industry movement of agricultural workers is with the construction industry (Whitby, Robins, Tansey and Willis, 1974)

Uc is the relative unemployment rate in construction industry to the general unemployment rate. Migration between two areas is related to unemployment in area i, relative to that in area j to which people are moving, relative to unemployment in the remaining areas. That is, migration is dependent on the conditions in the two areas and conditions elsewhere — on opportunities and intervening opportunities

DUa_{ij}	is the difference between the relative unemployment rate in agriculture between area i and area j
$\Delta DWa_{jit-1}, t$	is the change in difference between the agricultural wage rate in area j and area i between $t-1$ and t
Sa_{it}	is the supply of agricultural labour in area i at time t
Da_{it}	is the demand for agricultural labour in area i at time t
Aa_i	is the median age of the agricultural labour force in area i
ED	is the educational structure
R	denotes regional zero–one variables
P_a	is the index of agricultural prices
P_m	is the index of agricultural machinery inputs
T	is the time trend used as a proxy for productivity
ΔRPI	is the rate of change in the retail price and cost of living index
$PROF$	is the profits level
UN	is the degree of unionisation
NWP	denotes the national wages policy – zero–one dummy
CLF	is the civilian labour force activity rate
e	denotes random errors

Briefly, such a mixed model, which here is extended from a time-series supply-and-demand study of agricultural labour, states that the demand for agricultural labour is a function of the wage rate in agriculture, the price of agricultural machinery (capital), the price of farm products (goods) obtained in the previous year, and productivity. Change in the supply of agricultural labour over a time period depends upon wages in agriculture at the beginning of the period, and changes in wages during the period, the wage rate and unemployment rate in the construction industry at the beginning of the period and changes in these two rates during the period, plus in-migration and out-migration, regional dummies, age and education variables. The latter two variables are included because most recruits to agriculture are school leavers attaining the minimum school leaving age, while its greatest losses are from the 20–25 year age group (Heath and Whitby, 1970). Migration of agricultural labour between two areas, either to another job within agriculture or to a job outside agriculture, depends on unemployment differences between the two areas and change in the time period; wage earnings in agriculture in area i and area j at the beginning of the period and the change in the wage rates between the two areas during the time period; the wage rate obtainable by agricultural workers outside agriculture (i.e. in construction) and the change in the wage rate obtainable outside agriculture between area i and j from

$t-1$ to t; and the labour-force activity rate, and age and education structure of area i at $t-1$. In-migration is related to unemployment rate differences and changes; wages obtainable in agriculture in the two areas and changes in wages between the two areas over the time period; and the labour force activity rate. Wage rates are determined by the difference between supply and demand, and other variables justified on the basis of their influence on wage levels, independent of the forces determining labour supply and demand. Such variables considered relevant are the rate of change in the cost of living index, the level of agricultural profits, the level of unionisation in agriculture, and a dummy or zero–one variable for national wages policy.

This model is a dynamic time-series–cross-section model with demand, supply, in- and out-migration and wage rates as endogenous variables which can vary from one area and time period to the next. These are evaluated simultaneously and each can influence the other through the system over time. This model has not been evaluated in econometric terms, but it has potential application to planning in determining occupational migration not only over time, but also the rate between specific areas. Thus any change in exogenous variables over time and space will allow the spatial consequences of migration on population redistribution to be assessed, together with the areas which are likely to gain most and those origin areas which are likely to lose migrants as a consequence.

Conclusion

Despite much theoretical work on migration and analytical models – literary or mathematical – few planning applications of migration models in Britain have incorporated many of the general significant features. Only now are planning studies in academic institutions beginning to develop models which express many of the relevant features of theory, and which are related to unemployment, employment, income and growth – some of the major goals regional planners seek to influence. This situation has arisen because planners, in the past, have sought to analyse and interpret migration in isolation with other major variables – employment, unemployment, earnings and growth – which have themselves formed inputs to plans. There has been a general failure to realise and specify not only which variables influence migration and to what extent they do so, but also the extent to which, for instance, the changing employment level, itself caused by migration, influences and determines the level of migration. The next step is to identify policy instruments such as government expenditure and investment, national wages policy, aid to migrants and so on, and ascertain what can be inferred from the correlation between the effects of policy and the level of migration; that is, how far the correlation between the instrument and the target throws light on the effectiveness of policy. When the minimum variance strategy is used the correlation can be unity between the instrument variable (Ut) and the target variable (Zt), but it may be zero between Ut and Z_{t+1} in a lagged relationship (Peston, 1972). The danger of using cross-section models is that they are unrepresentative of the actual dynamic situation and the correlation coefficient may be zero in time-series models. The question remains of the extent to which the correlation between instrument and target variables provides information on the effectiveness of any policy adopted in practice. A perfectly successful migration policy may show zero correlation between changes in migration rates and the level of economic activity. This occurs in a situation where the correlation (R) between U_t and Z_{t+1} contains ranges where R is negative and the policy is not effective; R is negative and the policy is effective; R is positive and the policy is effective; R is positive and the policy is not effective (Peston, 1972).

Notes

[1] Regional Economic Planning Councils, created in 1965, are advisory bodies with one-third of members from local authorities, one-third from industry and trade unions and the remainder from prominent institutions in the regions.

[2] Regional Economic Planning Boards are comprised of civil servants — regional controllers of Transport, Housing and Planning and regional directors of the DOE, DTI, NAFF and Department of Employment. See Mackintosh (1968).

[3] Residence in 1960 compared to that in 1955.

7 Migration Data

Sources

Demographic methods are classifiable into three not necessarily mutually exclusive categories. These are:

(i) techniques through which data are collected;
(ii) techniques by which data are evaluated, adjusted, corrected or estimated;
(iii) techniques by which demographic data are analysed, including techniques of 'projection'.

Although this book is concerned mainly with the third category, with a statement of the theoretical and practical problems and theories requiring analysis and the major findings on migration, the results and appropriateness of techniques depend partly on the data under scrutiny. For this reason, this chapter is devoted to problems associated with data collection and adjustment.

Migration data can be utilised from two main sources: (i) a record system such as vital registration of births, marriages, deaths; continuous population registers; or the heterogeneous and increasingly vast system of records maintained in connection with a host of administrative tasks; and (ii) a field survey, which can be either a census or a special survey.

Parish registers provide historical record data up to 1838, when the Registrar General (England and Wales) took over the duty of recording births and deaths. This record system could be combined with the decennial census from 1801, which recorded, for the census day, details of the total population of every local administrative area, and the extent of net migration determined.

More recently, the vast systems of records maintained for administrative purposes have been used to provide data on gross migration. An early record system was the National Register set up in September 1939, by which every civilian possessed an identity card and a ration book. All moves and changes of residence, except temporary ones, had to be reported to the local registration office and the Food Office. The National Register ended with rationing. While data extracted from this record contained errors and biases, some useful analysis on the frequency of movement of migrants (Rowntree, 1957) was undertaken from it. In an earlier study by Newton and Jeffery (1951), national registration statistics were used to indicate gross in- and out-migration based on local authority areas, the volume of movement between localities, distance of moves to and from selected localities, and the age—sex structure of in- and out-migrants.

Prior to the cessation of the National Register, the National Health Service Executive Council's was created. This has provided a continuous population record since, but has never been used to provide information on migration. The NHS records each person who changes doctor and also records any change of address. The major objections to the use of this record system are the large under-representation of short-distance movement (changes of residence not requiring a change of medical practitioner), the fact that over 100 per cent of the population are registered with doctors, and the often considerable delay in leaving one area and registering with a doctor in another.

Electoral rolls have proved a popular sampling frame for migration, comparison of the list for one year being made with the preceding or succeeding list. The Social Survey estimates that the Electoral Registers are 96 per cent accurate, decreasing by ½ per cent each month after the qualifying date in October. The major disadvantage of the use of electoral information is its total exclusion of families which contain no electors. This error has decreased since the voting age was lowered to 18, but some migration of single persons takes place in the 16—18 year age group. The register may also contain temporary residents — owners of weekend cottages, businesses and so on. The use of electoral rolls is a tedious method of tracing migrants — necessitating the checking of additions to the list to determine whether these are in-migrants, voters coming of age, or existing residents previously excluded from the list. Names disappearing must be checked to determine whether the cause is the result of death, legal exclusion, failure to register or to have the name entered on the list, or out-migration. In the case of the latter, neighbours must be contacted to trace the destination of the out-migrant. Electoral rolls were used by House and Knight (1966) to study migration in the south Tyne in the sixties, and by the North Regional Planning Committee (1967) to identify in- and within-area migration.

The difficulty of tracing out-migrants remains the most serious limitation in the use of electoral rolls. This has led to the use of electricity board records to trace migrants, as almost 100 per cent of the population is now on a public supply system. It is a statutory requirement that notice should be given by a consumer leaving any premises. The meter is then read and a final account prepared and sent to the address to which the consumer has moved. This sampling frame was used by Rose (1958) in a study of distance of migration and socio-economic status of migrants; by the North Regional Planning Committee (1967) to gather data on out-movement from urban sub-regions in the North; and by the Standing Conference of Local Planning Authorities, Yorkshire and Humberside Region (1973) to study gross population movement — in, out and within the region and as a sampling frame for a questionnaire study of motives and reasons for migration. The chief deficiencies in this source of data are the exclusion of those on a pre-payment meter and the few households who do not have electricity. In 1966 in the North Eastern Electricity Board area, it was estimated that 83·7 per cent of households were covered by the final accounts system. The chief omissions are households (often individuals) in bedsitters on pre-payment meters — these are likely to be young people with a high probability of moving; and quasi households — families living with parents or in-laws; or those moving immediately upon marriage.

Other data sources have been used to analyse migration in Britain. Department of Employment annual estimates of interregional migration of employees was used by Oliver (1964) to explore the relationship of migration to the relative regional unemployment rates. This source has now been discontinued owing to increasing inaccuracies due to firms centralising the exchange of employment insurance cards. Data on particular sections of the population are more difficult to acquire, but have been used chiefly to look at occupational migration. Davies (1966) used the ratio of the number of job applications of medical practitioners to the number of job vacancies under the National Health Service to derive areas of latent migration potential — areas to which doctors would probably have moved in a free market economy if they had been allowed to set up their own practices. Trade union records have also been used as a sampling frame to derive information on the migration of particular occupation types (Willis, 1972a). Of course union coverage of a particular occupation can vary and does not provide 100 per cent membership except in cases of medical practitioners, architects, planners and the like, where job employment requires membership of a semi-legal official institute or association, or in unions which operate a 'closed shop'. This type of source has the advantage of identifying characteristics (occupation, age and so on) without requiring a questionnaire survey, or before a survey to determine migration takes place.

Some of the sources of migration data cited and used have been a variety of attempts to develop and utilise new sources of data which permit a longitudinal approach to the analysis of migration. Most of these efforts have been directed towards developing sources which embody the advantages inherent in the continuous population registers maintained by a number of countries, particularly in Europe — Norway, Sweden, Denmark and Holland (Thomas, 1938; United Nations Economic and Social Council, 1962; and Van Den Brink, 1954), but also in Japan. Like many sources of data their coverage varies as a result of the different national and administrative purposes and functions for which they are designed. The compilation and publication of migration data are not the sole purpose of maintaining population registers. In Japan population registers are used for security reasons, political elections, school enrolment registers, social and health insurance registers and many other legislative and administrative purposes in local government and agencies (Kono, 1971). Some population registration systems are designed solely to establish personal identity, and within these systems data is limited to that on age, sex, name and place of birth. More usually the system requires personal identification in terms of (some if not all) changing characteristics, of place of residence, marital status, occupation and names of children. The geographical basis of the system also varies; some record files are centralised, others held according to the place of residence of birth or place of residence of the family head. Sweden's continuous population register system applies to each community (Thomas. 1941). Every resident of Sweden is required to be registered and every resident is registered at any given time in only one community, residence being determined by fixed regulations and rules which give the individual a certain degree of freedom of choice. The registers are kept by pastors of the State Church in their function as civil servants. The basic register is a so-called community or parish book which is checked every year by a canvass and revised after each decennial census. Residents are registered in household groups. For each member information is given, as well as many other subjects, on surname and first names, sex, family status, birthplace and birth date, civil status, religious affiliation, nationality and citizenship, occupation, address in the community and place of previous residence if an in-migrant from another Swedish community or an immigrant from a foreign country. Changes affecting the status of a resident are recorded as they occur or when reported. Changes affecting the size of the population are always recorded in separate books before entries are made in the community book. These books are of births, deaths, in-migrants and out-migrants. In the books on births and deaths, births to resident mothers and deaths among residents are recorded, and notes are also made of other births and deaths occurring in the community. People presenting migration certificates from other Swedish communities (in-migrants) or who arrive from foreign countries (immigrants) with the intention of becoming residents are recorded in the in-migrant book. The out-migrant book lists residents who have taken out a migration certificate and subsequently departed from the community (out-migrants and emigrants). An out-migrant is not considered, however, until confirmation is received from his declared destination that he has taken up residence there. This system was introduced in the 1890s. The notification of pastors in communities of origin by pastors registering in-migrants, means, in theory, that out-migrants are numerically equal to in-migrants. From these various books tabulations are prepared each year for every community, but publication does not include details of factors involved in population change.

Despite some drawbacks, the continuous population register forms an important methodological concept and produces some useful statistics where they operate. Kono (1971) compared the results of measuring interprefectural and intraprefectural migration for a fixed period of one year from the data yielded by the 1960 Census of Japan with data from population registers for the same one year period. It is anticipated that registers, which record multiple moves, yield higher estimates than the census, which only records a single change of residence. On average, Kono found this to be true. At the national level, the two sources of data gave almost the same values for interprefectural migration, but significantly divergent estimates for intraprefectural migration. The prefectural distribution of the difference between the estimates revealed somewhat surprising and methodologically interesting results. The registration data for some of the prefectures showed a much smaller volume of migration than did the census data. The differences were larger for highly-urbanised and centrally-located prefectures than for remotely-located and less-industrialised prefectures. In addition to the provision of a time series of migration, the registration data are especially useful in providing information on gross migration and direction of migration; that is, information which is extremely useful in assessing general patterns of migration.

However, in proportion to its theoretical possibilities, this source has not supplied much data on migration. The data, as tabulated and published at present, have shown limited uses in the analysis of differential socio-economic and demographic characteristics of migrating and non-migrating persons. In theory, a continuous population register could produce valuable data, since a continuous system could collect up-to-date information, and since the register could facilitate the interaction of different types of data from various sources. Registration data has great potentialities for migration analysis. But Linder (1959) argues that no country has found a population register a satisfactory substitute for a periodic census, or system for registering vital statistics and monitoring international passenger movements for international migration.

Census data has and continues to be the most widely-used source of information on migration, both for calculating net migration (census survival rate methods) and exploring gross migration. Prior to 1961, early data on gross migration was limited to the analysis of present residence and birthplace (Friedlander and Roshier, 1966). The 1961 Census in Britain was somewhat of a landmark, by asking for the first time where each person had lived one year previously. This permitted gross population flows to be identified and determined between different areas. The 1966 and 1971 Censuses repeated this question, and in addition asked where a person was resident five years previously. But despite this recent phenomenal growth of information from the census on gross population flows, this information source continues to have grave disadvantages in the study of migration, although it is used with increasing frequency. In no sense does the census afford a longitudinal history, since other questions relate only to the census date. It is thus not possible to determine whether a job or occupational or marital change in status took place upon migration.

Moreover, as pointed out in a later section, even a complete migration count, as in the 1971 Census (although in most cases only a 10 per cent sample is processed), is only a sample of the cause-system underlying the migration. Continuing records are required at frequent time intervals to show changes and trends while they are taking place. If such records were available in Britain they would furnish more information on migration. The linking up of census questions for 1966 and 1971, on previous residence five years ago, is too wide an interval of time for anything conclusive to be drawn, and it overlooks moves within the time interval. The census questions concerning previous residence at a fixed point in time are more apposite to the study of population distribution than to that of migration: all moves are not recorded and the migration process is largely ignored. If data were available from special migration surveys on such things as individual residence histories, the scope for useful analysis of migration would be greatly enlarged.

Survey design

The problem of survey design initially centres around the type of variables to be measured — controlled or uncontrolled, dependent or experimental; factorial design and time-space design. Migration is a complex phenomena and it is rarely possible to deal with just one experimental variable and control all others. Survey design must ensure that the information collected is in a suitable form, or factorial design, so that comparisons can be made for each factor in turn and then for their various combinations and interactions. That is, the factorial design must be such for migration that it enables the study of several experimental variables in combination. Not only does this provide us with more information, but also with greater confidence in predicting the results under various circumstances. The various types of analysis suitable, whether analysis of variance or factor analysis are chiefly applicable to quantitative variables on an ordinal or interval scale, whereas many migration surveys have gathered information on a qualitative level merely on a nominal scale.[1] This problem will be returned to later in the measurement attitudes.

A cross-sectional survey design does not reveal anything about cause-and-effect relationships: it can only provide information about correlates. In an effort to overcome this, longitudinal or before-and-after designs have been developed. It has already been suggested that it is essential in migration and related studies that a longitudinal design be employed. Longitudinal survey designs have been pioneered by Taeuber (1968) in the United States. Such a design was employed in an analysis of smoking habits and cancer. The high urban—rural ratio of lung cancer risk has led investigators to consider the role of differential rates of cigarette smoking and speculate upon the role of air pollution in causing cancer (Taeuber 1968). The underlying rationale for these efforts is that the migration of human populations can be thought of as an unplanned experiment of nature. Longitudinal analysis is necessary to compare the morbidity and mortality experience of natives and migrants residing in the same areas and provide a study tool with which to assess the relative contributions of host and environmental factors in specific diseases. The problems posed for investigation in the US cancer survey required the classification of individuals with respect to their residence histories. Longitudinal histories provide a potential reference source for demographers engaged in the study of migration, and for planners concerned with community development or the direction of health and social welfare programmes, in addition to their use as baseline control data for planning epidemiological studies.

It is not possible, however, to attribute all the before-and-after differences to the effects of the variable under investigation until it is certain that without it such changes would not have occurred. With the passage of time and the introduction of new events, some differences may occur which cannot be attributed to the experimental variable. It is, therefore, necessary to have, in addition to the experimental group, a matched control group. This was used by House and Knight (1967) in investigating pit closure and mobility. The function of the control group is to show what would have happened to the experimental group if it had not been subjected to the experimental variable.

Decisions concerning the main and auxiliary methods of data collection, such as interviews, mail questionnaires and observational techniques, have to be made as well as the method of approach to the respondents (after selection through sampling procedures), including stated purpose of the research, confidentiality and anonymity. In a longitudinal approach, the documentation of decisions and attitudes tips the scales in favour of interview schedules rather than mail questionnaires in migration surveys. The great advantage of the interview in the hands of a skilled interviewer is its flexibility. The interviewer can make sure that the respondent has understood the question and the purpose of the research, and make ratings or assessments of attitudes, dwelling areas and so forth. The richness and spontaneity of information collected by interviewers is higher than that which a mailed questionnaire can hope to obtain. The chief advantage of the mail questionnaire is its cheapness, since it does not require a trained staff of field workers (who may also incur considerable travel and maintenance expenditure). Another advantage is that often a much larger sample can be covered for the same cost. But eliminating the interviewer means that the questionnaire has to be much simpler and that no additional explanations can be given and no probes requested. A mail questionnaire cannot hope to cover people of low intelligence or of very limited educational background. The greatest disadvantage of mail questionnaires, however, is the fact that they usually produce very poor response rates. The important point about these poor response rates is not the reduced size of the sample, which could easily be overcome by sending out more questionnaires, but the possibility of bias. This is because the returns are almost invariably not representative of the original sample drawn. Non-response is not a random process; it has its own determinates which vary from survey to survey. This is discussed later in the chapter with reference to migration data in the US census. To study response bias, the return data of every questionnaire must be known, since it has been found that respondents who send in their questionnaire very late are roughly similar to non-respondents. The presence of bias and the method of its introduction can be determined by comparing respondents with non-respondents on the original sampling list, or by comparing early respondents with late respondents in terms of their answers to the questionnaire.

Questionnaire and response problems

A great deal of effort has gone into questionnaire design among social scientists. Little of the information acquired and general principles established has been applied to migration questionnaires adopted for special *ad hoc* surveys. Response has, as a consequence, varied, but it has never been really high.

Oppenheim (1966) outlined three main problems of questionnaire design, after the type of survey — interview schedules or mail questionnaire — has been decided; the build-up of question sequences and the order of questions and other techniques within the framework of the questionnaire; the order of questions within each question — funneling, factual versus attitudinal opening; and the use of precoded versus free-response questions.

It is generally acknowledged that questionnaires must be attractive and interesting to the respondent, commencing with some easy and impersonal questions and not asking for details like age, family, occupation and so forth until rapport has been well established. Both the North Regional Planning Committee (1967) in its survey of mobility, and the Standing Conference of Local Planning Authorities, Yorkshire and Humberside Region (1973) in its migration study, avoided staccato questions such as age, occupation and marital status until the middle or end of the questionnaire. The former asked for views and reasons why respondents had moved before asking factual questions, and the response rate obtained was 70 per cent for a postal questionnaire. In contrast the questionnaire used by University College, London (Robinson, 1971), in its Housing and Mobility Survey, plunged immediately into factual questions on age, marital status, work status, qualifications, exact nature of job, details of housing including price, mortgage repayments and rent, income and so on, before moving on to more general and impersonal questions. If such a questionnaire were postal, the response rate would probably be low, but personal interview methods often raise this. Nevertheless, question sequences like those proposed by the UCL Housing and Mobility Survey are not likely to produce a helpful attitude on the part of the respondent.

All questions are either 'open' or 'closed'. A closed question is one in which the respondent is offered a choice of alternative replies. This was the method adopted by the Standing Conference of Local Planning Authorities, Yorkshire and Humberside Region, for nearly all questions, and also that adopted by Gerger (1966) in a study of migration associated with Vastervik in Sweden. The questionnaire employed in the latter study used closed questions with strict alternative answers offered on all questions elicited.

Closed questions in both these surveys were attitudinal as well as factual. The alternatives offered when asking questions on stimuli to migration or attitudes are very much part of the question and should be reported as such, for they guide the respondent's answers. The fact that this method directs the respondent's thoughts does not of itself make the questions in these surveys invalid or worthless. But, it is advisable to be aware of the method in interpreting the results. Closed questions are quicker and easier to answer than open questions and for this reason are generally more suitable where surveys are postal, as with the Standing Conference of Local Authorities, Yorkshire and Humberside Region, and the survey of business managers by House et al. (1968). Closed questions are often cruder and less subtle than open ones and the opportunity to probe is lost. The chief advantage of the open question is the freedom that it gives to the respondent. Once he has understood the intention of the question, he can let his thoughts roam freely, unencumbered by a prepared set of replies. This can give rise to a risk, in an interview or a reply, that what will be obtained is not so much a rounded and full account of the respondent's feelings, but rather just what happens to be uppermost in his mind at the time. Free−response questions are often easy to ask, difficult to answer and still more difficult to analyse. Answers, however, have a richness and quality not found in closed questions. Free−response and open questions were used, almost exclusively, by the North Regional Planning Committee (1967), Jansen (1968) and Willis (1970) in determining stimuli to migration and attitudes. For free responses, Lazarsfeld (1955) has outlined the questionnaire requirements, namely a good classification system of

(i) articulation − classification and questions to proceed in steps from the general to the specific, so that material can be examined in terms of detailed categories or broad groupings, whichever are the more appropriate for a given purpose;

(ii) logical correctness − in an articulate set of categories those on each step must be exhaustive and mutually exclusive;

(iii) adaptation to the structure of the situation − classification should be based on a comprehensive outline of the situation as a whole, an outline containing the main elements and processes in the situation, which it is important to distinguish for purposes of understanding, predicting or in policy-making;

(iv) adaptation to the respondent's frame of reference − classification should present as clearly as possible the respondent's own definition of the situation, his focus of attention and his categories of thought.

There are fairly standard types of structural schemes which have been developed in applied research for use in standard situations. In migration four schemes have been used, namely

(i) push-pull scheme used to study movement from *A* to *B*;
(ii) attributes—motives—influences scheme, used in the classification of reasons — motives of the individual, his attributes and attitudes;
(iii) technical properties—resulting gratification, used in assimilation studies in migration;
(iv) underlying reasons—precipitating cause scheme — used in classifying answers to the question, 'why did you move?' and 'why did you move at that point in time?'

The push—pull scheme was that adopted by the North Regional Planning Committee study, and the attributes—motives—influences scheme by House et al. (1968) in a survey of business managers and, more successfully, by Jansen in a sociological study of migration centred on Bristol. It is also important to adapt to the respondent's frame of reference. In giving reasons for moving a migrant may take some reasons for granted and not express them.

Reason analysis presents many problems in migration studies. A field operation involved in reason analysis consists essentially in asking respondents why they moved. Although this may seem a simple question, it is not feasible to ask it directly. A general 'why' question has been found to produce a congeries of answers as to why migrants move house. Rossi (1954), in a review of the problem, stated that some respondents answer in terms of the event which 'triggered' the move; others say why they moved to a particular area; still others answer with reference to changes that took place within their households (life-cycle changes), and so on. In one survey the question 'why did you move' was answered by 46 per cent in terms of the characteristics of their former home, by 26 per cent in terms of the new home, and by 5 per cent in terms of life-cycle changes. In the remainder of cases the decision was not the respondent's.

Migration questionnaires have not always adhered to this fundamental distinction and this has detracted from the value of results. Gerger (1966) separated reasons for moving into employment—income, housing, education, family—friends contact and amenity reasons, and attempted to assess the relative importance of each type. Within each of these groups, the alternative choices given in the closed questions as reasons incorporated both complaints about the old area and attractive features of the area of destination. It is not possible, therefore, to distinguish clearly in the migration process the decision to move and the decision to move to Vastervik, since only one reason could be chosen. The fact that a respondent answered in terms of his new area does not mean that his move did not involve important dissatisfactions with his old home area, and the fact that he interpreted the question in that fashion may only mean, at best, that he gave more emphasis to the attractions of the new area than to complaints about the old. We need to know not only what the respondent found attractive enough about his new residence area to move to it, but also what complaints led to the decision to contemplate moving and so on. House et al. (1968) posed business managers the question 'Please indicate your principal reason(s) for moving into the region' and offered as alternatives in the closed question reasons such as voluntary change of employment, marriage, family and personal ties, which left the choice to the respondent as to whether these reasons were complaints of the area of origin or specific factors of attraction to the North. This distinction between characteristics of the area of origin and characteristics of the area of destination are rarely distinguished explicitly by a migrant, even with a carefully worded question. The solution to this problem lies in a verbal explanation and an interview.

To account adequately for the respondent's action and structure of the situation, Rossi devised an accounting scheme for residential mobility. This consisted of

(i) complaints of previous dwelling and area, changing family structure, aspirations and values;
(ii) barriers to movement;
(iii) precipitants—events which permit or facilitate translation of complaint into action;
(iv) specifications—attributes of new home and area which the migrant is desirous of obtaining;
(v) attractions—features of the new home which made that dwelling and area more desirable than others considered;
(vi) information sources—means by which the new residence and area were brought to the migrant's attention.

All compaints and attractions were assessed by Rossi in terms of coverage, impact and effectiveness.

The problem of impact is important in migration. The whole population is exposed to many common stimuli to move, yet the impact varies between people and this determines effectiveness—the resulting number of migrants. Reasons for moving can be disaggregated into stimuli for the move (income, environmental conditions) and an attitude – the state of readiness or tendency to act or react in a certain manner when confronted with a certain stimuli. Gerger tried to measure the impact and importance of various stimuli in determining migration to Vastervik in Sweden. In Britain, attempts to measure the impact of complaints and attractions in migration have been limited. Wilkinson and Merry (1965) merely measured attitudes to moving on a nominal scale. House et al. (1968) and House and Thomas (1968) tried to derive ordinal rankings of reasons for moving. Knowledge of migration has not been advanced by asking such questions as the Standing Conference of Local Authorities, Yorkshire and Humberside, did, as follows: 'Please tick any factors which prompted you to move of your own choosing from the general area in which you previously lived'. Such a question provides no indication of the order of importance of each factor nor the strength of each stimuli or attitude. With every amenity or disamenity the individual has a strain—stress relationship (that is, the degree to which the migrant or his attitude is affected) providing an elasticity of environmental response.

Almost all migration surveys concerned with reasons for moving or attitudes to moving have not used interval scales of measurement. This raises the general problem of the interpretation of the results when objective assessments are wanted. It is dangerous to give such labels as 'frequently', 'moderately', 'often', 'occasionally', and so on to different grades, since they can be interpreted differently by different raters. Migration surveys should be more objective and try to measure reasons and attitudes for moving while adhering to the principles of scaling measurements. These have been outlined by Oppenheim (1966). Scales should exhibit unidimensionality or homogeneity, linearity and equal intervals or equal appearing intervals, reliability and consistency, validity and reproductibility. A score on an attitude scale might show, by means of a single figure which statements the respondent agreed with and which he disagreed with, revealing his place on the attitude continuum. Some attitude pools are, of course, not amenable to this kind of cumulative or progressive scaling — partly because they may not be unidimensional. But the majority of aspects of migration are amenable to the application of psychological scaling methods; for example, Likert's procedure for studying attitude patterning and exploring theories of attitudes, Guttman's method for studying attitude change and the hierarchical structure of an attitude, and Thurston's procedure for group differences. The problem is one of selecting the method most relevant to the problem.

Questionnaire surveys have concentrated exclusively on retrospective studies to gather information, rather than on approaching potential migrants before moving, assessing their complaints, and after moving, the attractions of the area of destination. This can give rise, in migration surveys, to errors which are probably greater than those occurring in a factual census. In longitudinal surveys of migration and residence history in particular, the accuracy of retrospective surveys depends on memory, which can be capricious and selective (Cartwright, 1963; Douglas and Blomfield, 1956). The coverage of events and the accuracy in reporting them depends principally upon

(a) the nature of the event — changes of residence with dates are recalled much better than work histories;
(b) the significance of the event;
(c) length of period the respondent is asked to recall — accuracy and coverage fall-off with time past;
(d) (to a considerable extent) the individual concerned;
(e) the circumstances under which the respondent is questioned.

Research on the reliability of worker-response indicates that work histories obtained by personal interview are, by and large, reliable (Palmer, 1942; Keating and Stone).

It is not possible to make any precise estimate of the error attached to the recall of past events in migration surveys that have already been conducted, except that error is greater in the case of changes in job than changes in residence, and that it varies directly with the number of jobs an individual has had and inversely with the length of time each job is held. There is a tendency on the part of those who have held a large number of jobs, each for a short period, deliberately to exclude or fail to recall some jobs. This error can be kept small in an interview by emphasising to respondents the importance of recalling even short-period jobs. Willis (1970) made internal checks on the consistency of workers' answers. Data of birth and age/year at leaving school were checked against year of first job; and all jobs and residence time-lengths were cumulatively added and compared to the length of time the person had spent in the labour force. A high degree of reliability was found.

Questionnaire surveys can be improved with greater resources, but the fundamental question still remains of how accurate the data should be and how much it is worth.

Quality of data

All things considered, it is unquestionably true that migration is the least satisfactorily measured of the three components of population change: natality, mortality and movement. Error in the data, whether from a record system or a field survey, results mainly from coverage and response errors. Deming (1950) listed nineteen main sources of error common to both complete counts and samples. Briefly these are: failure to state the problem adequately and decide what statistical information is needed; failure of the questionnaire; failure to recognise different degrees of canvass and fit questions to these; failure to define the universe with enough precision to define the frame therefrom; faulty instructions and definitions; bias arising from non-response; bias arising from late returns; errors in response — voluntary or involuntary; accidental variations in response; bias in response arising from interviewer; bias in response arising from auspices; blunders of the interviewer; careless and disorganised field procedure; bias arising from an unrepresentative date for the survey or of the period covered; ineffectual tabulation plans, such as too many or too few class intervals; errors in processing (coding, editing, tabulating, calculating and so on); faulty publication or interpretation of results; random sampling errors; and sampling biases.

Error in coverage can arise even in data which aim at complete counts. The US Census estimated that the 1950 Census undercounted by between 1.5 and 3.5 per cent. Shryock (1964), in his detailed study of migration in relation to the US Census, revealed the type of errors that can occur. Bias can occur in answers, and this led, in the 1940 Census, to migrants from surburban areas giving the central city as their place of origin. Shryock was also able to show from US censuses that variations in the non-response rate tend to be postively associated with variations in the mobility rate. Persons with mobility status not reported are more likely to be mobile than those with mobility status reported. The post-enumeration survey for the 1950 US Census found that there was a much larger proportion of movers among this problem group. Groups with high mobility rates also tended to have a high non-response rate on mobility status. The US Census found that one of the disadvantages of a mobility period as short as one year was that the number of non-responses tended to be fairly large relative to the number of movers of various types. There is, therefore, more uncertainty about such things as differential mobility rates and whether true net migration is plus or minus.

The British Census is not without errors. Gray and Gee (1972) estimated that the error associated with the age of the population was 5.7 per cent in 1951, 5.9 per cent in 1961 and 3.6 per cent in 1966. The error tended to increase with older age groups. They also suggest that the correction factor for the number of five-year migrants in the 1966 Census was 1.04. It was difficult from the 1966 post-enumeration survey to establish firm evidence as to the reason for the error, from the question 'usual address five years ago'. Gray and Gee suggest that it may have resulted from the form-filler giving his former address for himself and then wrongly answering 'same' for the rest of the family. What the form-filler probably meant was that they were at the same address as he was five years ago, whereas the question specified 'same' to mean the same address as one year ago. This source of error appeared to be more important than memory errors in giving rise to wrong addresses one or five years previously.

Bias arose, in the 1961 Census, from instructions not being strictly followed by some enumerators. Since migration data in 1961 and 1971 was derived on a sample basis, it was also subject to sampling error. Comparison of the true standard error with that obtained on the assumption of simple random sampling in the 1961 Census, indicated that the latter underestimated the true standard error by

(a)   47 per cent of the value, assuming simple random sampling of people with more than five years duration of residence;
(b)   183 per cent of the value for migrants within local authority areas;
(c)   245 per cent for migrants into and out of local authority areas.

The reason for this underestimation of the true standard errors of the various types of migration data (which did not occur to the same extent for data on other census topics collected on a sample basis) seemed to be that the clustering effect was generally much stronger for migration than for other topics. If one member of a household was a migrant, the probability of other members of the household being migrants was high. This contrasted with occupation, where different members of a houshold were unlikely to have the same occupation.

Enumerative and analytical studies

Migration surveys fall into two classes: enumerative and analytical. The North Regional Planning Committee (1967) survey of within, in- and out-migration was primarily enumerative. It set out to provide some elementary data on migration, to discover the age, sex, marital status and occupational status of migrants, enumerate the main flows of migrants, and, also, discover the reasons for migration. The majority of migration studies, like Wilkinson and Merry (1965), House et al. (1968), Jansen (1968), Gerger (1966) and Willis (1972a), are analytical, to obtain information to regulate and predict the results of the cause system that has produced the universe. In an enumerative survey, a 100 per cent sample without replacement represents the totality of the information on this problem. The sampling variance reduces to zero as the size of the sample is increased to 100 per cent. In analytical studies, action is directed at underlying causes that have determined the frequencies of various classes and will govern frequencies in these classes in the future.

In analytical problems interest centres on the causes of patterns and variations that take place from year to year, or from area to area, or from class to class. The reason for studying causes is to learn to control them. Deming (1950) pointed out that, for such studies, even a complete count is still only a sample of the product of the underlying cause system. For analytical purposes a small sample taken at frequent time intervals, by showing trends and changes while they are taking place, will furnish much more information than would be furnished at about the same cost by a much larger sample or even a complete count taken at wide intervals of time. When using the census for analytical purposes, even though the figures come from a complete count,[2] it is necessary to bear in mind that small numbers or frequencies in a cell are unreliable, in the sense of having a standard error just as if they had arisen in sampling, as indeed they did.

Deming has shown, where the aim is analytic to estimate p and q in the supply, that the coefficient of variation of the estimate is $\sqrt{q/np}$ for a sample size n. For enumerative purposes a complete count possesses no error of sampling, but for analytical uses a complete count ($n = N$) still has a sampling error with a coefficient of variation equal to $\sqrt{q/Np}$. A complete count gives all the information the lot is capable of giving concerning p, and if this is not enough information, then other lots must be studied. The problem in these circumstances, frequently met in practice, is when supply is not constant from one lot to another; in effect p varies indiscriminately. Under these circumstances no prediction can be made about future lots or migration.

A 25 per cent sample from a universe has a coefficient of variation only twice the minimum, and a sample of one in 16 has a coefficient of variation only four times the minimum. If there were 50,000 migrants associated with an area in an interval of time and the expected emigration rate was 2.5 per cent, there would be 1,250 out-migrants. Even if a complete count was made of the 50,000 migrants in the time period, this lot must still be treated as a sample. The observed 1,250 out-migrants are subject to statistical variability with coefficient of variation

$$\sqrt{\cdot 975 / (\cdot 025 \times 50{,}000)}$$

or about 3 per cent. This corresponds to a 3 sigma error band of about

8 per cent. An increase or decrease in out-migration might, therefore, not be evident. Tabulations in finer groups, such as age or occupation groups, would be even less meaningful. For example, if n is the expected number of cases to fall in a certain cell, the coefficient of variation of this cell will be $\sqrt{q/np}$ and if np is 100 or lower, the coefficient of observed frequency will be 10 per cent or higher. Cell frequencies of less than 100 have a high relative error, yet they can nevertheless be useful. Thus, unless the migration rates between two groups are striking, information available from one census is not sufficient to point one way or the other.

Conclusion

The degree of accuracy required of data is relative, and a function of the use to which the data are put. It is important to assess validity, reliability and precision of the data. Valid conclusions can still be reached from deficient data by either restricting generalisations to propositions which may be regarded as valid because of demonstrably limited error in the data or by adjusting and correcting the data so as to reduce error and make it usable. The major criteria for evaluating a data collection system are the coverage, comparability and quality of data it produces. It is quite likely that differences in research design of migration surveys and studies have accounted for many of the differing conclusions reported by them.

Notes

[1] This is measurement at its weakest level and numbers 0 or 1 and other symbols are used simply to classify a person or object. Reasons are classified as 'work', 'environment', etc.

[2] Migration questions in 1971 Census were asked of all the population, though processing is on a 10% random basis.

8 Regression Techniques in Migration

Introduction

The use of regression techniques within the framework of migration analysis has become increasingly fashionable, many research workers feeling that these techniques give rise to some promise in the estimation of factors influencing migration. Despite all the work undertaken so far, little that is new has emerged; and many inconsistencies and contradictory conclusions have arisen. In view of the quality of the methods employed to date, it will be argued here that any firm definitive statement on migration conclusions from regression is questionable. That is not to say that studies of this kind are of no use. On the contrary, they do serve to highlight the main variables; albeit the remaining spectrum of possibilities is forbiddingly large. In this chapter the primary issue examined is the usefulness of ordinary regression models in their present form as an aid to migration analysis.

Regression techniques have been used mainly because the tabulation of published migration data, including census data, is such as to preclude any extensive cross-classification of variables, such as occupational migration by age, sex, industry etc., to eliminate the influence of each variable upon the other and to determine the importance of each in the migration stream. Regression techniques can be used to estimate the structure of migration without cross-classification of variables.

General model

Regression analysis provides a method of testing the hypothesis of which factors are associated with migration; an analysis of the relations between a single criterion measure and one or more predictor measures. Like correlation, it indicates if two variables move together, but additionally it also estimates how. The equation, by which the best fit of a set of observations is obtained by ordinary least squares (OLS), takes the form

$$Y = \hat{\alpha} + \hat{\beta}_1 X_1 + \hat{\beta}_2 X_2 + \hat{\beta}_3 X_3 \ldots \ldots \hat{\beta}_n X_n$$

Of the infinite number of functional relations that might be established between X and Y, the subset of possible linear relations represents a very simple and manageable collection, and those engaged in migration research have usually restricted their explorations to it. There are, of course, many other ways in which Y may depend on X and these will be discussed later.

The regression coefficients indicate the extent to which a unit change in each exogenous (explanatory) variable is associated with increases or decreases in migration rates. $\hat{\beta}_1$ estimates how Y is related to X_1 if $X_2 \ldots X_n$ were held constant. The least squares line is generally written

$$Y = \alpha + \beta X$$

but it has been renamed here to emphasise that $\hat{\alpha}$, is our estimator of α, and $\hat{\beta}$ our estimator of the true β. Ideally the distribution of $\hat{\beta}$ should be concentrated around β, as close to β as possible. Thus an estimator should be unbiased, efficient and consistent. An unbiased estimator is one that is, on the average, right on target. $\hat{\beta}$ is an unbiased estimator of β because its expected value is β based on a probability distribution. Given an unbiased estimator of the population mean μ, other desirable characteristics are efficiency and consistency. The distribution of an estimator $\hat{\theta}$ is efficient if it is highly concentrated; that is, has a small variance. And a consistent estimator is one that concentrates completely on its target as sample size increases indefinitely.

Although regression has been used in analysing migration for some time, there has been considerable variation in results from such studies of the quantitative structure of migration behaviour. This is partly due to the fact that ecological correlations have been widely used in geographic, demographic and economic work on migration, not because investigators were primarily interested in correlations between the properties of areas as such, but with the obvious purpose of discovering something about the behaviour of individuals. Ecological correlations have been used simply because correlations between the properties of individuals are not available. Ecological correlations have meant that data analysed is the product of aggregates of different classes of migration in the total flow, and the product of aggregation of differing areas of regions, and differing time periods for change of residence. This has undoubtedly influenced the results. Aggregation problems in economic research are described by Allen (1959), Day (1963) and Buckwell and Hazell (1972). They are not explicitly dealt with here, being reserved for Chapter 10. This chapter deals with the problem of obtaining efficient, consistent, unbiased estimates of the parameters underlying migration structure, given that aggregation bias does not exist or has been minimised.

Assumptions of regression models

Early researchers did not appear to adhere to the assumptions of OLS regression models, in which it is assumed the probability function $p(Y_i/X_i)$ have the same variance σ^2 for all X_i; have the means $E(Y_i)$ lying on a straight line, known as the true regression line

$$E(Y_i) = \mu_i = \alpha + \beta x_i$$

where α and β specify the line and are to be estimated from sample information; and the random variables Y_i are statistically independent. The distributions of Y and e

$$Y_i = \alpha + \beta x_i + e_i$$

where e_i are independent random variables with mean = O and variance = σ^2, are identical, except that their means differ. The distribution of e is just the distribution of Y translated onto a zero mean.

If the strong assumption that Y_i are normal is added, since $\hat{\beta}$ is a linear combination of Y_i, $\hat{\beta}$ will also be normal. The distribution of $\hat{\beta}$ will usually approach normality even without assuming Y_i are normal, as sample size increases. The normal distribution is the only distribution which can be characterised by the mean and variance. With mean, variance and normality of the estimator $\hat{\beta}$ established, statistical inferences about β can be made. For the t distribution to be strictly valid, the distribution of Y_i must be normal.

The residuals are defined as

$$e_i = Y_i - \hat{Y}_i, \quad i = 1, 2, \ldots n$$

and are the observed errors if the model is correct. In performing the regression analysis certain assumptions have been made about the errors — that they are independent, have zero mean and constant variance, σ^2, and follow a normal distribution (for significance tests).

Bogue, Shryock and Hoermann (1957), in a regression analysis to explain the size and composition of migration streams, did not test for normality and linearity of data in using OLS. Later workers such as Ferriss (1965) and Olsson (1965) were careful to meet these assumptions or to transform the data to approach normality and linearity. Other researchers such as Tarver (1961) in an article 'Predicting Migration' failed to test for normality, linearity and multicollinearity in the data. For prediction purposes, multicollinearity does not hurt provided there is no attempt to predict for values of X and Z removed from their line of collinearity. But structural questions cannot be answered — the relationship of Y to either X or Z cannot be sensibly investigated. Tarver, unfortunately, was not predicting migration, but trying to explain its structural characteristics in terms of demographic, economic and social variables, and it is clear from the correlation matrix he presents that many of his independent variables were collinear. The problem of multicollinearity may be solved if there happens to be prior information about the relation of β to γ. For example, if it is known *a priori* that $\gamma = 5\beta$ then this information will allow the regression plane to be determined uniquely, even in the case of perfect multicollinearity. Unfortunately, in migration these relationships are not known.

Several ways have been suggested to avoid multicollinearity. The most obvious one is to exclude correlated variables; thus Willis (1972c) did not include variables which were highly correlated between spatial structure and socio-economic characteristics. Olsson (1965) noted that his independent variables were highly correlated and 'this would have caused difficult problems in a traditional regression analysis'. Olsson used a stepwise regression (forward)[1] as 'the stepwise technique has been partly designed for problems of this sort'. Tarver and Gurley (1965b) ignored multicollinearity and introduced two highly intercorrelated measures of education — median years of school and percent completing four or more years of high school — to account for county net migration rates in the United States, 1950 to 1960. Neither proved significant, contrary to expectations. Hamilton (1965) argued that this result could happen with any two highly-intercorrelated variates which are measuring essentially the same thing, unless a 'stepwise' procedure is used introducing potentially significant variates. Two highly-intercorrelated variates introduced together tend to eliminate each other.

The forward stepwise regression, however, can be shown to yield a less satisfactory result than applying standard multiple regression of Y on X_1, X_2 ... etc., for it not only provides a biased estimate of $\hat{\beta}_1^*$, but in the second step, by regressing the residual $(Y - \hat{Y}_1)$ on X_2, since X_1 and X_2 are not orthogonal, $\hat{\beta}_2^*$ will be a biased estimator of β_2. Any common influence of the two regressors on Y is attributed to X_1, robbing X_2 of its effect. Incredibly, Tarver (1961) used stepwise regression for the purpose of excluding variables that were merely linear combinations of others, without any concern as to whether the 'right' one (in the sense of one perhaps being a possible function of the other) was being excluded.

The final residual $Y - \hat{\beta}_1^* X_1 - \hat{\beta}_2^* X_2 \ldots$ will not be as small as in the standard multiple regression, since in the latter $\hat{\beta}_1$ and $\hat{\beta}_2$ were chosen by definition to make $Y - \hat{\beta}_1 X_1 - \hat{\beta}_2 X_2 \ldots$ a minimum, thus smaller than $Y - \hat{\beta}_1^* X_1 - \hat{\beta}_2^* X_2 \ldots$, unless X_1 and X_2 are orthogonal when the residuals coincide (Beale, Kendall and Mann, 1967).

If there are clear prior guidelines indicating that a few specific regressors are appropriate, then they should all be used right away in a full multiple regression, rather than a tested one at a time with any sort of stepwise approach. Where no prior guidelines exist and the number of regressors must be kept small to provide a more manageable model, then a stepwise technique may be reasonable. However, it should be borne in mind that the stepwise procedure tends to discriminate against regressors tested last, even if correctly applied; and if incorrectly applied, it discriminates even more (Goldberger, 1968).

To overcome the problem of multicollinearity, Riddell (1969) reduced his set of correlated explanatory variables by principal components analysis, which produces a new and reduced set of independent variables expressing the underlying similarities of the original variables. A new set of variates results from scoring the factors (or by multiplying the original standardised data matrix by the matrix of factor loadings). This new set of variates contains the underlying generality of the original data in reduced form, and most important, the new variates are statistically independent, that is orthogonal (Cooley and Lohnes, 1962). Employing factor scores as a new set of independant variables, the migration model takes the form

$$Y = \hat{\alpha} + \hat{\beta}_1 F_1 + \hat{\beta}_2 F_2 + \hat{\beta}_3 F_3 \ldots \hat{\beta}_n F_n$$

where $F_1 \ldots F_n$ are the scored factors.

The component model removes interaction effects and permits a realistic interpretation of the parameters (Kendall, 1957) and this is especially useful where the causal factors associated with migration are complex.

Problem of joint influences

Factors affecting migration are often joint influences giving rise to the problems described above. Interaction problems are very important in analysing the structure of migration. Hamilton (1965) argued that the joint influence of two or more highly-intercorrelated independent variates should be assessed. This can be done by the use of multiple–partial correlation techniques. The joint effect, unfortunately, is indivisible. It cannot possibly be unscrambled. The people who migrate most are high-income, educated people. Whether education or income is the more important causative factor no one can say. Age, education, occupation and income are related causal factors in migration. Neymark (1963) stated these factors should be seen as a collective process in stimulating migration, since socio-economic position is a determinant of education, intelligence and migration, and all the factors are interrelated. That is, factors should be considered jointly, since they are inextricably linked in determining migration. Willis (1972c) found it possible to recognise joint influences by using non-linear analysis,[2] and although they cannot be separated, an assessment can be made of the importance of joint as against single independent variables in explaining migration. A non-linear variable can take the form

$$Y = \hat{\alpha} + \hat{\beta}_1 X_1 + \hat{\beta}_2 X_1^2 + \hat{\beta}_3 (X_1 X_2) + \ldots \hat{\beta}_n f_n (X_1 X_2 \ldots X_m)$$

Willis considered single variates, squares and combinations of variables. Non-linear variables tended to improve the fit, the effect of the joint influence of two variables being greater than the variables considered separately.

A priori specification

Research studies such as that by Olsson (1965) gave a detailed theoretical outline of migration, although migration studies, in general, are often not based on sound theoretical statements about the process of migration. Gallaway, Gilbert and Smith (1967) specified migration between two areas as:

$$M_{ij} = \alpha_o + \beta_o (Y_j - Y_i) + \gamma_o D_{ij} + \lambda_o (U_i - U_j) + \epsilon_o$$

where $(Y_j - Y_i)$ = interstate differences in per capita income;
D_{ij} = miles between the largest cities of each state;
$(U_i - U_j)$ = difference between average 1955–59 unemployment rates in each state

This implies that migration from, say, New York into any two states the same distance away would be the same if per capita income levels and unemployment rates were identical in areas of destination. Only the size of the original state is included in the model, and nothing specified on the size and shape of areas of destination. This sort of migration pattern may exist but it seems unreasonable *a priori* without other supporting evidence. Indeed Goux (1962) stressed the importance of looking at the structure of space in which migration occurs, and Kulldorf (1955), Thomlinson (1961) and Luu-Mau-Thanh (1962) all developed models to assess the significance of spatial structure in determining migration rates. Willis (1972c) suggested that, while it is justifiable to disregard the structure of space in analysing net or composite in and out gross flows, when attempting to seek socio-economic relationships between migration flows from specific local authority areas to other neighbouring areas, the importance of spatial structure should be recognised. It is especially over short distances that the influence of boundary structure and spatial relations are particularly felt.

Moody and Puffer (1969) have pointed out that Lowry (1966) specified migration between two areas as

$$M_{ij} = k \cdot \frac{U_i^a}{U_j^b} \cdot \frac{W_j^c}{W_i^d} \cdot \frac{C_i^e \, C_j^f \, A_i^g \, A_j^h}{D_{ij}^m}$$

where U = unemployment rate
          W = wage rate
          C = civilian non-agricultural labour force
          A = stationed Armed Forces personnel
          D = distance

If either A_i or A_j equals zero, then M_{ij} will be zero. For large regions this is unlikely, but for smaller areas it is questionable as a good general specification of the structure of migration. Rogers (1967a) used a modified form of the Lowry model.

$$M_{ij} = k \frac{U_i}{U_j} \cdot \frac{W_j}{W_i} \cdot \frac{L_i L_j}{D_{ij}}$$

where L is the number of persons in the non-agricultural labour force, which is conceptually more satisfactory. It is very important, therefore, to have a sound theoretical model of the process being studied before any analysis is undertaken, as this can lead to inconsistent and nonsensical results.

Lagged responses

Migration is a function of economic, social and environmental stimuli, but as a reaction it is not immediate. The decision to migrate is somewhat lagged behind the economic and social conditions that originally stimulated it. Before the Second World War, it was estimated that the lag between a discrepancy in prosperity between two regions and the migration evoked by it was six months (Makower, Marschak and Robinson, 1938). Unemployment lags have been estimated to be three of four months behind production cycles (Haggett, 1971). The problem of lagged response is usually not taken into account in the specification of migration relationships. This is partly the result of the data; for instance, a census question asking for place of residence five years previously means lagged response is largely swamped. Some lagged response may be evident in one-year migration data, and is certainly evident in any continuous population register or survey data of migration histories.

Suppose the decision to migrate (Y_t) is dependent not only on current residential experience X_t, but also on residential experience in previous periods of time [3],

$$Y_t = \alpha + \beta X_t + \beta_1 X_{t-1} + \beta_2 X_{t-2} \cdots \epsilon_t$$

The above equation as it stands is difficult to deal with: multicollinearity is a serious problem. Simplications can be made, however. Distant history has less effect than the present on migration, so that the coefficients β in the above equation may be expected to decrease over time, perhaps exponentially

$$\beta_j = \beta \lambda^j \qquad j = 1, 2, \ldots$$

and λ being in the range $0 < \lambda < 1$.

Then a lagged model has the form

$$Y_t = \alpha + \beta X_t + \beta \lambda X_{t-1} + \beta \lambda^2 X_{t-2} \cdots \epsilon_t \tag{1}$$

and for the previous t

$$Y_{t-1} = \alpha + \beta X_{t-1} + \beta \lambda X_{t-2} + \beta \lambda^2 X_{t-3} \cdots \epsilon_{t-1} \tag{2}$$

Multiplying equation (2) by λ and subtracting from equation (1), most of the terms drop out

$$Y_t = \alpha^* + \lambda Y_{t-1} + \beta X_t + \epsilon_t^*$$

where
$$\alpha^* = \alpha(1 - \lambda)$$
$$\epsilon_t^* = \epsilon_t - \lambda \epsilon_{t-1}$$

This model will yield desired estimates of β, λ and α if ϵ_t^* is serially uncorrelated. The problem of multicollinearity has been largely overcome, but further difficulties remain if ϵ_t^* is autocorrelated.

This type of analysis was used by Greenwood (1970) to test the proposition that the more persons who have migrated from state i to state j in the past, the greater will be the quantity of information sent from j back to i and hence, *ceteris paribus*, the greater the current flow of migrants from i to j is likely to be. Greenwood was able to show that present migrants do have a strong tendency to move to the same localities to which persons from their home have previously migrated. Laber (1972) criticised Greenwood's model, finding, in the absence of equilibrating forces strong enough to remove the incentive to migrate, that it was not surprising to find current migration correlated with accumulated past migration. Laber thought that if adjustment is towards equilibrium, the migration stock will exert a negative influence on current migration. However, this seems to be merely confusing gross with net migration, and stochastic theory (see Chapter 9) shows that in an equilibrium situation gross migration will still occur between two areas although net migration is zero and no stock adjustment takes place.

Simultaneous equation bias

The essence of migration is the interdependence between variables. Often it is impossible to discover situations in which one variable may be taken as given and then observe the effect on the other. The failure to consider interactions between other economic and social structures and the set of migration variables studied results in simultaneous equation bias. Most migration studies explain migration using economic variables such as income differentials, unemployment rates and wage rates as explanatory variables. However, it is clear that there is a two-way interaction between economic variables and the level of migration; and that the level of migration over a period of time into and out of a region will have some influence on the economic variables. One of the hypotheses often presented on interregional migration is that out-migration, by diminishing the number of employable people without affecting a location's natural advantages, would eventually cause wages to increase and halt the tendency to net out-migration. The existence of this sort of two-way interaction gives rise to identification problems[4] and bias in the estimates of the structural parameters unless appropriate econometric techniques are used. To the extent that migration itself influenced the independent variables employed in the model, there may be simultaneous equation bias inherent in the estimates. Riddell (1969) thought migration to Freetown in Sierra Leone had a feedback mechanism which led to better information, which in turn led to further migration. He did not, however, recognise the possibility of simultaneous bias. Greenwood and Gormely (1971) recognised the likelihood of simultaneous equation bias but thought the problem was probably not serious in their study. Fabricant (1970) postulated a model of migration from i to j as a response to the positive expected excess demand for labour gap between i and j plus a barrier function. Fabricant tried to overcome or sidestep the problem of simultaneous equation bias by assuming that prices (wages) in the labour market are fixed by employers at the beginning of the period and do not change in response to *ex post* demands and supplies during the period; at the end of the period, sellers (employers) are assumed to reassess their prices in the light of *ex post* demands and supplies and alter their prices accordingly.

In the section on lagged variables it was pointed out that after multicollinearity had been overcome, further difficulties remained if ϵ_t^* was autocorrelated. When e is correlated with X the OLS estimator is no longer consistent (Christ, 1966). A mathematical explanation is given by Christ, but intuitively the reason for this inconsistency is clear. In explaining Y, OLS gives as little credit as possible to the error, and as much credit as possible to the regressor. When error and regressor are correlated, then some of the effect of the error is wrongly attributed to the regressor. This is likely to occur in Britain when non-economic attractiveness (such as social attractiveness, bright city lights, physical and climatic attractiveness) is correlated with the economic (income) variable for a region like the South East. If regions with high incomes also have high non-economic in-migration, while unattractive regions have lower incomes (and other non-economic indicators), regression of the economic variables on migration will yield a biased result.

A consistent estimator of β can be obtained if an instrumental variable can be found, a random variable Z, uncorrelated with e but correlated with X.

The most common example of correlation between error and regressor occurs when the equation to be estimated is part of a whole system of simultaneous equations. Since migration is a function of socio-economic variables and these variables themselves are a function of migration, it is obvious that migration is best analysed in terms of a system with which it interacts. A very simple model of migration, for example, may state

$$M = \alpha + \beta W + e \qquad (3)$$
$$W = M + I \qquad (4)$$

This relates migration M to an economic variable W. The parameters of this function to be estimated are α (the intercept) and β (the slope or marginal propensity to migrate). e is assumed to be independent with zero mean and finite variance. I is an exogenous variable determined outside the system of equations. Migration (M) and the economic variable (W) are endogenous variables determined within the model and influenced by I and e. The model is mathematically complete: there are two equations to determine two endogenous variables.

Figure 8·1 graphically describes the relationship between migration and the economic variable W with e the error term. The observed combination of migration M and the economic variable W will fall within the band around the migration function $M = \alpha + \beta W$ according to whether the error e is zero, greater than zero or less than zero. This satisfies equation (3). But any combination of migration M and the economic variable W must also satisfy equation (4)

$$W = M + I$$
or $$M = W - I$$

I might be distributed as in Figure 8·1. Since combinations of migration and the economic variable W determining M, must satisfy both conditions,

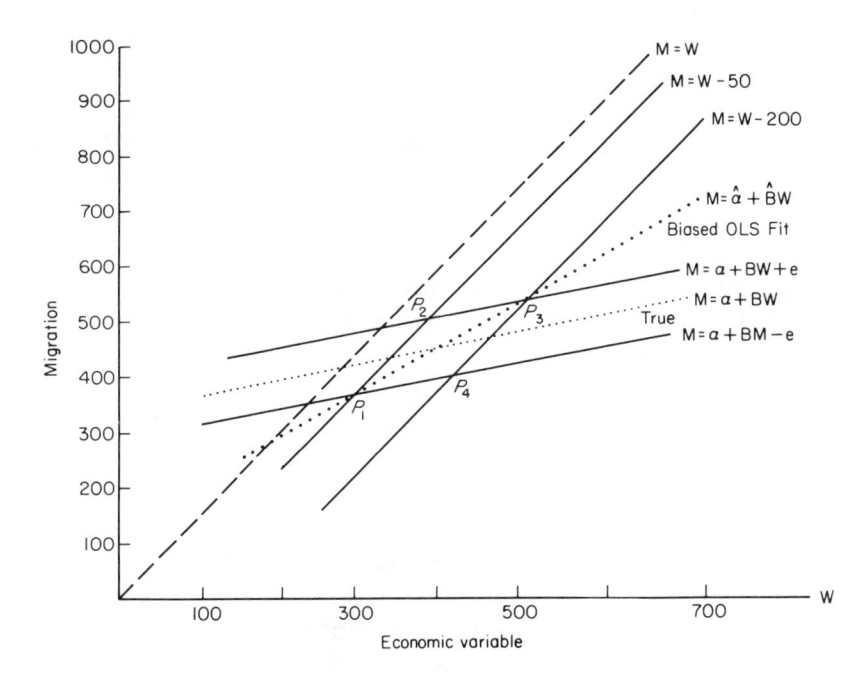

Fig. 8.1 The migration function and scatter of points around it

all observations of M and W will be within the parallelogram $P_1P_2P_3P_4$. An OLS regression on the sample of observations within $P_1P_2P_3P_4$ would fit a line $\hat{\alpha} + \hat{\beta}W$, which is clearly a bad fit compared with $\alpha + \beta W$, since it has a considerable upward bias. Increasing the sample size would make no difference; OLS is inconsistent.

A consistent estimator of β can be obtained if an instrumental variable can be found. I satisfies the two requirements mentioned previously, in this case — it is uncorrelated with e but since $W = M + I$, I affects W and the two are correlated. Thus a consistent estimator is

$$\frac{S_{IM}}{S_{IW}} = \hat{\beta}$$

where S_{IM}, S_{IW} are sample covariance.

An alternative method is to use indirect least squares (Christ, 1966). This is a useful method when W is correlated with e. W is regressed on a variable not correlated with e, that is I. This gives an unbiased estimator which is the same as that obtained using an instrumental variable.

Identification problem

The previous section on simultaneous equations set out some of the difficulties encountered in fitting a migration function to a scatter of observation of variables related to migration. Before becoming involved in identification problems, it must be asked whether the model is mathematically complete; that is, whether there are enough equations to obtain a unique solution for the endogenous variables. In general the model will be complete if there are as many equations as there are unknowns. It is only possible in systems to deal with models that are mathematically complete; that is, where there are enough equations to determine uniquely the endogenous variables in terms of exogenous variables and errors.

The purpose of *a priori* information, as well as providing a realistic model, is to rule out most hypotheses that are inconsistent with observed facts; for any set of observed facts can be explained in many different ways. Many hypotheses could be postulated, each of which, if true, would account for the given set of observations. The ideal is to find only one acceptable hypothesis after appealing to both the model and the facts; that is, one hypothesis consistent with both. A structure is identified with respect to a given model and a given type of data if, and only if, there is exactly one structure that belongs to both the data-admissible set of structures and the model (Christ, 1966). That is, a structure equation is identified if, among all the structure equations compatible with the data, there is only one that is also compatible with the restrictions imposed by the model on that equation. Both Walters (1968) and Huang (1970) give elementary examples of how under-identification occurs. It is sufficient to note here the close similarity of this problem to that of multicollinearity. In both case the relationship between the two variables to be measured cannot be determined by a unique plane through the points, because any number of planes would satisfy the observations. Identification is not primarily a statistical issue. If an equation is unidentified, even an infinite sample will not help; on the other hand, if an equation is identified coefficients can be estimated —approximately if the sample is small, or exactly if it is infinite.

After determining that the migration system is mathematically complete, by having as many structural equations as there are endogenous variables, so that the endogenous variables can be solved for in terms of the predetermined variables, it is necessary to ask whether prior restrictions on parameters of the model allow the equations to be identified. To be identified, an equation in a model of G linear equations must exclude at least $G-1$ of the variables that appear in the model. This is a necessary order condition. The rank condition for identification also exists. An equation in a linear model of G equations is identified if, and only if, at least one non-zero determinant of $G-1$ rows and columns is contained in the array of coefficients formed as follows: starting with the row and column array of coefficients in the model, omit all columns not having a prescribed zero in the equation in question, and omit the row coefficients of that equation. This is a necessary and sufficient condition, and if this rank condition is satisfied the order condition is also satisfied. The rank condition is more fully explained by Leser (1966).

An equation is just identified if the following order condition is satisfied (Christ, 1966):

$$K - J = H - 1$$

The number of known predetermined variables that influence it without appearing in it $(K - J)$ is one less than the total number (H) of jointly dependent variables that do appear in it. An equation is overidentified if the number $(K - J)$ of known predetermined variables that influence it without appearing in it is greater than the number of endogenous variables (H) appearing in it less 1. That is,

$$K - J > H - 1$$

An equation is unidentified because there are too few excluded exogenous variables (instrumental variables) to identify the equations. Such a system cannot be evaluated in a meaningful way. Assuming exact identification, the problems of multicollinearity must be avoided. This implies no linear dependence between exogenous variables, included and excluded from the first equation[5] and no linear dependence between endogenous and exogenous variables included in the first equation (except the endogenous variable determined by this equation, on the left hand side). These are estimation problems. An equation is over-identified because there are more instrumental variables available than is absolutely necessary, and the statistical problem occurs of how to use them all effectively. Over-identification thus occurs when there are more instrumental variables than are required to estimate the required parameters.

Two-stage least squares is the simplest solution to the problem of over-identification in selecting the best instrumental variable or variables to use. The computation of least squares is described in econometrics text books such as Goldberger (1964) and Johnston (1972). It has been applied in Britain by Willis (1971) to study income and labour participation and employment differences in the rural Northern Pennines.

Such a model, consisting of a series of equations relating migration to other socio-economic indices, and recognising that the value of these indices also depends on migration, is much more realistic than single equation models (Willis, 1972b). A systems equation model approaches more closely the dynamic processes through time which migration represents. Of course, completeness and identification problems do not exist in single equation models, provided that the equation is correctly specified as one endogenous variable as a function of several exogenous variables. Estimation problems for a single equation model reduce to the single condition that there be no linear dependence among the exogenous variables in the equation.

An identification problem and simultaneous equation bias may arise through lagged relationships between variables. For example, in a model of migration and unemployment, net out-migration from an area may result in unemployment, but unless this occurs in the same year the model will not be identified, that is, a lagged model must be used. If unemployment results in substantial out-migration in the same year and this causes secondary unemployment which reacts back in the same period, this poses no identification problem, but it does pose a probable equation bias problem; that is, OLS is an inconsistent estimator of such a model.

Identification is prior to estimation. Identification must be established before the estimation of the behavioural coefficients, since in the under-identified case there is no meaning in structural estimation. However, reduced form coefficients are always identified. In some instances — in, say, forecasting — one may estimate the reduced-form equation corresponding to the endogenous variable, the structural equation for which is under-identified. But structural estimation is only meaningful when the equation is identified.

Interpreting an estimated regression

The true effect of X_1 on Y is the fixed estimator β_1, but most regression estimates are derived from a sample so that $\hat{\beta}_1$ can differ from sample to sample. $\hat{\beta}_1$ can be shown to be normal, unbiased, with mean β_1. Confidence intervals can be established from the t distribution of β_1.

It is very important in migration studies to have sound theoretical statements of the influence of socio-economic variables on migration. The influence of some variables is uncertain and some research workers have used stepwise regression to try on a large number of variables they thought might possibly have some influence, in the hope of finding some relationship between a few. This is a very dangerous approach when the hypotheses are tested. If there are theoretical grounds for supposing X_1 and X_2 are related to Y, this can be statistically confirmed by a one-tailed test of the null hypothesis

$$H_0 : \beta_1 = 0$$

against the alternative

$$H_1 : \beta_1 > 0$$

If the t value is high and the null hypothesis is rejected (X_1 and Y are related to each other), this is straightforward. But if t values show the result — for example, X_2 is not statistically significant — some trouble is encountered, for this does not prove that there is no relationship between X_2 and Y. If there are strong theoretical reasons for supposing X_2 is positively related to Y and this belief is confirmed by a positive $\hat{\beta}_2$, statistical evidence is consistent with prior belief, although not as strong as the investigator would like. To accept the null hypothesis $\hat{\beta}_2 = 0$ and conclude X_2 does not affect migration would be in direct conflict with our *a priori* theoretical belief and statistical evidence. Prior belief would be reversed even though confirmed by statistical evidence. In such cases, if there are strong *a priori* theoretical grounds for believing X_2 and similar variables are related to Y, they should not be dropped from the equation. But if there are prior grounds for supposing X_3 is unrelated to Y (H_0 is true) but a weak relationship is observed (*t* value not significant), H_0 should be accepted as a reasonable judgement, since the relationship is easily explained by chance.

Prior belief is less important in rejecting a hypothesis, but it is still relevant. If X_3 was believed to be unrelated to Y but it was suggested that it should be tried, there is a 5 per cent chance of finding $H_1 : \beta_1 > 0$. When many variables are included just to see if there are any relationships the probability of no error is $(\cdot 95)^k$. Thus Tarver (1961) used 24 independent variables to 'explain' spatial mobility. When $k = 10$, the probability of no error is 0·60, making the probability of some error 0·40. When k is greater than 13 the probability of error exceeds that of no error. The probability of drawing a false conclusion therefore increases dramatically as more variables are included. It can be kept small by reducing the level of error for each variable tried on from 5 to 1 per cent, perhaps leaving variables with a hypothesised prior relationship at 5 per cent.

Classical statistical theory provides incomplete grounds for accepting H_0; prior belief and extra statistical judgement are also important. Statistical analysis must be tempered with good sense, prior understanding of the model, the assumptions and limitations of statistical techniques. In migration research there is a good case for using Baysian methods.

Residuals

If the migration model is correct, the residuals should exhibit tendencies that conform to the assumptions made or should not be contrary to these. It is important to examine residuals to determine whether the assumptions were right. Tarver (1961), Rogers (1968) and Fabricant (1970) were primarily concerned with R^2, and neither they nor Bowles (1970) considered observed errors of their models. Few studies have bothered to analyse residuals. Riddell (1969) recognised that the objective is not solely to produce the largest possible coefficient of determination, but rather to understand and explain the complex migration process. Thomas (1968) evaluated the use of maps of residuals from regression :

> The map of residuals from regression shows the spatial distribution of that part of the total magnitude of the dependent variable which is associated with phenomena other than those included in the analysis. Hence the selection of new variables by use of this tool involves identifying phenomena which show the same spatial patterns as the residual values.

Draper and Smith (1966) give an excellent account of the examination of residuals including the overall plot, time sequence plot, plot against $\hat{Y}_i$, plot against independent variables $X_{ji}, i = 1,2, \ldots n$, correlations among residuals, and outliers. Outliers are exceptionally extreme values which may suggest some points are atypical. Willis (1970) examined the residuals from a curvilinear multiple regression model of total gross in, out and within-area movement on Tyneside, and noted Longbenton as an outlier. Draper and Smith deal particularly with time-series plots. Autocorrelation or serial correlation causes difficulties, since OLS badly estimates the true regression. Time-series data can be transformed so that it does satisfy OLS assumptions by first differences or generalised differences (Christ, 1966). Migration records are such that time-series data is rarely available. The vast majority of regression studies of migration have used cross-sectional data. A fundamental assumption of regression analysis is that the population disturbance terms are not autocorrelated, and when cross-sectional data is used the residuals should be tested for spatial autocorrelation. This is rarely done. Cliff and Ord (1970) have shown under what conditions residuals may be tested for spatial autocorrelation. Willis (1970) tested residuals of migration models for Tyneside, using Cliff and Ord's proposed statistic

$$r = \frac{n \Sigma (2) w_{ij} z_i z_j}{W \Sigma (1) z_i^2}$$

where $z = x_i - \bar{x}$ where $x_1, x_2, \ldots x_n$ are sample values

$\Sigma (1)$ is equivalent to $\sum_{i=1}^{n}$

$\Sigma (2)$ is equivalent to $\sum_{j=1}^{n} \sum_{i=1}^{n}$, $i \neq j$

w_{ij} is the effect of area i on area j

and $W = \Sigma (2) w_{ij}$

Willis gave a nominal value of 1 if the ith and jth non vacant areas are contiguous and zero otherwise. Justification for this lies in the fact that the factors affecting the amount of migration interaction between two areas are imprecisely known, but clearly values could be weighted by distance, length of common boundary, etc. For in, and within-area migration on Tyneside, the models provided a good fit, with no spatial autocorrelation, but the model of out-migration had a large percentage unexplained subject to possible spatial autocorrelation.

Canonical correlation

Attempting to explain a migration matrix is a difficult task, since one area's out-migrants are another's in-migrants, and variables causing out-migration (push factors) must be considered simultaneously with variables associated with the area of in-migration (pull factors). Canonical correlation tries to account for multiple criteria (migration matrix) by multiple predictors (independent variables). Geometrically, canonical correlation can be considered as a measure of the extent to which individuals occupy the same relative positions in the p-dimensional space as they do in the q-dimensional space. Multiple regression is the special case where $q = 1$ (criterion to be explained) and $p > 1$ (predictors of the criterion). The algebraic representation and explanation of the calculation of canonical correlators and variates is fully explained in Cooley and Lohnes (1962), Anderson (1958) and Tintner (1952), to whom reference should be made. Briefly it involves the partitioning of a correlation matrix of the $p+q$ variables

$$R = \begin{vmatrix} R_{11} & \vdots & R_{12} \\ \cdots & \vdots & \cdots \\ R_{21} & \vdots & R_{22} \end{vmatrix}$$

into four sub-matrices where

R_{11} = intercorrelations of the p predictors
R_{22} = intercorrelations of the q criteria
R_{12} = intercorrelations of predictors with criteria
R_{21} = transpose of R_{12}

and their substitution into the canonical equation

$$(R_{22}^{-1} R_{21} R_{11}^{-1} R_{12} - \lambda_i I) b_i = 0$$

which involves determining the eigenvalues of

$$|R_{22}^{-1} R_{21} R_{11}^{-1} R_{12} - \lambda I| = 0$$

Vector a_i is obtained from

$$a_i = (R_{11}^{-1} R_{12} b_i) / \sqrt{\lambda_i}$$

The vector of coefficients b_i for the right-hand set is the characteristic vector associated λ_i, where $q < p$. Vectors a_i and b_i are applied to standard score vectors to obtain the canonical variates. The canonical correlation between the ith pair of new composites is $\sqrt{\lambda_i}$.

Canonical correlation has the particular advantage that it provides a description of the overall relationship between sets of dependent variables. It is based on the assumption that the variables utilised approximate normality, that they are independent and fixed. The problem of multicollinearity for both sides of the canonical equation becomes very severe when large numbers of variables are involved. Linear independence in each battery of variables becomes critical not only to avoid a singular matrix, but also to avoid the serious rounding errors involved when the determinant of the matrix approaches zero. One solution to this problem of multicollinearity is to transform both sets of data separately to their principal orthogonal axes and to use component scores, on the first 'n' eigenvalues greater than unity, as input for the canonical analysis. Component scores also have the advantage of being nearly normal as well as independent.

The largest λ_i is the square of the maximum possible correlation between linear combinations of the two sets of measurements $R^2_{c.max} = \lambda_1$. Bartlett (1941, 1947) outlined procedures for testing the significance of canonical correlations

$$\Lambda = \prod_{i=1}^{q} (1 - \lambda_i)$$

The χ^2 approximation for the distribution of Λ provides a test for the null hypothesis that the p variates are unrelated to the q variates.

$$\chi^2 = -|N - \cdot 5(p+q+1)| \log_e \Lambda$$

with pq degrees of freedom. The first root to Λ can be removed if the null hypothesis is rejected and the significance of $q-1$ roots tested. In general, with r roots removed,

$$\Lambda' = \prod_{i=r+1}^{q} (1 - \lambda_i)$$

and the χ^2 is distributed with $(p-r)(q-r)$ degrees of freedom.

Canonical correlation has been used to study occupational mobility in the USA (Klatzky and Hodge, 1971). Recently Willis (1972c) used canonical correlation to study migration flows between individual local authorities on Tyneside; in particular, to try and distinguish the importance of socio-economic factors of which they were a function and the spatial structure in which migrants are enumerated. The techique allows factors associated with different types of migration systems to be identified. The demographic dimension (population and density) was the chief variable associated with migration on Tyneside, accounting for 80 per cent of the variance. The general socio-economic factor was only positively associated with migration of the Newcastle sub-system, being negatively associated with intra- and inter-Tyneside migration of the other sub-systems. Higher occupation groups were negatively related to local movement over much of Tyneside, being bound up with Newcastle and its migration sub-system with Castle Ward RD, and Gosforth and Longbenton UDs.

Limitations of the technique are, however, severe for migration. Interpretation of canonical variates is difficult and the necessity of having a low degree of intercorrelation of predictor and criterion batteries within themselves requires the transformation of data to principal orthogonal axes. Interpretation is made doubly difficult by having to work back through predictor and criteria components to canonical coefficients and variables. The correlations between any two sets of variables are maximised, but the weights that give the maximum prediction are not necessarily the same as those that give maximum reliability. The chief limitation of canonical correlation is that the coefficients and variates are not like regression coefficients; they show the association and degree to which variables are related and not how variables are related. Cause and effect relations are irrelevant: it does not matter whether battery p affects q or vice versa, or both affect each other, or a third set of variables influences both. Hence canonical correlation cannot be used as a predictive technique, and is consequently a less powerful technique than regression.

Conclusion

It is difficult to believe that the highly complex pattern of inter-area migration can be adequately described by the set of extremely simple constructs that have been used to date. The interaction between cause and effect suggests that it is necessary, for analytic and predictive purposes, to specify a model of migration which takes into account the interactions between the various 'independent' factors involved in the process. Too many studies have attempted to explain migration by means of a single equation multiple regression model, and have found differing signs and insignificant coefficients on variables that *a priori* were thought to play a crucial role in the migrant's decision concerning his destination. Economic variables — income, unemployment, employment, (labour demand and supply) wage and earnings levels — have been particularly prone to resulting errors. A possible explanation for the conflicting and surprising results obtained from ordinary least squares single equation models, is that the parameter estimates possess simultaneous equation bias. Bias is likely to be particularly marked in studies employing some long-period measure of migration, since migration that has occurred over a long period of time is especially likely to have influenced the independent variables in the model. Consequently, it is important, that simultaneous equations models of migrations should be developed to improve model specification, analytical work, and the empirical estimation of parameters. Migration is a complex phenomenon requiring careful model *a priori* specification, the possible evaluation of non-linear parameters and variables, the incorporation of lagged responses, system evaluation, and great judgement in interpreting an estimated regression.

Notes

[1] For an account of stepwise regression see Draper and Smith (1966).

[2] Non-linearity applied only to variables and not to the parameters, i.e. α and β are still linear.

[3] Taeuber (1961) states residential mobility during a given time period is not independent of previous mobility experience. Persons who have not moved recently are less likely to move in future than those who have moved recently.

[4] This is the problem of identifying whether the observations will enable the simultaneous equations to be measured, i.e. the true structure of the migration relationship to be identified.

[5] If the equation is over-identified, some linear dependence between the exogenous variables is allowed, since there is a surplus of instrumental variables.

9 Stochastic Processes in Migration

Introduction

A stochastic process is one which develops in time according to probabilistic laws. Its future behaviour cannot, therefore, be predicted with certainty. Such a situation occurs widely in migration where migration processes are not deterministic. The probabilistic nature of migration results from both a failure fully to specify the system (because its full limits are not yet known) and the unpredictable character of much human behaviour. A stochastic model results when probability distributions are introduced into the model in place of mathematical variables, and equations in the model include random variables. Probabilities are then attached to the various possible future states. Simulation (discussed in Chapters 6 and 11) is one form of stochastic model.

Stochastic models serve a number of functions. They provide insight into and understanding of the phenomena in question in terms of the theoretical framework employed in model building, solving and testing. In Chapter 11 it will be seen that stochastic models are useful for predictive purposes. They can be used to forecast the consequences of migration in population distribution. This leads on to their use in the design of migration systems and their mode of operation. The design of migration policy and its operation would be greatly improved if a regional stochastic migration manpower model, incorporating government instruments, was available. Stochastic models have also made great contributions to the field of measurement in migration. For example, House and Knight (1966) measured turnover as the number of people leaving, entering or moving within an area per unit of time as a percentage of the average population during the same period. Large turnover values were taken as indicative of unstable areas likely to lose substantial population if this were triggered off by some mechanism. Stochastic models can show this measure to be inadequate, because it ignores the strong dependence of propensity to leave on length of residence. This dependence is such that an area with a large number of in-migrants and within-area migrants will have a misleadingly high figure of turnover. The conditions under which the House–

Knight index can be meaningfully used are very limited. Population turnover measures would be more meaningful if based on mean or median length of residence.

The dynamics of migration can only be adequately described in stochastic terms. The inherent uncertainty of migration means that its future cannot be predicted with certainty, but only in probabilistic terms. Stochastic models allow predictions to be made and one can also assess the likely error of the predictions. In formulating and analysing migration models, great use will be made of the theory of Markov chains in discrete time. Elementary accounts of the theory of Markov chains and processes can be found in Gray (1967), Kemeny and Snell (1960), Kemeny, Mirkil, Snell and Thompson (1959), Cox and Miller (1965) and Karlin (1966).

The basic model

We have seen (Chapter 4) that, in the life history of an individual, a number of 'decision' points occur at which the individual considers changing house and area of residence and job. At each of these points he may move to another job or house or remain where he is. This can be represented by a transition matrix

$$P = [p_{ij}]$$

$$\begin{bmatrix} p_{11} & p_{12} & \cdots & p_{1n} \\ p_{21} & p_{22} & \cdots & p_{2n} \\ \vdots & & & \\ p_{n1} & p_{n2} & \cdots & p_{nn} \end{bmatrix}$$

The diagonal probabilities p_{ii} of the matrix give the probabilities that no change is made (or alternatively that if a change is made it is to another house or job within the same area) and p_{ij} are probabilities of moving between areas. Additionally $p_{ij} \geq 0$ and $\Sigma_i p_{ij} = 1$, so that the matrix of transition probabilities, P, is a matrix with non-negative elements and unit column totals — a stochastic matrix.

Stochastic matrices have a number of properties:

(a) every stochastic matrix P has a latent root equal to 1;
(b) if P is stochastic, so is P^n for any possible integer n;
(c) all latent roots λ of a stochastic matrix satisfy $|\lambda| \leq 1$.

Aitken, using matrix theory, proved that a necessary and sufficient condition for $p_{ij}^{(n)}$ to tend to a limit independent of j, and hence for the limiting absolute probabilities to be independent of the initial condition of the system, is that $\lambda = 1$ is a non-repeated latent root of P and all other latent roots are strictly less than one in modulus.

A latent row vector [1, 1, 1, ...] is associated with $\lambda = 1$, and when a limiting distribution exists it is given by the latent column vector corresponding to $\lambda = 1$ scaled so that the sum of its elements is unity.

The basic model used in migration research is

$$p_i^{(1)} = P p_i^{(o)}$$

where p_i is a vector of absolute probabilities. Repeated application of this equation is equivalent to

$$p_i^{(n)} = P^n p_i^{(o)}$$

The matric P^n plays a fundamental role in the theory of Markov chains. It can be used to obtain the 'state' probabilities from the above equation; that is, the probability that a migrant is in a specific area or what proportion of the total population will end up in a particular area. They thus have an individual and collective interpretation.

The rest of this chapter discusses the theory of Markov chains in constructing probabilistic models of migration. It reviews initially studies that have used Markov processes to study labour, population, social processes and economic change, then discusses the theoretical framework upon which Markov chains are based, and suggests areas for improvement.

Markov models are primarily constructed to represent the changes which take place in the structure of population, the labour force, society or industry as time progresses. Social scientists and economists are often interested in characterising or summarising how social and economic processes and institutions have changed through time, as well as what paths they are likely to take in future time periods. Within this context the purpose of this chapter is to discuss the concepts of Markov chain processes that have been used in analysing problems where time-ordered data exists over some time span.

Applications of Markov chains

Although the basic concepts of Markov chains were introduced by A.A. Markov in 1912, their use by social scientists and economists is of relatively recent vintage. Solow (1951) and Champernowne (1953) applied this probabilistic approach to the analysis of income and wage distribution. Hart and Prais (1956) also employed the technique in an investigation of business concentration; Adelman (1958) used the same approach in analysing the size distribution of firms within the steel industry, and extended the work of Hart and Prais; and Preston and Bell (1961) used it to account for the distribution of the size of firms. In labour mobility, the work of Blumen, Kogan and McCarthy (1955) is classically cited; in addition, Prais (1955) applied the technique in measuring social mobility, and this work was developed in a demographic context by Matras (1960a, 1960b, 1966). The Markov framework has also been used to study fertility (Sheps and Perrin, 1964) and mortality (Chiang, 1968). Migration provides most examples, with studies by Muhsam (1961 and 1962), who also explains the theory non-mathematically and in simple terms, Rogers (1966), and Kelley and Weiss (1969). The 1960s saw a great proliferation in the number of studies using Markov concepts, and these are becoming increasingly fashionable. It is pertinent, therefore, to ask the contribution these have made to knowledge and assess the foundations – theoretical and empirical – upon which they are based. The popularity of the Markov model is derived from its appealing simplicity in describing dynamic processes. Users often acknowledge that the simple Markov process is a mechanical first approximation, but little effort has been made to appraise its appropriateness in migration, or to apply more sophisticated formulations in those cases where the simplest Markov assumptions are inconsistent with migration theory and economic theory.

Properties of Markov chains

Markov chains have fundamental but simple properties. In a finite set of independent trials, the joint probability of a possible set of events is given by the product of the respective individual probabilities. The simplest type of generalisation that can be made of independent trials is to allow the probabilities of the different possible outcomes of any trial to depend on the outcome of the immediately preceding trial, but on no others. For such a series of trials the probability of outcome E_{xr} is conditional on the actual outcome of E_{xr-1} which is obtained at the $(r-1)$th trial.

$$p(E_{x1}\ E_{x2}\ \ldots E_{xk}) =$$
$$= p(E_{x1})\,p(E_{x2}\mid E_{x1})\,p(E_{x3}\mid E_{x2})\ldots p(E_{xk}\mid E_{xk-1}) \quad (1)$$

The probabilities of different sets of joint outcomes can be defined from two families of probabilities — the initial probability distribution which governs the outcome of the first trial, and transitional probabilities for all possible pairs of outcomes, not excluding the case when $E_{xr} \equiv E_{xr-1}$. A series of trials subject to this specialised type of dependence is called a Markov chain. Generally, $p(E_{xr} E_{xr-1})$, the transition probability, is time dependent in the sense that it is a function of r, the number of the trial to which it refers. Many examples, however, have the simplification that transition probabilities are constant.

Homogeneity in time and space

Independence in space

There are theoretical grounds for believing that the Markov property will not hold exactly for many economic and social processes. These grounds arise from the fact that the class boundaries are drawn somewhat arbitrarily. For example, the seven social categories used by Glass and Hall (Prais, 1955) could be divided into more classes. Similarly, economic data (for example, on size and distribution of firms) is based on arbitrary classes. In migration, regional data is often divided into migration based on local authority areas. Alternatively, in migration or economic studies, some classes could be amalgamated to give a smaller number of categories. Kemeny and Snell (1960) have shown that if the states of a Markov chain are pooled, then the new chain does not, in general, have the Markov property. A necessary and sufficient condition for Markov chain $\{P\}$ to be aggregated into a smaller number of classes with respect to a partition $A = \{A_1, A_2 ... A_s\}$ is that for every pair of sets A_i and A_j, the probability of moving from each of the former components of the set to a different class is the same. That is, p_{kA_j} have the same value for every s_k in A_i. These common values $\{p_{ij}\}$ form the transition matrix for the lumped chain. Data collected from the 1966 Census on residential change within and between all local authority areas cannot be aggregated, for this condition is not generally, if ever, satisfied. This can readily be seen if a transition matrix is formed from the 1966 Census data (Willis, 1970). Moreover, Markov transition matrices obtained by aggregating across non-homogeneous (with respect to transition probabilities) individuals, may not bear any resemblance to the transition matrices possessed by the individuals (Morrison, Massey and Silverman, 1971). This means that, necessarily, the classes of a Markov chain cannot be arbitrarily re-arranged and retain the

Markov property. Rogers (1967c) has looked at the aggregation problem in demography in terms of space, people (age-groups) and time, and concludes that the consolidation conditions are probably never met in practice, although it is possible to derive schemes to approximate perfect aggregation as closely as possible. However, this suggests that even if there is one system of classification for which the Markov property holds true, this may not be the one which the researcher happens to have chosen as a starting point.

Independence in time

A great deal of quantitative research into the class structure of society has been carried out by social scientists, such as that by Glass (1954), Rogoff (1953) and Prais (1955). These looked at a son's social class in relation to that of his father, and Markov models applied to estimate the distribution by social class of succeeding generations. But neither the data set of Glass (1954), nor that of Rogoff (1953), allows a direct test of the Markov property. This property requires, in this example, that a son's class should depend only on that of his father and not on that of his grandfather. To test the assumption, records of family history are required over at least three generations. Similar problems occur in migration studies. Tarver and Gurley (1965a) have employed the theory of Markov chains in constructing a probabilistic migration model to project the future populations of census divisions in the United States. They recognised two limitations: the constancy of migration rates (that is, that future rates would correspond identically with those during the observed 1955–60 interval); and that migration rates prior to the observed five-year period have no effect upon future mobility. Both these assumptions in Markov models can be criticised. In particular, it has been recognised by Rider and Badger (1943) that 'the probability of moving within a specified time ... decreases as the length of maintaining the same residence increases'. Residential mobility and migration is not, in a given time period, independent of previous mobility experience. Persons who have not moved recently are less likely to move in future than those who have moved recently. This is a more general statement of Goldstein's (1954 and 1958) proposition that a small proportion of frequent migrants account for a high proportion of all migration. Willis (1972a) has shown that duration of residence and frequency of movement varies substantially between occupations and age group within occupations. In view of analysis of data on duration of residence and frequency of migration, mobility during a time period should be viewed as a stochastic process dependent upon previous mobility experience. In this way an individual in a given time interval is presumed to undergo a risk of migration that decreases as he continues to reside in the same community and/or house. This is an improvement upon Blumen, Kogan and McCarthy's (1955) division of the transition matrix into two parts, one representing 'movers' and the other 'stayers'. The conclusion must be reached, however, that in migration, and some other social processes, the probability of an outcome to a trial depends not only on the immediately preceding trial, but also trials $r-2, r-3 \ldots r-n$. Most Markov models of population growth and movement fail to take this into account.

This has significant implications for methods of data collection on migration. If a complete migration history were available for each person in the system, then this could be used to estimate the transition probabilities. In migration studies complete information is lacking because of the necessity of conducting expensive personal surveys, so that the main body of data is census material which records residential location one and five years previously.[1] Thus records give the current residence only at yearly intervals and/or five-yearly intervals. This would present no problem if the states of the system at successive years could be treated as a Markov chain. Unfortunately, this is the case only in rather special circumstances.

The basis of migration are decision points to move in time $m(T)$ and this is usually recorded (by census) on a yearly basis (η interval). Let $p_{ij}(\eta)$ be the probability that a person who is in area i at the beginning of the year is in area j at the beginning of the next year. It is assumed here that $\{m(T)\}$ is time homogeneous, so that transition probabilities $p_{ij}(\eta)$ do not depend on T. If there are exactly m decision points during the year, then $p_{ij}(\eta) = p_{ij}^{(m)}$. m itself is a random variable with distribution $p_m(\eta)$, so, following Bartholomew (1967),

$$p_{ij}(\eta) = \sum_{m=0}^{\infty} p_m(\eta) p_{ij}^{(m)} \qquad (i, j, = 1, 2, \ldots k) \qquad (2)$$

The matrix $P(\eta)$ can, therefore, be observed in practice whereas P cannot.

A condition for a system to be a Markov chain, which is both necessary and sufficient is that

$$p_{ij}^{(r\eta)} = p_{ij}^{(r)}(\eta) \qquad (r = 1, 2, 3, \ldots) \qquad (3)$$

where $p_{ij}^{(r)}(\eta)$ denotes the r interval transition probability for a Markov chain with transition matrix $P(\eta)$.

It can be shown that there are only two stochastic processes $\{m(t)\}$ for which (3) holds. The first is when decision points occur at regular intervals, and the second case is when $\{m(T)\}$ is a Poisson process. The latter implies that intervals between decision points are independently and exponentially distributed.

A transition matrix defines a Markov chain only if decision points occur either regularly or randomly in time. But migration is not a regular or random decision process, and in practice, therefore, Markov transition matrices do not give accurate predictions, tending to underestimate the elements on the diagonal. This is precisely what Blumen, Kogan and McCarthy (1955) found in their study of labour mobility using Markov chains.

One solution to this problem is to generalise the model so that each individual may have a different decision rate. Blumen, Kogan and McCarthy (1955) introduced heterogeneity in the process $\{m(T)\}$ by assuming that a certain proportion of the population were not mobile. These were the 'stayers', and the 'movers' were those whose mobility was postulated by a Poisson decision process model.

Blumen, Kogan and McCarthy (1955) thus expanded their original model of a modified probability process with provision for industrial attachment

$$P = S + (I - S)M$$

where
$$S = \begin{vmatrix} s_1 & 0 & 0 & \cdots \\ 0 & s_2 & 0 & \\ 0 & 0 & s_3 & \\ \vdots & & & \\ & & & s_n \end{vmatrix}$$

and s_1, s_2, ... is the probability or fraction of workers in each respective industry designated as stayers in the time period.

I   is an identity matrix.
M   is a transition matrix describing the behaviour of movers.

Hence $P^{(n)} = S + (I - S)M^n$

into a more general model

$$P = r_0 I + r_1 M + r_2 M^2 + \ldots + r_m M^m$$

where the movement pattern of those who moved x times is M^x, and this matrix is weighted by r_x, the fraction of the population exposed x times. $r_0 + r_1 + r_2 + \ldots r_m = 1$. In Blumen, Kogan and McCarthy's example,

$r_0 = \cdot 67$, $r_1 = \cdot 27$, $r_2 = \cdot 05$ and $r_3 = \cdot 01$; i.e. 67 per cent of the group have no exposure to movement, 27 per cent have one exposure, and so on. For a transition matrix of arbitrary order

$$P^{(n)} = r_0^{(n)}I + r_1^{(n)}M + r_2^{(n)}M^2 + \ldots r_{nm}^{(m)}M^{nm}$$

The probabilities $r_0^{(n)}$, $r_1^{(n)}$, $r_2^{(n)}$, ... $r_{nm}^{(n)}$ determine the number of exposures to the process, and the matrix M determines the patterns of movement of those who have been exposed.

Blumen, Kogan and McCarthy were able to show, for a homogeneous group with respect to exposure to a movement pattern, in which exposure probabilities were constant over the entire time period and where exposure had no effect on further chances of exposure during the period, that if each individual time period is divided up into an arbitrary large number of time intervals then the probabilities, r_x, are those of a Poisson distribution.

$$P = e^{-a}\left(I + aM + \frac{a^2}{2!}M^2 + \ldots\right)$$

where a is the average number of exposures in any year of time interval.

$$P^{(2)} = e^{-2a}\left(I + (2a)M + \frac{(2a^2)}{2!}M^2 + \ldots\right)$$

The coefficient of M^x in the resulting series is

$$e^{-2a}\frac{(2a)^x}{x!}$$

Blumen, Kogan and McCarthy found that, for a given transition matrix, important differences arose between the two models: the simple Markov model and the Poisson model, i.e. a comparison in BKM notation between P^n and $P^{(n)}$. The differences became marked and more substantial if the time periods increased in number. The differences between P^8 and $P^{(8)}$ was that the simple Markov model understated the probabilities on the main diagonal for transitions of higher orders or powers. It was also clear that $P^2 \neq P^{(2)}$ or $P^n \neq P^{(n)}$. The BKM approach improved the 'fit' of the model to data when population was divided into movers and stayers. How well such a model describes mobility can be determined only by estimating the parameters of the model from actual data and testing observation against hypothesis. It is often not possible, on data available, to distinguish between the two models $\{P'(r=1)\}^8$ and $P'(r=8)$ for the decision point process. For predictive purposes they are identical, but data on individual case histories is necessary for a full explanation of the processes.

Other generalisations of this basic model can be made. More elaborate stochastic processes could be introduced to account for the decision points if existing ones were inadequate and the matrix P could be allowed to become time-dependent. This latter possibility offers the most fruitful reward in migration studies, and is explored in the following section. If data can be obtained on individual migration and job histories, the scope for useful model building will be greatly enlarged.

Dynamic stochastic models and duration of residence

The accuracy with which it is possible to predict the distribution of a population within a system of states at some future time depends upon the degree to which the system obeys the Markovian constraints. One of the chief restrictions of Markov chain theory is that only the state of the system at time t determines the state of the system at time $t + 1$. A second constraint is that the matrix of transition probabilities is constant for each time interval of transition $(t, t + 1)$. This states the probability that an individual will move from a state S_i at time t to state S_j at $t + 1$ is the same as the probability of transition from S_i to S_j between times t_n and t_{n+1} for all $n = 0, 1, 2, ...$ This property is called the axiom of stationarity.

Myers, McGinnis and Masnick (1967) formulated migration as a stochastic process governed by probabilities that are non-stationary. They assume that migration risks, expressed as probabilities, are not constant over time and that they decrease as a person continues to reside in the same location and becomes socially and culturally integrated into the community. Accumulated residence seems to generate inertia: the longer a person remains in a given location, the lower should be the probability that he will leave it. In the McGinnis model, the set of elements in each location at each point in time is sub-partitioned with respect to duration of residence, which can be assumed to have unit value equal to that of time. Each time specific matrix $P(t)$ was broken down into an ordered sequence of submatrices $dP(t)$, with respect to duration of residence d. For each diagonal element, $dp_{ii}(t)$,

$$dp_{ii}(t) > d - 1 p_{ii}(t) \qquad d < \infty$$

and $$\lim_{d \to \infty} dp_{ii}(t) = 1$$

This states that, given sufficient residence, any location becomes an absorbing state. Two further axioms complete the proposed system. One requires that probabilities remain stationary for each specified residence group. The other requires that the proportion of movers from a location S_i who go to a particular location S_j, remain invariant in duration of residence in S_i.

The merit of this approach to a Markov process is that it permits the transition matrix to change according to the duration of residence structure of the population. The same approach can be taken with respect to population characteristics other than duration of residence – for example, occupation, income and social status – where these have been demonstrated to be relevant in producing differential rates of migration.

A fully-fledged model has not been developed along these lines because individual histories of movement are the only source of data for this type of analysis and such data had not been gathered in sufficient quantity to assure reliable within-cell probabilities of movement. Empirical data produced for 1,700 individuals by Myers, McGinnis and Masnick (1967) supported the view that probabilities of movement decline with increasing duration of residence for each year. Morrison (1967), in a random sample of 5,000 records from Amsterdam, and Zeist in the Netherlands demonstrated that within age categories the probability of migrating declined as duration status increased, but the exact form of the relationship differed from one age to another, suggesting that age was an interacting variable. The decline in the probability of migrating, as duration of residence increases, increases with age.

The restriction that probabilities are invariant through time is unjustifiable in the analysis of migration. Evidence favours a non-stationary formulation which postulates a linkage between previous residential experience and future mobility prospects. But a model of the form proposed by Myers, McGinnis and Masnick assumes that all moves entail the dissolution of ties with the place of origin, and place the migrant in the category of 'newcomer' within the place of destination. This is clearly unrealistic. Any migration model should also reassess the probabilities of moving to specific areas from a particular state in the light of migration into the area. Return migration accounts for a large proportion of all migration. An individual moving to an area will have a high probability of moving again, since duration of residence is short, and a high probability of moving back to his area of origin.

The character of available data has precluded research in this important field in migration processes. Higher order Markov chains have tended to be concerned with adjusting data to fit the Markov property through transformations, or altering the Markov chain to fit the data — for example, by the incorporation of mover—stayer parameters (Goodman, 1961) or a Poisson process.

Higher order Markov chains

The Markov property states that the outcome of each trial depends solely on the outcome of the immediately preceding one, symbolically

$$P(t_n = S_i \mid t_{n-1}, ..., t_{n-j} = S) = P(t_n = S_i \mid t_{n-1} = S_j)$$

which states the probability that any state S_i occurs on sequence t_n is independent of all other states in the sequence except that one which occured on t_{n-1}. This tends to make the length of each trial period crucial. Where independence does not exist in time, which is common in migration, it will be meaningful to change the Markov property itself. Transition probabilities can be made functions of any number of previous states, or symbolically

$$P(t_n = S_i \mid t_{n-1}, ..., t_{n-j} = S) = P(t_n = S_i \mid t_{n-1}, ..., t_{n-a} = S_j)$$

where a is any positive finite integer $\leqslant n$.

For example, a second order Markov chain expresses the relationship for a state between two time periods: the probability of moving from S_3 to S_4 depends on the probability of moving from S_2 to S_3

$$(S_2 \ S_3) \rightarrow (S_3 \ S_4)$$

All possible relationships at a nominal level (link or no link) are

	S_1	S_2	S_3	S_4
(a)		0	0	
(b)		0	1	
(c)		1	0	
(d)		1	1	

(a) expresses no relationship between $(S_2 \ S_3)$; (b) allows movement to S_3 not dependent upon S_2; (d) specifies that movement from $(S_2 \ S_3)$ is dependent upon the probability of moving to S_2.

A 2×2 matrix for a second order Markov chain would have the form

$$\begin{array}{c c} & t = 2 \\ t = 1 & \end{array} \begin{pmatrix} & S_1 S_1 & S_1 S_2 & S_2 S_1 & S_2 S_2 \\ S_1 S_1 & \alpha & \beta & 0 & 0 \\ S_1 S_2 & 0 & 0 & \gamma & \delta \\ S_2 S_1 & \epsilon & \eta & 0 & 0 \\ S_2 S_2 & 0 & 0 & \kappa & \lambda \end{pmatrix}$$

This states probabilities. An individual in the first time period moving from S_1 to S_1 has the option in the second period of remaining in state S_1 (probability α) or moving to state S_2 (probability β). An individual moving from S_1 to S_2 in the first period has a probability γ of moving back to S_1 or remaining in S_2 with a probability of δ. Similar probabilities can be calculated for moving $(S_2\ S_1\ S_1)$, $(S_2\ S_1\ S_2)$, $(S_2\ S_2\ S_1)$ and $(S_2\ S_2\ S_2)$.

If a third order Markov chain for a two-state model were considered, the matrix would be 8 × 8 instead of the 4 × 4 matrix for a second order chain. Obviously as the number of states increases and dependence increases back in time, the size of the matrix increases very rapidly. The complexity of the problem for analysis may be reduced, however, if the various matrices are found to have particular properties deriving from the zero elements they contain.

The equilibrium distribution

One of the greatest problems facing the application of stochastic processes and, specifically, Markov chains to demographic studies, and migration in particular, is a lack of understanding of the concepts involved, and this has resulted in unrealistic interpretations in consequence.

For example, Willis J. (1968) stated, in a review of techniques for analysing population growth and movement; 'The concept of the "equilibrium" distribution is a useful index with which to differentiate various mobility patterns', and that a Markov chain 'when projected to its equilibrium state provides an abstract index which can be used to compare movement patterns of different cohorts'. Ignoring births and deaths for the moment, take a numerical example of migration between two regions:

$$P_1 = \begin{bmatrix} 0\cdot 9 & 0\cdot 1 \\ 0\cdot 2 & 0\cdot 8 \end{bmatrix}$$

and this renders an equilibrium row of P_1^n (2/3, 1/3). Changing the migration pattern, say to

$$P_2 = \begin{bmatrix} 0.85 & 0.15 \\ 0.30 & 0.70 \end{bmatrix}$$

in which the probability of migrating between areas is increased, rends a common row of P_2^n (2/3, 1/3), i.e. the new mobility pattern leads to the same ultimate distribution as the old

$$P_1^n = \begin{bmatrix} 2/3 & 1/3 \\ 2/3 & 1/3 \end{bmatrix} = P_2^n$$

In other words, it is impossible to infer from the distribution of population what mobility pattern must have got them there. The same conclusion would hold if births and deaths were included. There are an infinite number of mobility patterns which can produce the same equilibrium distribution: the equilibrium distribution reveals nothing about the migration pattern from which it evolved. This is a problem of identification of parameters — the model is not restrictive enough for the values of parameters to be determined.

The equilibrium distribution is independent of the initial distribution: it is a property of the migration matrix only. Yet the initial distribution of population can have considerable influence in the first few initial time periods of the process, after which the equilibrium vector is approached as a geometrically decreasing sequence.

A very simple first order stationary Markov process example may be given (after Lee, Judge and Zellner, 1970):

$$P = [p_{ij}] = \begin{array}{c} \\ S_1 \\ S_2 \\ S_3 \\ S_4 \end{array} \begin{bmatrix} S_1 & S_2 & S_3 & S_4 \\ \cdot 60 & \cdot 40 & \cdot 00 & \cdot 00 \\ \cdot 10 & \cdot 50 & \cdot 40 & \cdot 00 \\ \cdot 00 & \cdot 10 & \cdot 70 & \cdot 20 \\ \cdot 00 & \cdot 00 & \cdot 10 & \cdot 90 \end{bmatrix}$$

This indicates a strong tendency to remain within a given state from one time period to the next, and the most probable outcome, excluding remaining in the same state, is that individuals move one state at a time to a neighbouring state. This type of behaviour is characteristic of migration where this occurs chiefly between neighbouring areas, or occupational mobility that is mainly between similar occupation groups. The equilibrium or stationary vector for this matrix is

(·0189 ·0755 ·3020 ·6036)

but different starting vectors generate different patterns of aggregate data. The patterns of changes in the aggregate data for four starting states are shown in Figure 9·1.

All of these examples show a population decrease, increase or increase followed by decrease. It is also possible for an area's proportional share of total population to decrease initially and subsequently increase. For example, in the case

[1]   (0·20 0·30 0·50) $\begin{pmatrix} 0·8 & 0·1 & 0·1 \\ 0·1 & 0·9 & 0·0 \\ 0·0 & 0·2 & 0·8 \end{pmatrix}$

the following distributions arise

[2]   0·19   0·39   0·42
[6]   0·22   0·55   0·23
[11]   0·27   0·58   0·15
[∞]   0·286 0·572 0·142

In practice, initial population distributions do not show such concentrations of population, but similar time paths can result from more even distributions. In all cases, however, the largest fluctuations occur in the early cycles of the model, the equilibrium distribution later being approached asymptotically and without fluctuations. In looking at migration between 23 Tyneside local authority areas in 1961–66, fluctuations in future time paths of vectors were noted by Willis (1970). Areas could be classified by type of proportional change. Central Tyneside local authorities (excluding Tynemouth), from Newcastle-Gateshead east to the sea, and including Longbenton in the north and the coalmining areas of Houghton-le-Spring and Hetton, all recorded a steadily-declining proportion of the national population. Outer areas, including the 'cocktail areas', recorded a fluctuating proportion – an increase (substantial for some areas such as Tynemouth, Castle Ward, Bolden, Felling, Ryton, Whickham and Chester-1e-Street RD) – followed by a decline in their proportion of population. Despite subsequent decline, a number of these areas retained a greater proportionate share of the national population than their initial (1961) distribution. Only the rest of England and Wales recorded a steady unfluctuating increase.

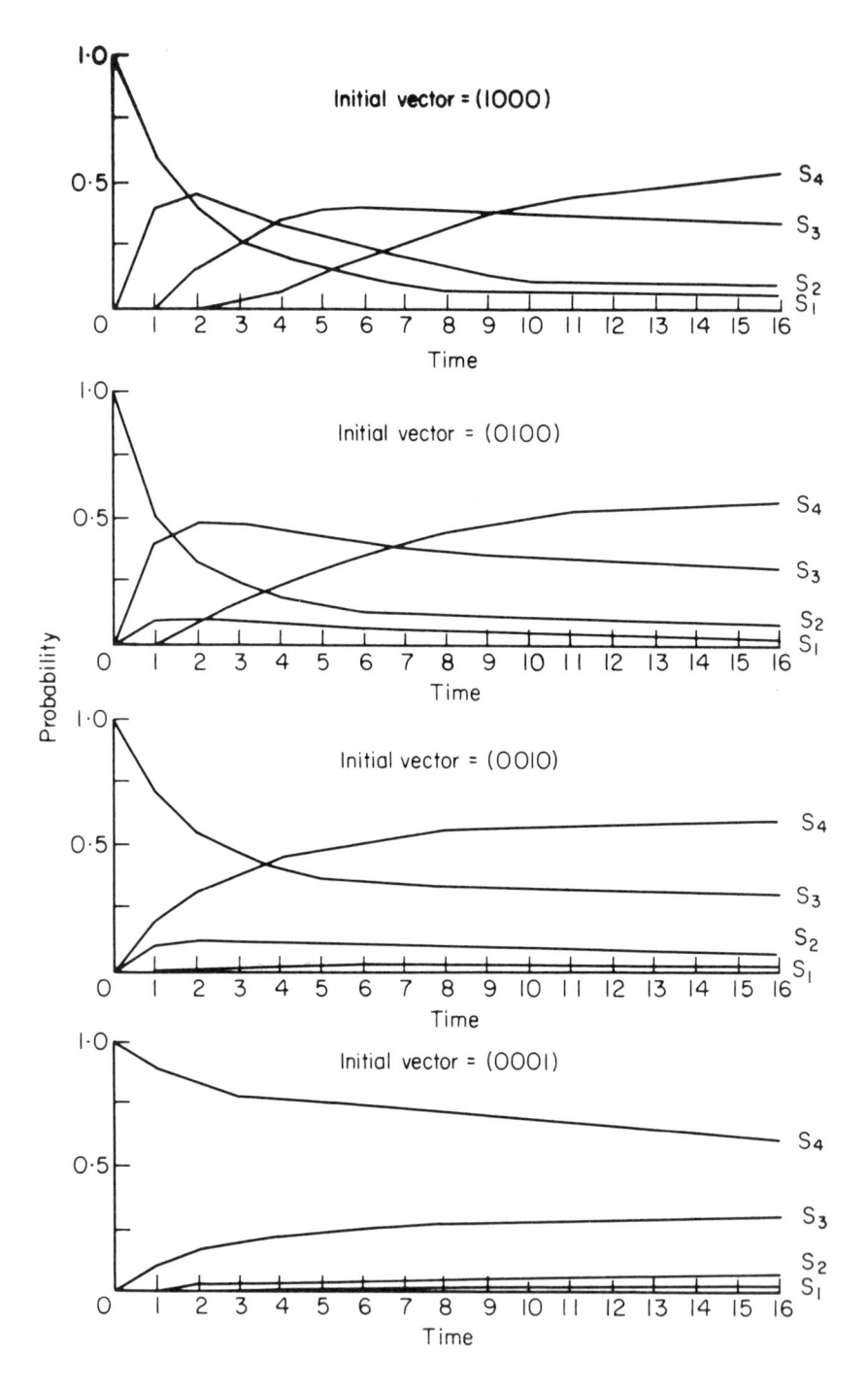

Fig. 9.1 Alternative initial vectors and time paths

The unsuccessfulness of attempts to explain migratory movements mainly on the basis of themselves and their short-term effects is only partly due to the shortcomings of existing methods and models. If continuity is assumed in the migratory pattern, the distribution of population at any given moment can be considered only as a very transitional stage which should, therefore, not be used as a standard of comparison with the next distribution, nor with the equilibrium distribution. Muhsam (1961) maintains that, for this reason, it is difficult to explain the difference between the distribution of a population at the beginning and the end of a short period of observation in terms of concrete economic and social forces. It is equally as difficult to explain the migration matrix in terms of these economic and social forces deduced from the distributions. Only the equilibrium distribution should correspond with economic and social facts. Population change and movement, as observed during a given time period, are just one step in a long series of similar steps, each of which can, in many respects, only be understood in terms of the final distribution to which they would lead if perpetuated for a sufficiently long time and without major modification.

Prediction and goodness-of-fit

One of the objectives of using a Markov model is to provide a basis for predicting the outcomes of future migration events. Lee, Judge and Zellner (1970) have shown that the chi-square statistic can be employed to test whether the observed proportions or aggregate data are 'usual' or 'unusual' outcomes, given that it is assumed that the observations have been generated by a first order Markov process. The chi-square test can be applied to the maximum likelihood estimates from aggregate data of the transition probabilities for, say, the periods involved when $t = 3, 4, \ldots 16$. The observed aggregate distributions are compared with the predicted proportions from the estimated probabilities. The chi-square test is also applicable to micro migration data — recording all movement between areas in one year. Predictions from this actual transition matrix can then be compared with observed proportions in following years.

Guthrie and Youssef (1970) evaluated the levels of significance of chi-square tests of hypothesis for orders zero to three within a fourth order Markov model, for both the two- and three-state case. Results were consistent with asymptotic theory only when samples were quite large.

If outcomes are deemed quite unusual on application of the χ^2 test, it can be tentatively concluded that the data may not be generated from the assumed process. On the other hand, if on the basis of traditional sampling theory test procedures, the result is consistent with the hypothesis that the aggregate data are the outcomes of the Markov process, then Markov theory that has been developed can be used to provide additional information.

Mean migration times

This additional information on migration is of passage times typical of migrants, and can be derived from the transition matrix. The probability matrix, P, provides a great deal of information about the Markovian migration process. From this matrix it is possible to study the length of time it takes an average individual to move from state i to state j.

Theory developed for regular Markov chains can be used to portray mobility patterns in transition matrices. If P is a regular transition matrix, the matrix $Z = (I - (P - A))^{-1}$ is the fundamental matrix for the Markov chain determined by P. I is an identity matrix and A is an equal row matrix P^n. The mean first passage matrix M is given by

$$M = (I - Z + EZdg)D$$

where D is the diagonal matrix with diagonal elements $d_{ii} = 1/a_i$
where a is the limiting probability vector
       Zdg is the Z matrix with all off-diagonal entries set equal to zero
       E is a matrix with all elements equal to one

For a regular Markov chain, the first passage time is a function the value of which is the number of steps before entering s_j for the first time after the initial position s_i (Kemeny and Snell, 1960).

First passage times have been calculated for migration between California and the rest of the United States (Rogers, 1968), and by Brown, Odland and Golledge (1970) to analyse functional distance in order to define migration fields. Brown and Longbrake (1970) calculated mean first passage times to evaluate place utility functions. They found mean first passage times by neighbourhood type to be

	I	II	III	IV	V
I	1·66	5·28	24·92	11·39	326·35
II	2·08	4·62	24·71	10·61	327·23
III	2·45	5·47	20·02	9·23	326·86
IV	2·60	5·32	22·80	7·81	323·05
V	2·92	4·99	21·83	7·49	312·80

Zones were: type I — middle-class family households; type II — upper middle-class households; type III — lower economic status, sound rented two-family dwelling units; type IV — lower economic status, unsound rented multi-family dwelling units; type V — downtown commercial zone.

In this example, for a person in zone I, the mean number of time periods before moving to zone II is 5·28; before moving to zone V, 326·35. The mean number of time periods before moving back to zone I, after leaving, is 1·66.

Theory developed for absorbing Markov chains can also be used to provide information on migration and on regular Markov chains. By using such theory it is possible to determine, on average, the length of time it will take for the process to be absorbed and, on average, how many times the process will be in each non-absorbing state (Kemeny, 1959).

Willis (1970) analysed an absorbing Markov chain of local authorities on Tyneside, plus the rest of England and Wales, by making one state, the rest of England and Wales, s_j, into an absorbing state. This was done by replacing the jth row of P by a row with one in the jth component and zero otherwise. Starting at any state other than s_j, the new process behaves exactly like the old one up to the first time that state s_j is reached. Since the original chain was an ergodic chain, it was possible to reach s_j from any other state. The new chain is an absorbing chain with a single absorbing state s_j. For an absorbing chain the process will eventually reach an absorbing state no matter where it started, hence s_j is sure to be reached no matter what the starting state is. The fundamental matrix for an absorbing chain is

$$N = (I - Q)^{-1}$$

where

		r states	s states
$P =$	r	I	0
	s	R	Q

where I is an $r \times r$ identity matrix (representing absorbing state(s))
O is an $r \times s$ zero matrix
R is an $s \times r$ matrix
Q is an $s \times s$ matrix

The entries of N give the mean number of times in each non-absorbing state for each possible non-absorbing starting state. In terms of the original chain, these qualities represent the mean number of times in each of the states before reaching state s_j for the first time. From 1961—66 migration data starting at Newcastle, the mean number of times (five-year periods) a migrant was in Newcastle was 2·54; in Gosforth, 0·13; in Newburn, 0·30 (overspill); in Castle Ward, 0·29; in Hebburn, 0·02; and so on. Mean passage times have the usual interpretation for the individual process, but do not seem to have a natural interpretation for the collective process. The mean number of times a migrant was likely to stay in an area (his starting area), before moving to other areas and finally being absorbed, was found to be low for Gosforth (1·53), Longbenton (1·92), Whitley Bay (1·70), and Castle Ward (1·56). Starting areas for which the mean number of times a migrant was likely to stay there was large included Tynemouth (3·25), Gateshead (3·02), South Shields (4·55), Felling (3·21) and Washington (4·01). Furthermore, it was possible to discern from the N matrix, that people moving out from larger urban centres (for example, from Gateshead to Felling, Gateshead to Whickham, Newcastle to Newburn, Castle Ward to Longbenton, South Shields to Bolden; that is, migrants to traditional overspill areas) were, on average, likely to spend less time in those areas than migrants moving in the opposite direction.

The first passage times for a regular chain are quite similar to absorption times for an absorbing Markov chain. They both have variances which are in general large compared to their means. Since the standard deviations of the first passage times are of the same order of magnitude as the means, the means should not be taken as typical values. However, the relative size is of interest. Results should be interpreted not as absolute values, but as showing the relative importance and position of areas in the spatial extent of migration and in a migrant preference over time.

The mean time before being absorbed can now be calculated from the N matrix. If the matrix is considered an absorbing Markov chain with a non-absorbing state, and C an s component column vector with all entries one, then the vector NC has as components the mean number of time periods before being absorbed for each possible non-absorbing starting state. Mathematically, it is equivalent if all entries in a row are added. Table 3 records the mean time required, starting in states $s_1, s_2, \ldots s_n$ before being absorbed in s_j. This is called the mean first passage time from s_i to s_j. Migrants from Castle Ward take 3·16 periods before being absorbed and those from Whitley Bay 3·34. On the other hand the mean number of time periods before absorption for migrants starting from Felling was 6·83 — more than twice as many. The mean first passage time gives some indication of the connectivity of each area.

A theorem states that, for an ergodic Markov chain, the mean recurrence time for state s_i is $1/a_i$, where a_i is the ith component of the fixed

Table 3

Migration passage times

	NC mean first passage time into England and Wales outside Tyneside	Mean recurrence time
Newcastle upon Tyne	5·07897	351·7
Tynemouth	5·30534	588·9
Gosforth	3·81312	2,403·8
Longbenton	4·99696	1,663·8
Newburn	5·38389	1,481·4
Seaton Valley	5·09781	1,730·1
Wallsend	5·79124	2,109·7
Whitley Bay	3·34448	1,172·3
Castle Ward	3·15586	1,233·0
Gateshead	6·44892	1,039·5
South Shields	6·10290	1,180·6
Blaydon	3·99224	2,061·8
Boldon	3·85950	2,083·3
Chester-le-Street UD	4·65354	2,197·8
Felling	6·82594	1,923·0
Hebburn	6·64539	6,849·0
Hetton	4·13994	5,464·4
Houghton-le-Spring	3·91262	1,814·8
Jarrow	5·79373	6,097·5
Ryton	4·50922	2,840·9
Washington	5·76570	2,732·2
Whickham	4·83605	1,709·4
Chester-le-Street RD	4·68249	962·4
Rest of England and Wales		1·016347

Note: both times are in terms of the base time (five years) used to compile the transition matrix for 1961–66 probability vector for the transition matrix. The mean recurrence time is defined as the mean time required if we start in, say, state s_i before returning to s_i. We must return on the first step or go to some other state and from any other state we know we will eventually reach s_i. The mean recurrences are given by the reciprocals of these probabilities. In the North East, the mean time for a migrant returning to Newcastle and Tynemouth from starting at these local authorities is much less than that for starting elsewhere. As it is, no one leaving any local authority area would return in their lifetime. Obviously this is not exact, since much migration is return migration. But the mean recurrence times give an indication of return migration time according to the transition probabilities (in this case of a first order Markov chain).

Conclusion

Stochastic processes are a valuable and often much-overlooked aid to analysing migration processes. Once the process has been tested for goodness-of-fit and accepted, many extremely useful analyses can be undertaken. Some of these have been mentioned, such as mean passage times and equilibrium distribution. Markov theory provides a tool for analysing both the consequences of migration and isolating the migration patterns and types themselves from the migration matrix. Some conclusions using specific data are obviously suspect in absolute terms — such as recurrence times, using 1966 Census data. If existing methods and results are challenged, it must be on grounds of data inadequacy. Complete information is lacking because census records only give place of residence at five-year intervals (also yearly, but these are discontinuous in time). There is no record of changes that have taken place during these intervals. This would present no problems if the states of the system at successive intervals could be treated as a Markov chain. Nevertheless, where data is inadequate results may still be valuable in providing a view of the relative importance and position of areas in migration and in a migrant's system of preference. It is, therefore, possible to build models capable of describing mobility patterns which have been observed, but if data can be obtained on individual case histories in migration and labour mobility the scope for useful model building will be greatly enlarged.

Note

[1] See the 1961, 1966 and 1971 Censuses. The usual question is, 'Was the person's usual residence one year ago (five years ago) the same ... ? If no, write also usual address on ... '.

10 Spatial and other Multivariate Techniques

Vector and standard distance analysis

The areal representation of static characteristics in demography, such as total population, density, sex and age structure, housing and occupational composition, birth, fertility, morbidity and death rates, can be adequately satisfied with choropleth maps, or by the use of proportional circles, cubes, squares, bar diagrams, pyramids and so on. Migration is a demographic characteristic no less than birth and death rates, but infinitely more difficult to measure and represent adequately in a special context. The techniques most frequently used to portray migration streams are arrows or lines of varying width from areas of origin to destination (House and Knight, 1966), circles and spheres to indicate magnitude of movement to and from areas, and bar diagrams to show the proportion of the population involved in migration, or to show deviations from the average (House and Willis, 1967).

The difficulty in using lines to portray migration was first recognised by Thornthwaite (1934), when he attempted to depict interstate migration streams in the United States. Even with the use of coloured flow lines, he found the graphic representation too unwieldy to show movement from each state to every other state. If there are n areas to and from which migration is recorded, the theoretically possible number of streams is n^2 or $n^2 - n$ if within area migration is ignored.

Individual vectors have been used to depict migration. Hägerstrand (1962) used lines to record all movement out of dwellings in one single year (1935) from the parish of Asby in Sweden. Movements within and to areas outside the parish were shown, but not movements in, and Hägerstrand concluded, 'This straightforward picture is not very clear of course, but it gives a rather striking impression of how complicated the flow is and also how large the turnover must be'.

Individual migration through time can probably best be illustrated diagrammatically (Hägerstrand, 1962) as a flow through a system of stations; but where there is a large quantity of data, there has been a general search for methods to reduce it to terms that can be usefully interpreted.

Price (1948) provided one solution, in a study of 1935–40 internal migration among nine census divisions, by computing 72 vectors, assessing the direction and distance of each. However, here the amount of data based on only nine census divisions of the United States was becoming unwieldy in diagramatic form. Wolpert (1967) extended this type of analysis, and computed and graphed, for 1955–60, the median centres of in-migration, out-migration and net-migration by direction for the 100 largest Standard Metropolitan Statistical Areas in the United States. The mass of data produced still needed to be evaluated visually and subjectively with both of these methods.

Bachi (1958, 1961, 1965a, 1965b) attempted to reduce large masses of raw and often unwieldy statistical geographical data into a few summary values expressing the broader aspects of the migration distribution over space, and the general trends of migratory movements. The main characteristics of a special distribution are (i) location (ii) dispersion (iii) main direction (iv) asymmetry and (v) concentration. Bachi's work has largely focused on the first three aspects.

Location can be measured by the centre of gravity of the distribution, which is a point that minimises the sum of squares of the distances to the points of distribution. Alternatively, the median centre can be calculated; this is a point from which the sum of the distances of the points of the distribution is minimal. Both measures are easily calculated on an electronic computer; the former by the use of Pythagoras' theorem (Randall and Willis, 1969).

Given the location of the points of residence of each of the n individuals after leaving a specific area or before moving into the area, the location of an individual being indicated by co-ordinates $X_i\ Y_i$, the co-ordinates of the centre of gravity of the set are

$$\bar{X} = \frac{\sum_{i=1}^{n} X_i}{n}, \qquad \bar{Y} = \frac{\sum_{i=1}^{n} Y_i}{n}$$

Bachi (1965b) has indicated that dispersion can be measured as 'the standard distance' or the quadratic average of the distance of each point from the centre

$$d = \sqrt{\frac{\sum_{i=1}^{n} \{(X_i - \bar{X})^2 + (Y_i - \bar{Y})^2\}}{n}}$$

Using the centre of gravity, Bachi (1965a) traced in the USA the shift caused by interstate migration between the centre of place of birth and centre of place of residence of migrants at censuses. The average birthplace—current residence move in 1870 was 582 km., rising to 641 km. in 1890, falling to 442 km. in 1940 but rising again to 482 km. in 1950. The main direction of the shift had constantly been to the West. Calculating 'standard distances', Bachi found internal migration had been one of the factors causing the continuously increasing dispersion of the population. Applying these techniques to Israel, Bachi (1965b) found that internal migration had no practical influence on population dispersion, and that in certain periods internal migrations of new immigrants had been more centripetal than centrifugal. He found that the policy of population-spreading and enlarging settlement areas has been reached mainly by influencing the distribution of new immigrants at their arrival in Israel. Despite the subsequent centripetal tendency of new immigrants in their internal migrations, their first settlements are much more widely spread than the settlements of old immigrants.

The technique was further developed by Tarver, Gurley and Skees (1967) and Tarver and Skees (1967), who computed, for 38 State Economic Areas in the South-Western United States, migration vectors in total people—miles and average number of miles for in, out and net movement, using both rectangular and spherical (polar) co-ordinate systems. A comparison was made of the different types of vector representation of migration, and the accuracy of vectors based upon rectangular and polar co-ordinates. Rectangular distance was computed from the formulae (people—miles out-movement),

$$X_{oi} = \sum_j M_{ij} (X_j - X_i)$$

$$Y_{oi} = \sum_j M_{ij} (Y_j - Y_i)$$

where X_{oi} is the X direction people—miles co-ordinate of all persons moving from the ith SEA into the other 37 SEAs; Y_{oi} is the Y direction people—miles co-ordinate for the out-migrants from the ith SEA; and M_{ij} is the number of migrants moving from the ith SEA to the jth SEA; $X_j - X_i$ measures the distance between SEA$_j$ and SEA$_i$ in the X direction, and $Y_j - Y_i$ measures the corresponding distance in the Y direction. Vectors for each of SEAs were thus calculated by multiplying the number of people moving from each SEA to every other SEA by the distance they moved in the X and Y direction, and then summing the SEAs. Vectors for in-migration were calculated on a similar basis. The length of the resultant vector was obtained from

$$d = \sqrt{X_i^2 + Y_i^2}$$

and the angle from the expression

$$\phi = \tan^{-1} \frac{Y_i}{X_i}$$

Using a polar co-ordinate system, the law of cosines for the side of a spherical triangle states that, the cosine of a side is equal to the product of the cosines of the opposite sides, plus the product of the sines of the sides and the cosine of the angle between the sides. From this the expression may be formed

$$\cos(D_{ij}) = \sin(a_i)\sin(a_j) + \cos(a_i)\cos(a_j)\cos(\Delta\lambda)$$

from which D_{ij}, as an angular value (each minute equal to one nautical mile), is derived. The expression

$$\cos(\phi_{ij}) = [\sin(a_j) - \sin(a_i)\cos(D_{ij})] \div \cos(a_i)\sin(D_{ij})$$

was used to obtain the angle.

Tarver, Gurley and Skees concluded from US data that the spherical co-ordinate system was more accurate than the rectangular, due to the curvature of the earth and the fact that much migration is in an east–west direction in the USA over long distances resulting in large errors.

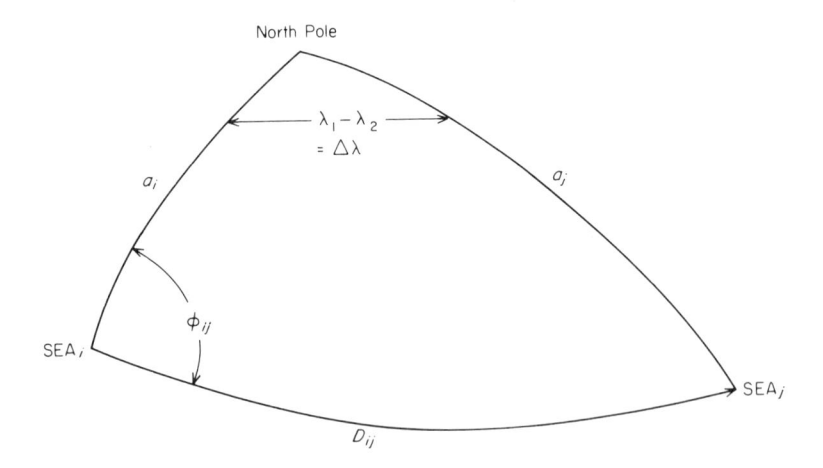

Fig. 10.1 Spherical triangulation method used in computing the distance and angle between each pair of SEAs

Theoretically, three-dimensional trigonometry represents the curvature of the vectors; any error in longitude and latitude representation of polar co-ordinate vectors is due to the deviation from the ideal population centres of areas and not from the curvature of the vectors.

Willis (1968) used the rectangular co-ordinate system in a study of British migration data, since migration distances are small in Britain compared with the US and there is also a more rapid decline of migration rates with distance. These two factors, together with the error resulting from the inaccurate measurement of population centres of areas, from which migration is measured, are likely to be greater than the difference between the spherical and rectangular systems.

Willis used a similar formula to that of Tarver and Skees to compute migration vector distance

$$d = \sqrt{\frac{\sum_{i=1}^{N}(m\,D_{ij}\,\sin\phi)^2 + \sum_{i=1}^{N}(m\,D_{ij}\,\cos\phi)^2}{\Sigma\,m}}$$

where D_{ij} is the distance between area i and j;
        m is the number of migrants between i and j;
        N is the number of local authorities to which or from which migration takes place.

This statistic measures distance in the dominant direction; that is, other directions are eliminated in the calculation so that gross out- or in-movement is so many kilometres in the given direction.

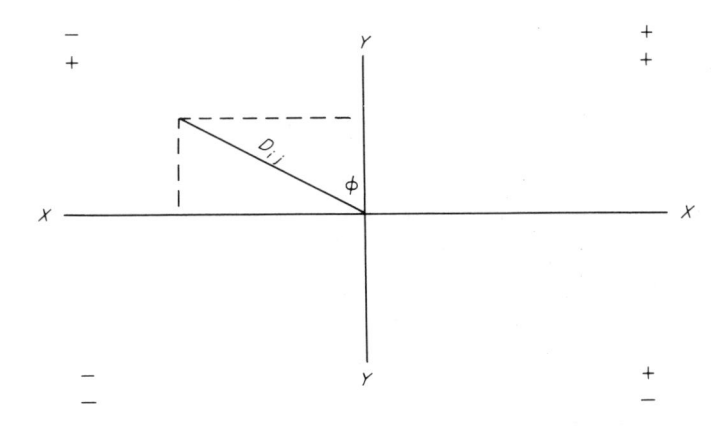

Fig. 10.2 Rectangular co-ordinate system for computing distance and direction

The resultant dominant vector direction is obtained from the above equation by summing all the sines and cosines (Willis 1968, 1969, 1970) and then obtaining the angle.

$$abs \sum_{i=1}^{N} (m\, D_{ij} \sin \phi) + \sum_{i=1}^{N} (m\, D_{ij} \cos \phi)$$

Angles (degrees) cannot be summed individually. The reason for this can easily be understood from Figure 10·3.

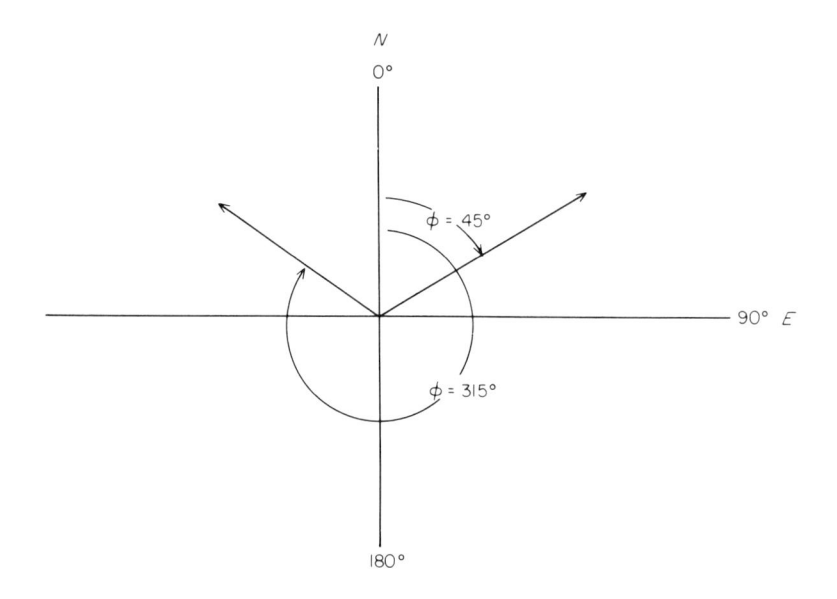

Fig. 10.3 The summing of angles to obtain migration direction

If two migrants moved the same distance in the two directions indicated in Fig. 10·3, a summation and division of angles by number of migrants (315 + 45)/2 would result in a dominant direction of 180°. This is in the opposite direction to the two migration vectors!

Depending upon the quadrant in which the angle falls, 180° is added to the angle or the angle is subtracted from 180° or 360° in the calculation of vector direction, (Randall and Willis, 1969). In Fig. 10·3 the individual angle is 360° − ϕ.

The results of this type of vector analysis depend upon the configuration of the boundaries over which it is undertaken; that is, direction is influenced by shape and relative position. Analysis in North East England suffers from the boundary between England and Scotland[1] and the coast to the east. Nevertheless, the technique is valuable particularly in areas such as the English Midlands and in the USA to produce summary values of direction of migration streams. Interesting results based on distance were obtained for North East England (Willis, 1970) by measuring 'standard distance', or average dispersion of migration out of and into an area, and migration vector distance: the average distance of movement along the dominant direction vector. Newcastle was the only area on Tyneside to which in-migrants moved, on average, farther than out-migrants. Migrants to and from the larger urban centres (Gateshead, South Shields, Tynemouth, Newcastle) moved on average nearly the same distance, whereas from the smaller local authority areas out-migrants moved on average twice as far as in-migrants moving into the same area. This suggests that while large urban centres lose population to surrounding areas they attract proportionately more long-distance in-migrants and lose proportionately less long-distance out-migrants than small surrounding urban centres.

Taylor (1968) criticised the type of analysis presented by Tarver, Gurley and Skees as being dependent upon the relative frame of reference; that is, it would not show a direction bias if movement was of a centre-wards or dispersion nature (assuming the same number of migrants moved the same distance in a diagonally opposite direction). Another frame of reference is needed to show this bias. While no vector direction or length could be derived, the form of the distribution could still be measured by 'standard distance' or by an index of oblongity. Bachi (1965b) defined the latter as

$$\lambda = \frac{\sigma x'^2 - \sigma y'^2}{\sigma x'^2 + \sigma y'^2}$$

Standard distance is invariant to rotation of the axes of co-ordinates, but σx and σy are not. If co-ordinates are rotated in the range $-45° \leq \alpha' \leq 45°$ by the simple method

$$X' = x \cos \alpha - y \sin \alpha$$
$$Y' = x \sin \alpha + y \cos \alpha$$

where x and y are the original co-ordinates and the rotation being through α degrees, one of the standard deviations will be minimised while the other is maximised, indicating the spread in the two directions. The oblongity index, therefore, lies in the range between -1 and $+1$ with zero indicating a completely random distribution or a uniform outward movement from a centre. Note that standard distance d equals

$$d = \sqrt{\sigma x'^2 + \sigma y'^2}$$

while the axes of $\sigma x'$ and $\sigma y'$ lie at an angle α' to the original co-ordinates, enabling the main direction of the distribution to be indicated.

Eigenvalues and eigenvectors

The use of a migration matrix itself describing movement between areas, and the use of distance and vector analysis, is limited; the former by the necessity to make subjective evaluations between array elements, and both by the difficulty of recognising structured patterns of movement and interrelationships between systems and subsystems. The complexity of migration flows causes difficulties in structuring relationships between movement and area.

Preliminary analysis may help interpretation, eliminating some flows by comparing the actual migration with the expected migration from a model. A crude model similar to the $P_1 P_2 / D$ hypothesis (Zipf, 1946; Anderson, 1955) may have the form

$$M_{ij} = k \frac{P_i P_j}{P}$$

where P_i and P_j are the total populations of areas i and j respectively;
P is the population of the whole area under consideration; and
k is a constant M/P — average number of migrations per capita.

Alternatively, more sophisticated models may be used. Goodman (1963) suggested some statistical methods for the preliminary analysis of transaction flows, to eliminate the effects of the 'size variable' before examining how other possible explanatory variables may affect transaction flows.

In migration a number of different nodes and types of movement are involved: migration between pairs of places represents a great range of functional types of movement. Linkages within subsystems of migration are strong, but there are important connections between different migration systems and types. The cartographic, distance, and vector representation of migration data create a better visual impression, but do not resolve superimposed migration patterns into separate types. A map and graphic representation of data, and subjective appraisal, allow few opportunities for manipulating its information directly to extend knowledge about migration. In migration it is important to transform pieces of cartographically-portrayed information into numbers capable of being manipulated mathematically: it is only by manipulating a migration matrix that we are able to uncover patterns and relationships in complex situations where many variables enter a problem and compete for our attention (Gould, 1967). The use of eigenvalues and eigenvectors permits the elimination of the noise of random flows and allows us to focus on the basic characteristic of the system.

Every square matrix has an equation (a polynomial of the same order as the matrix) associated with, or characteristic of, the matrix. Eigenvalues are the latent roots of these equations. The characteristic equation of a square matrix A is defined as

$$det \mid A - \lambda I \mid = 0$$

where I is the identity matrix and λ is the scalar matrix (Gould, 1967; Bellman, 1960; Christ, 1966). Associated with each eigenvalue is a vector the values of which may be obtained by substitution after solving n equations

$$(A - \lambda I) X = 0$$

where X is an eigenvector and λ is an eigenvalue 1 to n. From this it may be seen that

$$A(X_j) = \lambda_j (X_j)$$

X_j at this point are orthogonal.

The result of these computations is to produce a linearly transformed set of variates $X_1, X_2, X_3 ... X_n$ (latent vectors) called 'principal components' of the original variates, which are mutually independent and can, therefore, be considered separately. An important property of eigenvalues is

$$\lambda_1 + \lambda_2 ... + \lambda_n = \sigma_{11} + \sigma_{22} ... + \sigma_{nn}$$

Because of the decreasing order of variance associated with the principal components, it is possible that only one or two of the variates are needed to summarise the whole of the variability and co-variability of the original variates. The objective of the analysis is thus the parsimonious summarisation of a mass of observations (Seal, 1964). Eigenvectors might be regarded as an ultimate development in the use of orthogonal functions to describe patterns of arrays of data (Stidd, 1967). They have an advantage over those orthogonal functions expressible by simple formulas in that they are derived from the data being studied and strongly resemble the important features of the data, so that the first several eigenvectors contain a much higher percentage of 'variance' than would be contained in an equal number of ordinary orthogonal polynomials. Matrix transformation is necessary where the matrix is not square. If the original matrix is A_{nm}, then

$$A_{nm} \times A_{mn} = AA'_{nn}$$
$$A_{mn} \times A_{nm} = AA'_{mm}$$

where AA' is a symmetric matrix.

For an unsymmetrical matrix the eigenvalues associated with the rows are not the same as those associated with the columns. Thus in- and out-migrants are evaluated separately.

Eigenvalues of absolute migration during 1961–66 on Tyneside show the migration surface to be convoluted, representing a departure from an even migration surface (equal unit flows between elements i and j of the array). The ratio λ_1/λ_2 is an indication of this. The larger the ratio, the more even the migration surface. λ_1/λ_2 was about 3·0 for in- and out-migration on Tyneside and this compares with 3·12 for Gould's (1967) ridge and valley λ_1/λ_2 ratio. For out-migrants the ratio was slightly smaller than for in-migrants. This signifies out-movement to be more uneven over Tyneside than in-movement. (Willis, 1970).

Eigenvalues and eigenvectors revealed that local migration on Tyneside was more differentiated spatially within the area than migration from outside the Northern region to areas of Tyneside, or migration from Tyneside localities to areas outside the Northern region. Interregional migration was much more undifferentiated by local authorities on Tyneside: the migration surface was much more even. Areal differentiation in local movement exists to a much greater extent than in interregional migration in Britain. This method of analysis has the advantage that it does allow indices of migration:

$$\lambda_1/\lambda_2 \quad \text{or} \quad \lambda_1/\lambda_2 + \lambda_3 + \ldots \lambda_n)$$

to be calculated and comparisons between areas and types of migration are therefore possible.

Clustering analysis

Eigenvalues and eigenvectors form the basic mathematical component of a number of multivariate techniques including clustering analysis. Clustering analysis is concerned with producing homogenous areas or groups of individuals according to some criteria, by analysing certain statistical variations among individuals and grouping these criteria where the patterns of variations show the most similarity.

Clustering procedures vary in the methods by which new groups are formed at each step, and this can affect results (Fisher and Van Ness, 1971). Ward's (1963) method has proved the most popular and has been used to derive homogenous areas for planning purposes (Willis, 1971), and to classify standard metropolitan labour areas to indicate the degree of similarity between areas in terms of their pattern of migration and their housing and labour market conditions (Hadjifotiou, 1971). Ward's procedure relates a number of variables associated with an individual to such variables associated with other individuals, in such a way that linked groups of variables and individuals may be built up in an orderly sequence to form a complete linkage tree. Each pair of items or observations, and subsequent groups, are joined so that the least possible increment in the error sum of squares is made (or the minimum amount of within-group variability relative to the total data matrix variation) at each step in the sequence. Ward's grouping procedure is based on the premise that the amount of information available is greater when a set of n members is ungrouped. The first step is to group two individuals, which, when effected, will reduce by one the number of subsets, while producing the least increase in the error sum of squares from the within group variance. The number of subsets is systematically reduced ($n, n-1, \ldots 1$) and a 'hierarchical grouping' results. Hierarchical groupings are particularly useful for classification purposes and 'identifying' types of migration, migrants and associated areas.

Hadjifotiou was able to show through clustering analysis the differing associations between migration rates, type of population, housing conditions and labour market conditions over England and Wales. She also found clustering useful in providing a classification which could be used as a sampling frame for choosing particular areas for detailed questionnaire investigation in contrasting or in similar type areas. By relating migration flows between pairs of areas, weighted by shape, size and distance, it may be possible to test the hypothesis that migration usually occurs between similar areas.

Mention was made of aggregation bias in the specification of stochastic models. Aggregation bias is a common problem associated with linear programming models; each activity considered is assumed to be homogenous in all its uses. Markov chains too assume homogeneity in activities considered. The more aggregated the unit under consideration, the greater will be the likelihood that the homogeneity condition does not hold. Aggregation bias exists when the sum of the solutions for each subset does not equal the solution of the entire set, or the total obtained by weighting the solution for the representative group (Miller, 1966). This occurs where the aggregate migration or production functions of the grouped types or enterprises are no longer representative of the migration or production function of individual migrants or economic enterprises.

The individual provides the best accounting unit for analysis, but this requires large amounts of data on the characteristics of each person and the use of micro scale areas; which in practice is impossible to handle. It may be possible to reduce the number of units or areas by aggregating individuals or very small areas according to a set of sufficient conditions. A set of such conditions is provided by Day (1963) for aggregating firms in economics, but similar conditions would hold in analysing occupational labour migration. Aggregation without bias is possible where individuals or areas are: (a) technologically homogenous – each unit serves the same type of production, uses the same resources, and is subject to the same constraints; (b) institutionally homogenous – constraints on individuals and areas must be proportional to aggregate constraints; (c) pecuniously homogenous – expectations of individuals or areas in net returns are proportional to the average expectations of the group they represent. These conditions apply to dynamic as well as static situations – individuals or areas cannot be aggregated if they enjoy differing rates in salary scales or differing rates of economies of scale to migration. Buckwell and Hazell (1972) used clustering analysis to maximise these conditions and minimise aggregation bias. The use of clustering analysis to minimise aggregation bias in stochastic models of migration has not been explored, but as a technique offers promise in tackling this particular problem associated with probabilistic models and, also, regression models; for example, cross-sectional models based on areal data. In general, an exact total migration relation is obtained by aggregating migrants with weights proportional to individual marginal propensities to move.

Factor analysis

Linkage structure in the pattern of migration flows can be isolated by factor analysis, from the viewpoint of origins and destinations. Factor analysis has become the generic term for a variety of procedures developed for the purpose of analysing the intercorrelations within a set of variables. The numerous descriptions of the technique that are in existence are easily accessible, so it is pointless describing it here. The technique is described by Harman (1960) and Cooley and Lohnes (1962), and applications of it by Berry (1966), Goddard (1970) and Wilkinson (1973).

Factor analysis, through rotation procedures, concentrates on significant patterns of variation or common factors and ignores all other influences. Factor analysis has the advantage of allowing origins and destinations of migration to be identified. It has been used to study migration patterns between local authority areas on Tyneside (Willis, 1970) and, more recently, flows between standard metropolitan labour areas (Hadjifotiou, 1972). As a result, in both studies specific migration networks between small groups of specific areas were identified. It is a useful tool, as far as migration is concerned, for describing flows, but it is worth summarising, following Hadjifotiou, a number of difficulties attached to its use. Factor analysis is based on the correlation matrix of the variables. Correlation analysis measures the similarity of the flow patterns but ignores the total number of people involved, weighting large and small flows equally. Factor analysis will, therefore, reveal a number of different migration patterns, which may not be the most important in terms of volume of migrants. Direct factor analysis has been suggested as a method to overcome this problem, in which the original data is the basis of factor groups and is not used to produce a correlation matrix. Also, by using correlation to measure the similarity of the flow composition, it is possible that the factor groupings may identify 'negative' patterns based on a common distribution of zeros or low values, rather than patterns of 'positive' movements. The identified factors must be checked against the original data to overcome this problem. There is the problem, with any factor analysis, of the threshold value adopted to define groups from the factor scores and loadings. Some workers have taken these values as ± 0.50 for factor loadings and ± 1.00 for factor scores (these represent the destinations and origins respectively of the migration flows). Low values will result in the inclusion of a large number of areas, and too high a score might eliminate so many areas that migration networks are oversimplified.

Two further problems are inherent in any factor analysis. One is the problem of how many factors to preserve for further analysis (in rotation procedures). Statistical considerations alone are not completely satisfactory, since the number of significant factors then depends on the size of the sample. Kaiser (1960) made a practical suggestion for deciding how many factors to use by recommending the use of those factors with corresponding latent roots greater than one. This rule only applies if unities are used in the diagonal, and this forms another problem: whether to use unity or some other criterion or value as the communality estimate. Alternative diagonal elements for communality estimation might be the squared multiple correlation coefficient, maximum absolute row value, or other diagonal elements specified by the user. Each has its advantages and disadvantages.

Factor analytic identification of networks and motives for moving provides a useful adjunct to additional types of analysis and may provide some additional insight into the basis of migration and motivation, but rarely provides the sole method or approach.

The measurement of mobility

This chapter has been concerned with both describing and measuring mobility. It is convenient, when comparing migration patterns, to have some measure of mobility as a yardstick of judgement. Three types of pattern spring to mind. The easiest to define and the most recognisable pattern is a completely immobile pattern with no movement between areas. It is less easy to decide some measure of migration characteristic of a mobile situation. Migration may be thought of as random and independent of previous area, and in such a case the columns of P will be identical. Actual migration could be compared with this situation. Maximum movement takes place when each migrant has a different area from his previous one. For a transition matrix these three types of migration are represented by:

$$\text{(a)} \begin{bmatrix} 1 & 0 \\ 0 & 1 \end{bmatrix} \quad \text{(b)} \begin{bmatrix} \cdot 5 & \cdot 5 \\ \cdot 5 & \cdot 5 \end{bmatrix} \quad \text{(c)} \begin{bmatrix} 0 & 1 \\ 1 & 0 \end{bmatrix}$$

Most migration patterns are likely to be intermediate between the first and the second case. For transition matrices the determinant of P is a useful index and is 1 for a perfectly immobile migration (case (a)); zero for a migration pattern where flows are independent and regular (case (b)) and -1 when the maximum amount of migration occurred (case (c)). These measures are less satisfactory when larger matrices are considered, since whenever any two columns of P are identical the determinant will be zero, implying perfect mobility. It is also difficult to decide the structure of a large matrix to represent maximum migration.

Muhsam (1961) suggests that all matrices with the same characteristic vector can be represented as a weighted average of the identity matrix and the matrix with identical rows, which transforms any given distribution immediately into the equilibrium distribution. Thus, all paths that a population can follow to reach a certain equilibrium distribution can be ordered, and a quantitative index attached to each of them. The identity matrix is at one end of the range, with the mobility of the population at its minimum, and the equilibrium distribution is reached after an infinite number of steps; while at the other end of the scale, with an equilibrium matrix, equilibrium is reached by one step, but mobility is very high. The numerical value attached to a given path shows at which position the given matrix stands between these two extremes. An example is given of migration probabilities, based on the 1950 US Census, between the north and east of the country and the south and west,

$$\begin{bmatrix} 0.990497 & 0.009503 \\ 0.009085 & 0.990915 \end{bmatrix}$$

of which the characteristic vector is (0·4888   0·5112).

The degree of mobility expressed by this migration matrix could be appreciated by comparing it with extremes — low mobility leading to the equilibrium distribution in an infinite number of years, and that of high mobility which would produce equilibrium in one step. The actual migration matrix can be obtained as a weighted average of the matrices representing these two extremes.

$$0.0186 \begin{bmatrix} 0.4888 & 0.5112 \\ 0.4888 & 0.5112 \end{bmatrix} + 0.9814 \begin{bmatrix} 1 & 0 \\ 0 & 1 \end{bmatrix} =$$

$$\begin{bmatrix} 0.990497 & 0.009503 \\ 0.009085 & 0.990915 \end{bmatrix}$$

The first matrix is the equilibrium matrix, the actual matrix raised to the nth power. The second matrix is the identity matrix. The actual migration matrix is nearer to the identity matrix, and it is in fact only 1·86 per cent of the scale, between the two extremes. However, this value can at present be calculated only for a 2 x 2 matrix, which limits its actual value and usefulness as an index.

All matrices admitting the same characteristic vector can also be considered as powers of one another. The identity matrix is then the zero power and the constant row matrix the infinite power, so it would be difficult to define a benchmark from which powers could be determined. But a matrix which is the square of another brings the distribution of a population to equilibrium twice as quickly as the other matrix. However, since it is difficult to define fractional powers of matrices (Waugh and Abel, 1967) which would be needed, Muhsam prefers the weighted average model.

Any measure which attempts to summarise the contents of the transition matrix into a single number is bound to result in an oversimplification. A more detailed picture of the migration occurring can be obtained if we replace the single number by a set of numbers.

A measure of mobility is to determine the eigenvalues and eigenvectors of P. When $\lambda_1, \lambda_2, \ldots \lambda_m$, the latent roots of P, are non-zero and all distinct, then from matrix theory P can be expressed in the form

$$P = H \Lambda H^{-1}$$

where $\Lambda = \text{diag } \lambda_i = \begin{bmatrix} \lambda_1 & & & & \\ & \lambda_2 & & & \\ & & \lambda_3 & & \\ & & & \ddots & \\ & & & & \lambda_m \end{bmatrix}$

and H is the matrix with columns given by the m latent column vectors of P written in order. The first few eigenvectors and eigenvalues contain the significant dimensions of migration in the P matrix, but a point is rapidly reached where this set of measures contains more elements than the transition matrix itself.

Prais (1955) proposed a set of measures considering the main diagonal of P; that is, considering only whether a move takes place and ignoring the kind of move. The duration of residence in an area j has a mean $u_j = 1/(1 - p_{jj})$. An immobile society will have large means, and in a mobile society means will be small. Prais suggested standardising the means by expressing them in terms of the means for a standard population, which he took to be a perfectly mobile society with the same equilibrium structure as the given population. This measure was

$$U_j^* = (1 - p_j)/(1 - p_{jj}) \quad (j = 1, 2, m)$$

These measures, unlike eigenvalues, depend only on the diagonal elements of P, and the information contained in off-diagonal elements is not utilised. Off-diagonal element information can be utilised by enlarging Prais's set of measures, by considering P^T for $T = 2, 3, \ldots$. The quantity $P_{jj}^{(T)}$ is the probability that an individual in area j is also in area j, T time periods later. This probability will be near 1 in an immobile society and small in a mobile population. Dividing this probability by $P_j = \lim\limits_{T \to \infty} P_{jj}^{(T)}$, Prais's immobility ratios are derived. As with eigenvalues and vectors a set of measures is obtained, rather than one index, and Bartholomew (1967) has suggested that these measures are alternative ways of presenting information contained in P rather than summary measures of mobility.

Various measures of migration are needed for different purposes and call for different approaches. A few have been presented in this chapter. Adaptation of other ideas might prove a fruitful exercise, although one must guard against a rigid mechanical translation of techniques and strive to develop concepts meaningful to migration. The use of rates and indices keyed to a particular type of analysis must be guarded against. This may arise from the fact that most data on migration has been obtained from secondary sources and censuses not under the direct control of the investigator. It may be instructive at this stage, given our reservations on many techniques expressed in the last three chapters, to pose the question: Has the ingenuity in the construction of theories and techniques not outrun the capacity for collection of relevant observations?

Note

[1] The 1966 Census recorded no movement between individual local authorities on either side of the boundary.

11 Estimating and Projecting Migration

A comprehensive survey of migration estimation and projection is beyond the scope of this chapter, yet no book covers the subject (which is regrettable), and the limits of the field are undefined. Literature on migration projection and estimation is fragmented rather than scarce, with articles in various journals investigating specific problems. This chapter reviews some of the major methods of migration estimation and projection, and work done in this field. The desire for accurate forecasts of future migration, together with the monitoring of current trends, is acute. This arises from the rapid increase in importance of migration as a contributor to population change, as disaggregation from studies of relatively closed national population systems to analyses of essentially open areas within multiregional systems proceeds. At local levels, migration assumes primary fundamental importance over fecundity, fertility and nuptiality, and divorce, remarriage and mortality rates (see Cox, 1970) for determining population trends.

Methods of migration estimation

There are a number of major methods for estimating migration. These differ in concept, orientation and operation and can be broadly classified as either direct or indirect. Direct methods are based on current and past data of demographic characteristics and rates. Indirect methods relate migration to the economic, social and political indices, such as statistics on employment, investment, income, exports, or school enrolments, and are based primarily on regression and correlation analysis (Isard, 1960). Indirect techniques for estimating migration have now been superseded by direct methods as more reliable demographic data have become available.

Included among traditional direct methods are cohort-survival models, which focus principally on the age–sex distribution of a population at a given time. Data are analysed in terms of appropriate age–sex specific rates of fertility and mortality. The cohort-survival method has provided the conceptual framework for a number of studies of migration such as that by House and Knight (1965), *Migrants of North East England*, analysed by age and sex, and Jackson (1968) for population change in the Cotswolds. Several local authorities in England and Wales — for instance, Durham County Council (1969) — have also used cohort-survival on a sub-regional basis to study migration.

The cohort-survival methods of estimating migration gives rise to two fundamental problems in time and space. These will become obvious in the description of the two major variants of this residual method, which are:

(i) the vital statistics method, which employs actual birth and death statistics of each area to allow for natural increase or decrease; and

(ii) the survival rate method, which, as it is generally applied, employs national life table survival rates to allow for mortality and national birth rates (for female age groups), to allow for natality.

True net-migration is the difference between the total number of persons entering an area during the inter-censual interval (decade or quinquennium), and the total number of persons leaving the area during the same period. Total net migration equals surviving in-migrants and in-migrants who die, minus surviving out-migrants and out-migrants who die.

Siegel and Hamilton (1952) have demonstrated how the vital statistics formula makes allowance for those migrants both in and out, who die after migrating. From

$$\Sigma M = (\Sigma P_1 - \Sigma P_0) - (\Sigma B - \Sigma D) \quad (1)$$

Siegel and Hamilton have shown

$$M = M_i - M_0 = L_i + D_i^a - L_0 - D_0^a \quad (2)$$

and that

$$D = D_n + D_i^a + D_0^b$$

where ΣB and ΣD, respectively, symbolise the total number of births and deaths occurring to residents in the area;

ΣM, the balance of all movements into and out of the area;

ΣP_0 and ΣP_1, respectively, the total population at the beginning and end of the period;

M = $M_i - M_0$ = exact net migration;
M_i = in-migrant sub-cohort;
M_o = out-migrant sub-cohort;
L_i = in-migrant sub-cohort enumerated final population within area;
D_i^a = in-migrant sub-cohort deaths within area;

L_o = out-migrant sub-cohort enumerated final population outside area;
$D_o{}^a$ = out-migrant sub-cohort deaths outside area;
D_n = non-migrant sub-cohort deaths within area;
$D_o{}^b$ = out-migrant sub-cohort deaths within area. While not important, $D_o{}^b$ is included for the sake of completeness.

In Britain, the requisite vital birth and death statistics are not available for local areas on a cohort basis. But even if individual returns on births and deaths could be obtained, the vital statistics method requires that rates are calculated for each local area investigated, which is cumbersome. Where vital statistics for local areas are not used, accuracy is lost, but by the use of survival rate methods painstaking work is avoided.

Survival rate methods present a number of problems. Do survival rates and birth rates (usually national rates) reflect accurately the mortality and fertility of the population of a local area? Do the survival rates, even if correct, really measure the number of deaths in an area if one takes into account the occurrence of migration (US Bureau of the Census, 1951)? Three survival rate methods can be employed to estimate migration. The 'forward survival rate' formula has the form

$$M = P_1 - rP_0 \qquad (4)$$

or $$M = P_1 - P_0 + (1 - r)P_0 \qquad (5)$$

for an aging cohort, where r represents the survival rate, and $(1 - r)$ the mortality rate, which is the complement of the survival rate. For new-born cohorts the equation would also include a birth rate, estimated from fertility rates of women by age groups, and a survival rate applied to the number of births.

The 'reverse survival' rate has the form

$$M = P_1 - P_0 + \frac{(1 - r)P_1}{r}$$

and the 'average survival' rate (an average of the forward and reverse methods) is expressed as

$$M = \frac{(1 + r)}{2r}(P_1 - rP_0)$$

According to the forward survival method, the population at a given age at the beginning of a decade (quinquennium etc.) is multiplied by an appropriate survival rate to obtain an estimate of the population ten years older than would be present at the end of the decade if no migration occurred. This number of expected survivors is then compared with the actual population in the age group at the end of the decade, to determine the amount of net migration. Forward survival is the method most often used and is that adopted by House and Knight (1965) and Durham County Council (1969), but it is easily shown to be unrealistic in determining true net migration.

Equation (5) is similar to equation (1) for ageing cohorts (births are excluded here since they make the argument more complex) in that $(1 - r)P_o$ has been substituted for D. But this substitution is not a valid one. The number of deaths in an ageing cohort P_o is represented by $(1 - r)P_o$, and this is equal to

$$D_n + D_o{}^a + D_o{}^b$$

and not $\quad D_n + D_i{}^a + D_o{}^b$

as the substitution assumes.

The difference, $D_o{}^a - D_i{}^a$, is the difference between the deaths of in-migrants and out-migrants. The forward survival method implies that no persons who die during the period (including those who move and then die) have migrated.

The forward method, therefore, assumes that all migration takes place at the end of each period over which the survival rate is carried forward. This gives rise to errors in 'time'. The distinction between the vital statistics method (recording true net-migration) and the forward survival rate method is the difference between the deaths of in-migrants and out-migrants. This difference may not be negligible, and for each area will depend on the distribution of its in- and out-migration to other areas. Depending on the distribution of migration to and from each area and its occupational structure, there could be considerable differences in death rates between in- and out-migrants (Cox, 1970, p. 146). If all in-migration occurred instantaneously at the beginning of the decade, and all out-migration instantaneously at the end of the decade, or vice versa, the maximum possible migration estimate error in using the forward survival rate is the total number of deaths among in-migrants or deaths among out-migrants, according to when migration occurs in time. Much migration is related to economic fluctuations in the economy, although different areas are often subject to different economic conditions or varying intensities of similar economic problems. It would seem, therefore, that an average method could be applied more generally throughout all areas, since the maximum possible error is the average of deaths among in-migrants and deaths among out-migrants. The average survival method gives the same results as the vital statistics method if one-half of the implied net number of deaths among migrating cohorts occurs after migration. This method implies an even flow, or an approximately even flow, of migrants during a given time period. Obviously this method is superior to the forward method, in that mortality is allowed to affect migrants between the base year and every interval (decade or quinquennium) for which the analysis is undertaken. The average method was adopted by Willis (1971) in a study of population in the Northern Pennines. Under extreme conditions, and particularly at ages subject to high mortality, errors in using these census survival rate formulae could in some cases exceed considerably the difference between the three estimates and provide inaccurate results. This is more likely in areas that have an unbalanced age structure.

Given perfectly enumerated data, the vital statistics method provides an exact measurement of demographic change in local areas. Census survival rate methods, in contrast, suffer from census errors, and from the inability of survival rates and fertility rates to measure deaths and births occurring in an area exactly. Tarver (1962) advocated using the formula which most accurately duplicates 'vital statistics' deaths over all ages, to obtain the most precise intercensal net migration estimates by age groups. Many demographers have recognised that errors in census enumeration and in the registration of births and deaths (in the United States) have been reflected in errors of estimated net-migration by both vital statistics and census survival rates (Hamilton 1966, 1967).

Price (1955) called attention to the fact that neglecting to consider the difference between national, regional, and local survival rates could lead to large absolute and also relative errors. Some adjustment of rates is necessary to allow for variations between local and national mortality and fertility rates. Neighbouring local authority areas in Britain can have very different vital rates; for example, after adjusting for age-sex structure, 20 per cent or more difference between the local and national birth rate is not uncommon (Registrar General, 1970). There is more variation in birth than death rates, however. Craig (1970) considered several possible indicators of the variation of local to national mortality rates, in terms of frequency of collection and publication, areas covered, and age—sex breakdown, when estimating net migration. Standardised mortality ratios are produced decennially, covering counties sub-divided into county boroughs, urban areas and rural areas (aggregates) (The Registrar General, 1967). Where the quinary breakdown is not given, the rates can be averaged and smoothed before being used to adjust the national mortality rates to comparable local rates. Adjustment for spatial variations in birth rates is more difficult, with detailed age—sex breakdowns only for regions and conurbations. Regional birth rates can be used, but these are likely to underestimate the number of children born in some localities, and overestimate those in others. This problem can be partly overcome by applying total population local (age-corrected) differentials to all fertility data, for female birth-producing cohorts in the 15—45 age group, from the Registrar General's Statistical Review. This is admittedly crude, but no other measure for local areas is feasible at present (Willis, 1971). Failure to account for local variations in vital statistics and the occurrence of migration in the time period under consideration, overshadows the detailed conclusions on net-migration of House and Knight (1965) and Jackson (1968). Jackson partly overcame some of the difficulties by using vital statistics to study births; and, for net-migration of ageing cohorts, by restricting national mortality estimates to age groups less than 55 years old, where the difference between national and local mortality was likely to be low.

Interregional cohort-survival models

The shortcomings of traditional methods of estimating migration have been documented (Rogers, 1968). Cohort-survival models are manifestly dynamic, but have an aspatial structure. Spatial differences are measured only in so far as the analysis is repeated for each of the geographical units in the study area; but space and time should be considered simultaneously to explain the processes of migration. Only by considering such an integrated system in space as well as time can the effects of migration on the demographic structure of neighbouring areas be assessed. Cohort-survival models of the traditional form provide no evidence on the repercussions of any change in migration associated with one area on the demographic events in surrounding geographical areas.

Rogers (1968) tried to overcome this problem by defining an interregional cohort-survival model of the form

$$\begin{bmatrix} W_1^{(t+1)} \\ W_2^{(t+1)} \\ \vdots \\ W_m^{(t+1)} \end{bmatrix} = \begin{bmatrix} S_1 & M_{21} & M_{31} & \cdots & M_{m1} \\ M_{12} & S_2 & M_{32} & \cdots & M_{m2} \\ \vdots & & & & \vdots \\ M_{1m} & & & & S_m \end{bmatrix} \begin{bmatrix} W_1^{(t)} \\ W_2^{(t)} \\ \vdots \\ W_m^{(t)} \end{bmatrix}$$

where W is a vector for each area denoted by subscript of the population in the rth age group at a specified time
S for each area denoted by subscript equals

$$\begin{bmatrix} 0 & 0 & b_1 & b_2 & b_u & 0 & 0 \\ {}_1d_2 & 0 & 0 & & \cdots & & 0 \\ 0 & {}_2d_3 & 0 & & \cdots & & 0 \\ 0 & 0 & 0 & & \cdots & {}_{n-1}d_n & 0 \end{bmatrix}$$

b_r = the number of births that survive to the end of the unit time interval, in the rth childbearing age group.
$_rd_{r+1}$ = the proportion of people in the rth age group who survive to the $r+1$ age group after the unit time interval.

During each unit interval of time a certain fraction of the ith region's population, in a given age group, r, migrates to region j and enters the $r+1$ age group there. A series of migration matrices M_{ij} can be constructed, which, when applied to the age distribution at i, will migrate the requisite number of people from region i to region j and survive them into the next age cohort. M_{12} is a matrix which expresses the proportion of migrants from region 1 to region 2 by age groups. M_{21} is a similar matrix of cohorts from region 2 to region 1.

This model is simply a tool for the manipulation of data and contains nothing conceptually fresh. The process of change can be isolated from the main body of the population. For example migration can be derived from

$$W^{(t+1)} = (S + M) W^t$$

where W, S and M are defined above,

to equal $MW^t = W^{(t+1)} - SW^t$

Since inter-area cohort migration data is not generally available, the heart of the problem is the estimation of the probabilities that structure the transition matrices. Generally these area matrices, or super matrix of spatial cohort migration, are not directly soluble and must be estimated according to some criteria of goodness-of-fit. The problem of estimating a migration matrix is taken up in the following section.

Matrix estimation

Ideally the researcher would like to have micro-information over each period on actual movements of individuals from one state to another. Unfortunately, a common constraint in local population analysis is the absence of data on movements between areas. More likely data reflects the end result of such movements, this data being in the form of proportions or market shares — macro-data — such as resident population in each area from the population census. This is a case of 'limited information'.

It is impossible to infer from a distribution of a population, X_1, what mobility pattern must have got them there. There are an infinite number of mobility patterns that can produce the same equilibrium distribution or a given distribution from an initial distribution. These can be determined by linear programming. The problem is to find a matrix P, given x_o and x_1, such that $x_o P = x_1$, where x_o and x_1 are population distribution vectors at time t and $t + 1$. For example, to determine P such that

$$(4 \quad 3) \begin{bmatrix} p_{11} & p_{12} \\ p_{21} & p_{22} \end{bmatrix} = (6 \quad 1)$$

the vectors could be probability vectors if summed to 1·0, but the argument remains the same. From the above example the following equations are derived:

$$4p_{11} + 3p_{21} = 6$$
$$4p_{12} + 3p_{22} = 1$$

Constraints are now introduced such that

$$0 \leqslant p_{ij} \leqslant 1{\cdot}0$$
and $\quad p_{11} + p_{12} = 1{\cdot}0$
and $\quad p_{21} + p_{22} = 1{\cdot}0$

Thus $4 - 4p_{12} + 3p_{21} = 6$
$\quad\quad 4p_{12} + 3 - 3p_{21} = 1$

Therefore $4p_{12} - 3p_{21} = -2$
$\quad\quad\quad\quad 4p_{12} - 3p_{21} = -2$

and it follows $p_{12} = \dfrac{3p_{21} - 2}{4}$

from which $p_{12} = \tfrac{3}{4} p_{21} - \tfrac{2}{4}$
and $\quad\quad\quad p_{21} = \dfrac{4p_{12} + 2}{3}$

192

from which $p_{21} = \frac{4}{3}p_{12} + \frac{2}{3}$

Therefore $\frac{2}{3} \leqslant p_{21} \leqslant 1.0$

$0 \leqslant p_{12} \leqslant \frac{1}{4}$

A linear programming graph solution can be drawn for such a 2 × 2 case

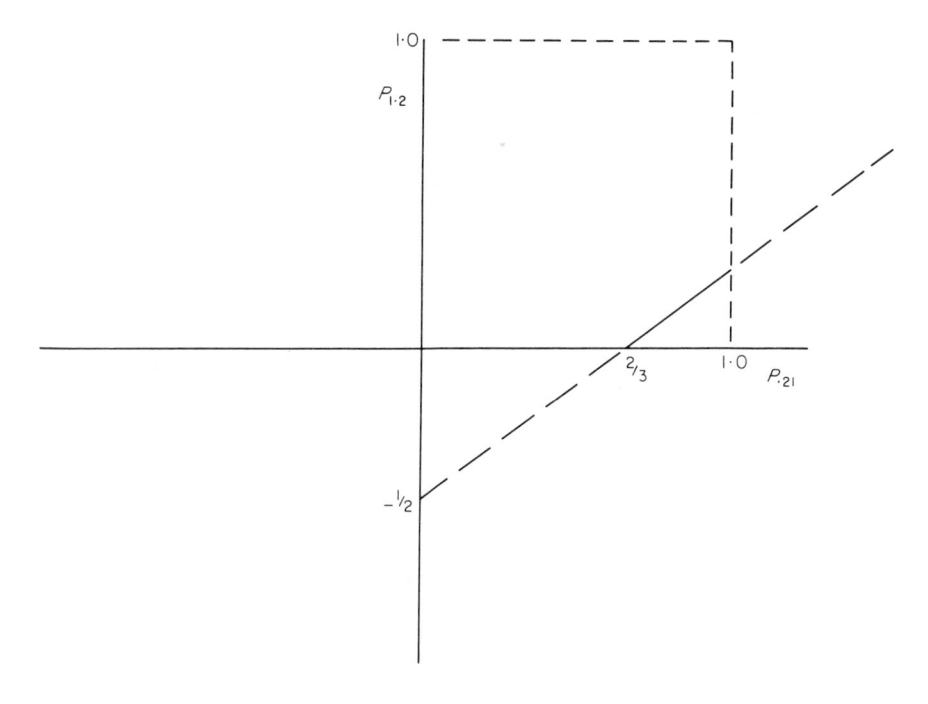

when $p_{21} = 0$ $p_{12} = -\frac{1}{2}$
when $p_{12} = 0$ $p_{21} = \frac{2}{3}$

Since p_{ij} must be $0 \leqslant p_{ij} \leqslant 1$ only values on the continuous section of the line are solutions, but even here there are an infinite number of solutions.

Thus when

$p_{12} = 0$ $p_{21} = \frac{2}{3}$ therefore $p_{11} = 1$ and $p_{22} = \frac{1}{3}$

$p_{12} = 0.2$ $p_{21} = 0.93$ therefore $p_{11} = 0.8$ and $p_{22} = 0.07$

$p_{21} = 0.8$ $p_{12} = 0.1$ therefore $p_{22} = 0.2$ and $p_{11} = 0.9$

The broken line describes the relationship between p_{12} and p_{21} and solutions for matrices with no stochastic constraints. For Markov stochastic matrices it is of interest to note that if a matrix is chosen from the programming model with $\lambda_2 > 0$, then the equilibrium distribution from

$x_0, x_1, \ldots x_n$ will be reached in n steps. If a matrix is chosen such that the second latent root equals zero, then x_1 will be the equilibrium distribution. A matrix with $\lambda_2 < 0$ will reach equilibrium in n steps with oscillating distributions.

Basically the problem is one of estimation of the transition probabilities in Markov chains, although it is possible to derive actual numbers as well as proportions. An excellent review of the state of the art of estimation in micro and macro Markov models is to be found in Lee, Judge and Takayama (1965) and Lee, Judge and Zellner (1970), where detailed mathematical and Monte Carlo analyses of theoretical models are undertaken and reported. The common model for most applied studies may be written as

$$w_{jt} = \sum_{i}^{r} w_{it-1} \, p_{ij} + v_{jt} \qquad \begin{array}{l} j = 1, \ldots r \\ t = 2, \ldots T \end{array}$$

where w_{jt} is the proportion of the system in state j at time t, there being r states and $T-1$ time periods, and v_{jt} is a random error component. The transition probabilities P_{ij} are assumed constant over the time span analysed, which means that if 1951, 1961, and 1971 population data are used to evaluate p_{ij}, the migration estimates derived will not be very realistic. However, for data on a yearly basis — such as data on numbers of farm workers from the annual June agricultural census over five years — more realistic migration patterns can be determined, and the change in these every few years can be assessed.

In matrix notation, after Lee, Judge and Takayama (1965),

$$y_i = X_j \, p_j + v_j$$

that is,

$$\begin{bmatrix} y_1 \\ y_2 \\ \vdots \\ y_r \end{bmatrix} = \begin{bmatrix} X_1 & 0 & 0 & \cdots & 0 \\ 0 & X_2 & 0 & \cdots & 0 \\ \vdots & & & & \\ 0 & & & & X_r \end{bmatrix} \begin{bmatrix} p_1 \\ p_2 \\ \vdots \\ p_r \end{bmatrix} + \begin{bmatrix} v_1 \\ v_2 \\ \vdots \\ v_r \end{bmatrix}$$

Where y_j is a $(T \times 1)$ vector of observations reflecting the proportion in state j in time t, X_j is a $(T \times r)$ matrix of realised values of the proportion in state i in time $t-1$, p_j is a $(r \times 1)$ vector of unknown transition parameters to be estimated, and v_j is a vector of random disturbances with properties

$$E(v_j) = 0$$
$$E(v_j v_j) = \sigma_j^2 \, w_{jj}$$

The only given relations on the data are

$$\left. \begin{array}{l} w_t \cdot 1 = 1 \\ w_t \geqslant 0 \end{array} \right\} \quad t = 1, \ldots T$$

where 1 is an r component column vector of ones. The desired constraints on the transition probabilities are

$$1 \geqslant P \geqslant 0$$
$$P.1 = 1$$

although to estimate actual numbers of migrants these constraints must be omitted.

Rogers (1967 b) religiously estimates migration between California and the rest of the United States by: (i) an unrestricted least squares estimator; (ii) a minimum absolute deviations estimator; and (iii) a restricted least squares estimator. The first can be estimated by regression techniques; the latter two require a mathematical programming formulation. Rogers recognises that unrestricted least squares estimation permits the occurrence of inadmissible estimates — negative elements; so this particular analysis seems hardly worth undertaking. In the case of transition probability estimates, it additionally allows probabilities greater than unity. Telser (1963) suggested setting negative elements equal to zero or unity and adjusting the matrix to compensate for this change. This modification is somewhat doubtful, since resulting estimates are generally unreliable. This is due to the approximately singular nature of the matrices, causing extreme sensitivity to rounding errors.

Rogers then uses a weighted, unrestricted least squares estimator, and it is hardly surprising that non-admissible estimates are still derived, for the non-negativity and not greater than one condition of the estimated transition probabilities p_{ij} are still not necessarily satisfied.

Although attempts have been made to adjust the basic least squares technique for admissibility, the modifications are somewhat arbitrary and resulting probabilities are no longer guaranteed to satisfy the least squares criteria. To enable both the equality restriction $P.1 = 1$ and the inequalities $1 \geqslant P \geqslant 0$ to be explicitly included in the formulation, the problem was specified by Lee, Judge and Takayama (1965) and by Theil and Ray (1966) as a typical quadratic problem. The objective was to minimise the error sum of squares,

$$\sum_{t=2}^{T} v'_t v_t$$

with respect to the above linear constraints.

Rogers (1968) used restricted least squares evaluated by the standard simplex version of the quadratic programming alogarithm. Consideration of the restrictions on the probabilities by the restricted least squares method results in estimates being admissible, but the efficiency of the restricted least squares estimator has been questioned (Zellner, 1961; and Hocking, 1965) and the weighted restricted least squares estimator was developed. When a matrix weight function was introduced into the least squares objective equation, this was found partly to overcome the problem of heteroscedasticity.

All these techniques have been concerned with the gradual evolution of the use of least squares criteria for estimating the transition probabilities of the postulated Markov chain underlying the process being investigated. Other published techniques differ in the criteria used to derive optimal estimates, and some of these are presented by Lee, Judge and Zellner (1970). Among these, the minimum absolute deviation (MAD) procedure, has been used by Rogers (1967b) to estimate population change. A MAD estimator is not as efficient as a minimum variance estimator. The advantage of this technique, however, is its computational simplicity. The problem can be formulated as a linear program, and the estimates resulting from the procedure are normally distributed except for those estimates close to the limits of the allowed probability values. The quality of results was found to be highly dependent on sample size, improving as the sample size grew.

It is difficult to compare analytically the various techniques of transition probability estimation. Lee, Judge and Cain (1969) derived the following ranking of procedures based on random walk experiments: weighted restricted least squares, unweighted least squares, restricted minimum absolute deviations, and unrestricted least squares. The MAD and unweighted least squares techniques were found to be approximately equal. Another study by Lee, Judge and Zellner (1968) resulted in the following rank ordering of methods: Bayesian, maximum likelihood, weighted least squares, least squares. All techniques improved with larger sample sizes.

Rogers' (1967b, 1968) attempt to estimate migration operators from interregional population distributions suffers both from the small sample size, coupled with the unreliability of estimates of population in California and the rest of the United States every year over a decade; and the fact that the analysis was confined to migration between these two areas only. This lack of population data is a hindrance to the use of this type of technique in Britain, except for cases and sectors where annual censuses are taken, such as in agriculture. Rogers suggests that a migration matrix can be found if natural increase from t to $t + 1$ is subtracted from the population distribution at the time $t + 1$. The equation used for estimation by one of the above techniques is

$$\begin{bmatrix} w_1{}^{t+1} \\ w_2{}^{t+1} \\ w_1{}^{t+2} \\ w_2{}^{t+2} \end{bmatrix} = \begin{bmatrix} w_1{}^t & 0 & w_2{}^t & 0 \\ 0 & w_1{}^t & 0 & w_2{}^t \\ w_1{}^{t+1} & 0 & w_2{}^{t+1} & 0 \\ 0 & w_1{}^{t+1} & 0 & w_2{}^{t+1} \end{bmatrix} \begin{bmatrix} g_{11} \\ g_{12} \\ g_{21} \\ g_{22} \end{bmatrix}$$

If the square matrix is W, the reliability of least squares estimates based on this equation is mainly dependent upon the size of $|W'W|$ which reduces to

$$= \{w_1{}^{t+1} \quad w_2{}^t \quad - \quad w_1{}^t \quad w_2{}^{t+1}\}^4$$
$$= \{w_1{}^t \quad w_2{}^t\}^4 \quad \{w_1{}^{t+1} \;/\; w_1{}^t - w_2{}^{t+1} \;/\; w_2{}^t\}^4$$

The ratios will in most practical cases be rather similar, so that $|W'W|$ is close to zero (determinant close to zero), which implies an unreliable method. Relatively high birth rates (relative to immigration rates) will exacerbate this tendency. The nearer the solution is to equilibrium: $W_{n-3}, W_{n-2}, W_{n-1}, \ldots$, the less the proportional change in the distribution vectors (w), and consequently the less the information which can be derived from the system of resulting equations. In such cases the determinant of $|W'W|$ will be zero or close to zero.

Rogers chose only two regions for this analysis — California and the rest of the United States — two very contrasting areas in terms of population growth. In other areas of the USA and many regions in Britain, there will be little or no differential in proportional population change between areas. In such cases the transition matrix will be difficult or impossible to estimate. Of course, although this technique can be used to estimate net flows, or minimum flows to effect the changed distribution of population, gross flows may be many times net flows, but these cannot be estimated. An infinite number of different gross flows can incorporate the net flow (to effect desired distribution change), so that the actual gross flow cannot be determined.

All of the previous estimation techniques have had one assumption in common, that the transition probabilities are constant over time. When this assumption is relaxed, the task grows from finding one set of probabilities, to finding nearly as many different sets as there are time periods. Such a problem would be difficult to solve if some relationship between probabilities in successive time periods is not assumed. If variables other than time are assumed to influence changes in probabilities, the determination of the relevant independent variables and the exact form of the relationships must be hypothesised.

Some recent studies, such as that by Hallberg (1969), assumed the availability of micro-data. He predicted the future transition probabilities by regression analysis, but assumed there existed a time series of known transition probability matrices. It was possible to fit, with these matrices, a least squares regression equation of various exogenous factors explaining the transition probability values. The result was used to predict probabilities in future periods, but some estimates were inadmissible. Hallberg suggested setting the inadmissible estimates equal to the closest permitted value (zero or unity). The remaining estimates were then adjusted so they still summed to unity. However, micro-data is generally not available. Dent (1967) suggested a technique for estimating non-stationary probabilities from macro-data restrictions. The method is dependent on heuristic rules for bounding the movements of individual transition probabilities between successive periods, the rules being determined by the application. The objective function was expanded to include the effects resulting from time dependence. At the same time a consideration was made of external influences. Quadratic programming was found to be required for solving most problems.

Certainly, in migration P_t should be looked on as being dependent upon previous period probabilities and other observed variables such as income and wages. If proportion data were used from say the annual June agricultural census over a sufficiently long period, the time could be separated into groups. Constant probabilities over each group (say every five-year span) could be estimated by existing procedures. There would then exist sets of transition probabilities, and relations between them could be found by time dependent estimators (after Hallberg, 1969; Dent, 1967; Miller, 1952; and Lipstein, 1965) and the pattern of change could then be applied within the groups to find different probabilities for each year. This involves drawing inferences from sets of constant probabilities.

The estimation and prediction of non-stationary probabilities are crucial to the development of migration theory and empirical work. While various system formulations may be readily constructed, the actual derivation of solutions can be extremely complicated; but solutions are critical for testing the theory, and are the foundations upon which further theoretical work is built. The use of non-stationary probabilities, and their value in prediction, for migration studies, appears to be the most pertinent field for immediate analysis.

Projecting migration

The preceding techniques are the principal methods by which migration can be estimated in the absence of any actual data on the phenomenon itself. There still remains the problem of forecasting or projecting the future levels of migration. A major reason why comparatively little work has been done on forecasting migration is the poor documentation of relevant data. This dearth of information has slowed the development of analytical techniques to handle flows, and consequently migration planning is inhibited.

Isard (1960) tried to forecast moves by a ratio method, where migration is not seen as an isolated phenomenon, but related by some ratio to independent projections of employment and other variables. The relationship was determined by co-variance analysis. Durham County Council (1966) employed a similar method to project migration from each of their local authority areas, by estimating future employment opportunities on the basis of suitable land available for new industry. The difficulty with this type of projection is the uncertainty of the relationship between migration and employment and other variables in the future, and the accuracy with which the exogenous variables are projected. These techniques are characterised by the use of a base period, the experience of which is then extended forward into the forecast period. Typically projections work with time and forecast variables only, but this does not hold true in migration. Migration projections tend rather to seek to explain the changes occurring in the base period than merely to extend them forward at an assumed rate. Obviously, the critical factors with projections are the choice of base period and the shape of the curve fitted to the base and forecast periods.

Lowry (1966) reports the efforts of Blanco and produced a modified Blanco–Lowry model

$$dMi = \alpha_o + \beta_1 dP_i + \beta_2 dQ_i + \beta_3 dA_i + \beta_4 d E_i + \beta_5 d I_i + \mu$$

where dM_i = net migration,
 dP_i = natural increase of labour force,
 dQ_i = net change in demand for labour,
 dA_i = change in military personnel,
 dE_i = change in those engaged in higher education,
 dI_i = change in median family income.

The final model treats internal migration as a movement in time between place i and the rest of the nation. Variable dE is omitted because it correlates with dQ, and dI is removed because of its peculiar behaviour. Lowry thought the forecasting power of this model to be high, provided the exogenous variables can be projected. The interaction between migration and jobs also affects the size of the labour force when the natural increase of already-attracted migrants is considered. Employment forecasts fed into the model will give a consistent forecast of future migration, provided the cross-sectional parameters are suitable for time series inference. Lowry points out the danger of having confidence in their stability. They refer to absolute changes in the determinants rather than relative changes; for example, a nationwide recession would result in a forecast of out-migration for every area of the country, even although in actual fact no change occured in international migration.

Masser (1970) attempted to predict migration between the conurbations of England in 1965–66 by means of gravity and a Lowry model using coefficients derived from the analysis of 1960–61 material. The analysis was designed to assess the extent to which the 1965–66 flows between the six conurbations could be predicted by these means, given the 1965–66 values for the independent variables, adjusted where necessary to take account of changes in wage levels during the period. It was observed that the projected results involving the coefficients determined in the 1961 Lowry model gave a better overall fit than the predicted results of either the gravity or the Lowry models based on the 1966 data. Masser then concludes that the predictive value of the models was very high indeed. His results however, suggest that the nature of the factors affecting migration had changed, and the failure to derive as good a model from actual 1965–66 data hardly inspires confidence in the model's predictive value for 1970–71 or 1975–76 migration.

For prediction purposes there is little to be gained by the use of existing regression models to predict migration. There are only minor differences between the results obtained by a gravity model and those obtained by the Lowry model (Masser, 1970) and the gravity model has the added advantage that all its independent variables are either virtually constants, like distance, or change relatively slowly over time, like population, whereas it is also necessary to predict wages and unemployment differentials in the Lowry model.

While it is true that more demographic models are of a cross-sectional nature, in having variables which vary more from one individual to another than they do in time, the element of time must nevertheless be considered in any migration projection. Most migration models are cross-sectional with exogenously-determined variables, although in forecasting migration we are intimately concerned with time.

There is an important difference between pure cross-section and pure time-series models, and this emerges when lagged variables are considered. In a pure time-series model the observations are in a natural (chronological) order, but in a cross-sectional model the observations typically have no natural order. The cross-sectional case has no analogy to the lagged value in the time-series case. It is possible to think of a dynamic version of the pure cross-section model. This turns out to be a set of equations like a cross-section model, but lagged one period; the equations describe period $t - 1$ and do not involve period t at all. The variables are not only predetermined, they are also exogenous. Each equation in a 'dynamic' cross-section model constitutes a complete model in itself. If data are available for several periods, then there will be T distinct pure cross-section models, one for each period from 1 to T. If each parameter has a constant value throughout all periods, then the model is a mixed time-series and cross-section model.

Essentially, regression (econometric) methods seek to develop models that reflect the causal relationship between socio—economic variables. Once these relationships have been adequately measured during the base period, they then provide a means of forecasting. The major difficulty encountered with such forecasts is that it is necessary to have adequate forward measures of all the explanatory variables used, if reliable forecasts are to be produced. This is necessary for both pure-time and cross-section models. Thus the danger with econometric models is that they may simply transfer the forecasting problem to other variables. The usefulness of forecasts based on econometric models depends on the precision with which the explanatory variables in the model can be specified in the forecast period.

The immediate point to note is the inadequacy of existing regression models of migration projection. This will be reconsidered later and suggestions made for improvement. Meanwhile, simulation models will be reviewed as an aid to forecasting. Traditionally, most migration predictions have been based on estimated relationships among economic aggregates. This approach to the problem of forecasting has not proved altogether successful, for not only do many statistical difficulties arise in aggregating anything but the simplest relationship (Allen, 1959) among and about elemental decision-making units, but also, without a reasonable model of the same economic system stated in terms of the behaviour and interaction of the elemental decision-making units themselves, it is not possible to aggregate up without the possibility of loss of accuracy of representation. This problem could be overcome if the relationships to be aggregated are linear, but the behaviour of decision-making units is known to abound in non-linearities and discontinuities. Predictions would be more successful if they were based on knowledge about the elemental decision-making units — how they behave, interact and respond to situations. Migrants by the act of moving influence other factors, and in turn there is a feedback effect on the original component from reactions of these other units. The relationship between the characteristics of a component (a person) of the socio-economic system and its behaviour could be called the 'operating characteristics' of the component, and what the micro-analytical approach to model building and forecasting attempts to do is to learn something about the operating characteristics of the components of the system so as to predict more accurately the behaviour of the system.

A simulation model contains components (people), which correspond to micro-components of the real socio-economic system. The model also contains variables that relate to components. Input variables are external to the component, but act on it and influence its behaviour by means of wage levels, unemployment and so on, which influence the decision to move or stay. Status variables are internal to the component — age, sex, level of education — and the value of these and input variables influences the behaviour of the component during the time period. The output during the time period may alter the values of the status variables at the start of the following period. Output is derived from the interaction of inputs and status variables. A simulation model must also contain relationships if it is to generate predictions. Relationships specify how the values of different variables in the model are related to each other, or how they are otherwise generated. Of primary importance are the relationships defined as operating characteristics — the relationship of the output variable to status and input variables. Operating characteristics cannot be directly observed in the real system, but must be inferred, and they can be of any form that research indicates to be appropriate. The relationships linking outputs of a component to prior inputs and status variables are based on probabilities of the occurrence of certain outputs. Thus the probability that a given individual will die in a given period can be estimated from what has actually happened in past experience, and this can be used in the model with the assumption that death will continue to occur according to the estimated probabilities. Most output updates status variables of the same unit and/or becomes inputs to other units. Thus if an individual in t marries, his status variable alters in $t+1$ and his operating characteristics — probability of leaving an area — also change. The resulting response of the units to various stimuli can be measured, and such measurements can be aggregated up to give projects of the aggregates which are of interest. From the point of view of accuracy, simulation has not yet established itself as a technique. However, it does seem to offer some promise, and several simulation studies have been applied to the

United States labour force, an interesting example being that by Orcutt et al. (1961).

Morrill (1965) devised a probabilistic model to simulate rural settlement and migration in Sweden. Migration and location decisions are subject to error or uncertainty. People may not know the correct decision, or may be unable to distinguish between almost equally good alternatives. Some kind of random decision, like coin-tossing, is required to make a decision in the face of such uncertainty, and simulation provides for random choice limited by strong forces. Morrill's general model, for the location of town settlement and local migration, was subdivided into a model for conditions of new settlement and a model expressing conditions of existing rural population. The former sub-model generated initial migration from outside through a point or points subject to given defined areas, time periods, technological state and migration volume, with appropriate probability conditions of moving various distances. The assignment of central places was subject to minimum size for eligibility, hinterland requirements, already existing places, and the reasonable weighting of areas according to transport advantage and so on. Migration probability conditions were subject to differential attractiveness of areas, and all probabilities were unique and recomputed for each time period, so that areas with a greater initial population became more attractive. Where there were conditions of existing rural population, differential probabilities of areas for attracting activities were calculated, based on existing settlement and transportation links, taking into consideration local transportation improvements and the like. Country-to-town migration was also considered. There was a slight tendency for the simulation of towns to be more regularly spaced than actually occurred. The extent to which the original towns, both in reality and in the model, restricted and channelled the ultimate develoment of the current distribution, was striking. The simulation correctly matched typical distances travelled by migrants, but the failure to take into account the strong dependence of migration upon previous moves or contacts resulted in a more regular migration field than that observed. This was probably the major deficiency in the model.

From a practical point of view, results can be obtained easily and rapidly by simulation on a computer. If the objective is simply to obtain a quick answer to a specific solution, simulation will usually be the best method of attack. On the other hand, if the primary interest in stochastic models is to gain insight into the workings of the socio-economic phenomenon of migration, simulation is less satisfactory. Simulation provides solutions only for specific cases, whereas in essence interest is usually in general solutions; and as such the economy and clarity of a simple formula makes problem-solving worthwhile even if it is an approximation.

General stochastic models of migration have centred on Markov chains. These were more fully discussed in Chapter 9, as a method of analysing the current movement of a variable in order to predict its future movement. A demanding assumption of the Markov chain model is that the probability of occurrence of a particular outcome in any one trial of the sequence does not change throughout the entire sequence: the transition probabilities are assumed to be stationary. In migration, stationarity assumptions appear untenable in most cases. Changes in exogenous variables — wage rates, housing costs, demand for labour — are likely to result in non-stationary transition probabilities. Migration probabilities can be tested for stationarity (Anderson and Goodman, 1957). If the null hypothesis cannot be accepted and transition probabilities are not constant over time, Hallberg (1969) suggests a method, based on multiple regression techniques, of replacing the constant transition probabilities with probabilities which are a function of various factors affecting the endogenous variable. In a study of changes in frozen milk product manufacturing plants, Hallberg obtained results using this method which were more acceptable from a predictive standpoint than results obtained from the traditional Markov model. Additional work clearly needs to be done to determine the appropriate structural system from which the transition probabilities are generated, as well as the appropriate form of the structural equations. Problems associated with the estimation of (stationary) transition probabilities by regression have already been mentioned, and equally apply here; these are the problems associated with obtaining positive elements in the array

$(p_{ijt} \geq 0$ for all i, j, t) and the constraint

$$\sum_{j=1}^{n} p_{ijt} = 1 \quad \text{for all } i \text{ and } t.$$

Cross-section models

The previous section led back to a reconsideration of regression models. Here the special features of dynamic stochastic cross-section models are considered. Migration models which have been presented in the literature are generally neither dynamic nor stochastic, stochastic but not dynamic, or occasionally dynamic but not stochastic. It can be appreciated that what is required is a dynamic stochastic model, which is the most interesting case.

Migration by individuals from one area to any other takes place because of a desire to increase real income in terms of extra consumption and saving. The level of an individual migrant's consumption of goods and services depends on his decision to move to a particular area and on the new income he obtained in the first period (earnings and non-monetary income). The relationship is a lagged one, with consumption dependent upon new income that has been previously earned or accrued. The income from migration is made up of a systematic exogenous part from earnings, w_{it}; a systematic property and non-monetary income from free public goods and so on – that is, the product of the current interest rate, r_t (discount rate); and the net value of this (property and services) at the end of the preceding period $p_{i,t-1}$; plus a random part. Non-pecuniary returns cannot be evaluated and discounted like fixed investment and property income to the migrant until the end of each time period. The simple model may be written as:

$$\begin{aligned} c_{it} &= \beta m_{i,t-1} + \gamma + \epsilon_i + \mu_{it} & i &= 1,\dots N \\ m_i &= p_{i,t-1} r_t + w_{it} + v_{it} & i &= 1,\dots N \\ M_t &= C_t + Z_t \\ M_t &= P_{t-1} r_t + W_t \\ C_t &= \beta M_{t-1} + M\gamma + U_t \end{aligned}$$

where c_{it} is the individual's consumption after moving and $m_{i,t-1}$ is the migrant's lagged income after moving.

Aggregate consumption after migration is assumed to depend linearly on the decision to migrate and the new lagged income M_{t-1} and an aggregate disturbance U_t which is equal to $\sum_i u_{it}$. Aggregate income accruing from the decision to move, M_t, is equal to aggregate consumption C_t plus aggregate non-consumption expenditure, Z_t, which is exogenous. Aggregate income after migration is also equal to non-earned and property income $\sum_i p_{it-1} r_t$ plus aggregate earned income $\sum_i w_{it}$

and
$$\sum_i w_{it} = W_t$$
$$\sum_i p_{i,t} = P_t$$

with
$$\sum_i \epsilon_i = 0 \quad \text{and} \quad \sum_i v_{it} = 0$$

This pure cross-section model is described by the first $2N+3$ equations, where N is the number of individuals moving. The model is very crude but is by way of illustration only. Exogenous variables in the model are r_t, C_t, $Mt, c_{it}, m_{it}, i = 1,\dots N$. Variables Z_t, W_t and w_{it} are assumed exogenous with statistically independent disturbances. The model is unrealistic in the sense that non-earned income does not primarily affect migration, but most migrants have some idea of non-pecuniary returns to moving.

In this pure cross-section model every temporally predetermined variable is exogenous. M_{t-1} and P_{t-1} are predetermined, since they are independent of all disturbances in the current and future periods, and exogenous, since they are independent of all disturbances in the current period. $m_{i,\,t-1}$ is exogenous, and this means that the first equation of the model explaining consumption is a complete single equation model in terms of parameters, disturbances and exogenous factors. If data were available for several time periods there would be T distinct pure cross-section models, one for each time period, from 1 to T. If each parameter has a constant value through time and two more equations are added

$$p_{it} = m_{it} - c_{it} + p_{i,\,t-1} \qquad i = 1,\ldots N$$
$$\qquad\qquad\qquad\qquad\qquad\qquad t = 1,\ldots T$$
$$P_t = \sum_i p \qquad\qquad\qquad t = 1,\ldots T$$

then the model becomes a mixed time-series and cross-section model with $(3N + 4)T$ equations.

This latter equation states that non-earned income at the end of the period is equal to non-earned income at the beginning of the period, plus accumulation of savings and non-monetary benefits. Now the cumulation of non-earned monetary and non-monetary income depends on the cumulation of non-earned monetary income in the past, and net change in non-monetary benefits in the period. This means $m_{i,\,t-1}$, M_{t-1}, and $p_{i,t-1}$ are predetermined at time t, but they are no longer exogenous because the forces determining them have now been incorporated in the model by making it a time series model. The disturbances in the model u_j and v_i are not now independent of all the values of M_{t-1}, $m_{i,t-1}$ and $p_{i,t-1}$ for all $i = 1, \ldots N$ and for all $t = 1, \ldots T$, but the variables Z_t, W_t and w_{it} are both predetermined and exogenous as before.

Little research using this type of model has been done to estimate and predict the new levels of consumption, earnings, and unearned income accruing from migration. It would be of considerable interest to evaluate the growth in non-earned income from migration, how this is growing over time, and its contribution to total real income. The development of dynamic stochastic cross-section models of migration has a unique role to play in migration research. The integration of spatial migration with economic variables, the effect on these variables of migration, and the adequate treatment of this situation in time-series has been, and continues to be, the most neglected sector of all.

12 Conclusion

The aim of this chapter is to bring together, in terms of policy and research implications, some of the material presented in earlier chapters. Essentially the case is one of determining how migration – forces and impediments – with government policy impinges on the demand and supply of migrant labour; and how the problems to which migration gives rise can be analysed with appropriate techniques. It is an attempt to inquire into the effects of migration on areas and groups and draw some conclusions for planners and policy makers. The major problem in outlining the effect of migration and policy on aggregate resource demand is to know when to stop. Some policies have a direct and obvious impact: a Regional Employment Premium will, *ceteris paribus*, increase the demand for labour in lagging regions and lower the net out-migration rate. Other policies have a direct but less obvious effect: an incomes policy which allowed increases in the pay of low paid workers – particularly those in lagging regions – would raise earnings in those areas relative to earnings in more prosperous regions. This would reduce the pull of the latter regions from the viewpoint of the potential migrant, but it would encourage entrepreneurs to substitute capital for labour in lagging regions.

The demographic effects of migration from whence economic effects flow, are of two sorts. Migration modifies the absolute rate of population growth – in-migration usually increases population growth and out-migration reduces it. Migration also tends to change the age composition of the population, and to modify the labour force even more, since a disproportionately large share of migrants are of working age.

The effects of migration in relation to the individual are most certain if rational decisions and returns to factors reflecting marginal conditions are assumed. Chapter 2 has shown migration to be a form of private investment which entails benefits, costs and a rate of return. This approach is helpful in pinpointing the factors influencing migration. It allows the incorporation of purely economic variables, such as salaries and employment opportunities, into a wider view of the complex migrational decision. These were explored in Chapter 4 on the motivations underlying an individual's utility function. These variables, such as psychic costs, relate to strength of ties in area of origin, and difficulties of adjustment to the area of destination. Ties are strengthened (and migrational costs increased) through family establishment; that is, marriage and the presence of school-age children. Adjustment costs tend to be higher, the greater the inter-area differences between origin and destination. Personal characteristics exert important influences on the individual's decision to migrate. Among these characteristics are age and level of education. The probability that a labour force member will migrate decreases as the migrant's age increases, since older persons have a shorter expected working life over which to realise the advantages of migrating, and this makes the rate of return on migration lower for them. Job security and family ties are also more important for older persons than younger ones, and these further discourage persons over 45, particularly from long-distance migration. Education reduces the importance of tradition and family ties and increases an individual's awareness of other localities. The continual flow of migrants into and out of an area, subject to either net in- or out-migration, is not inconsistent with theory or policy, but reflects the movement of those on career paths and also the different evaluation in terms of non-monetary income people derive from living in certain areas. From the individual's point of view, it is quite consistent to move to an area where his marginal revenue product (wage) is lower, provided that his total real income is increased through additional non-monetary gains.

Planners and policy makers, however, are rarely concerned about migration at this micro scale. Interest is rather centred on the aggregative macro effects. After moving to a job or area where the marginal return to a migrant's labour is increased, his productive capacity is increased and, therefore, his value to the community. The aggregative effects of net-migration are likely to be an increase in output per worker if, through increasing the size of the market, the division of labour is augmented. If, however, the required increase in the division of labour does not take place, and if the increase in population is not accompanied by a proportionate increase in the factors of production utilised by the labour force, output per head will fall. Migration from rural areas has the effect of reducing the division of labour in those areas, so that output per head falls relatively more than the decline in population. This arises because, for example, the cost curves facing the production of various goods and services in rural areas are decreasing cost curves (Whitby, Robins, Tansey and Willis, 1974) — so that migration into the area, if this occurred, would have the opposite effect of increasing returns to scale. Migration, to increase output in a region, must intensify the expectation of entrepreneurs in that area, that their markets will expand and stimulate induced and autonomous investment, and also extend time horizons. If investment does not occur in an area of in-migration, output per worker and real income of its residents will fall.

Migration into an area can spare that area some of the cost of producing its own population and labour force, but only if an area's population is at an infra-optimum size. Large towns and conurbations in Britain are in excess of optimum and operate on increasing cost curves for many services such as housing construction costs, and supervision and management of housing services. Even though migration can reduce an area's costs of producing population by natural increase,[1] domestic savings are still required to equip in-migrants. Either the *ex ante* rate at which capital is formed in an area must rise, or capital that might have been used to improve the infrastructure and facilities for the resident population must be diverted into equipping the in-migrants. If neither occurred, or neither one nor a combination of them was followed by government, in-migration into an area would, if policy permitted, be accompanied by an increase in *ex ante* offsets to savings which was not matched by a corresponding increase in *ex ante* savings. Local price inflation in some markets would result, the amount depending upon the extent to which agents of production were initially underemployed, and upon the degree to which the increase in demand for agents of production was incident upon those in relatively short supply. The chief local effects in Britain of this phenomena have been in road transport and housing, where in-migration into certain areas has not been accompanied by changes in the propensity to save. Consequently traffic congestion has been ensured, and overcrowding has occurred in the housing market. The result has been a commitment on the part of local authorities to invest more in housing and, as a result, less on other services. If in-migration stimulates an increase in the rate of investment, however, the real rate of growth in output and income would rise even more than had been anticipated, since conventional depreciation charges tend to exceed necessary replacement outlays and this excess expands when the rate of investment accelerates.

One real effect of migration is that it can and does give rise to inflation by increasing aggregate demand in certain areas. The most obvious example is the effect on house prices and land values in certain areas as a result of migration: an increase in the South East and on the South coast, and a relative decline in many remote rural areas. On a local scale, temporary migration and second homes increase prices in selected rural areas. Migration also gives rise to increasing costs if in-migrants are paid more than they are really worth (through a national wages policy, for instance), or trade unions keep wages at a higher level than that compatible with full employment. With unemployment the government will undertake deficit spending, resulting in upward pressure on prices, followed by rising wage demands. On a national scale this was experienced by Israel after the Second World War (Lerner, 1958).

In-migration to an area is one of the possible initiators of a self-perpetuating inflationary process, as demonstrated by Borts and Stein (1968), who showed how autonomous migration (migration not in response to economic variables in the system, but occurring because of climate, for example) can produce a permanent divergence in growth rates. Where labour grows more rapidly, so capital must grow more rapidly in order to maintain uniformity in the rate of return on investment. Shifts of this type induce a movement of capital between regions. By itself population migration sets in motion, within the framework of Borts and Stein's model, the forces that lead investment to exceed savings. The reason is that the migration induces the growth rate in income, savings and the stock of capital to rise to the new higher rate of growth of the labour supply. In adjusting to this new growth rate of the stock of capital, investment must grow more rapidly than the stock of capital. This conclusion is independent of the possibility that migrants bring capital with them, for this would imply capital movement is autonomous. If this does not occur in a dynamic equilibrium situation (returning to our inflation argument), and if in-migration makes local investments more attractive, the increase in investment expenditure might make total expenditure too great and establish the excess demand that sparks a self-perpetuating inflationary process. Local government, seeing additional infrastructure equipment – houses, schools and so on – is needed, may provide these by spending new money in the hope that this will draw the necessary resources away from other uses in which they were fully employed initially. The needs of in-migrants to areas like the South East do not create any demand until the in-migrants have money to spend on items such as housing. If they get the money by earning it, they thereby increase supply and there is no problem. Indeed inflationary pressure is reduced by their marginal propensity to save since some of their earnings are not used for consumption. But to the extent that in-migrants demand facilities such as housing immediately, by borrowing from others in the area and thus decreasing the area's marginal propensity to save, inflationary pressure is created. This also occurs when an increase in demand by in-migrants is accompanied by an interregional flow of funds (whether owned by the migrants or not). But this depends on whether monetary and fiscal policy permits this to happen. Governments can control private investment through planning and other controls just as they can control public investment. If this occurs inflation may be avoided. However, migration can still produce a self-perpetuating inflationary process even when there is no excess demand, full employment has not been reached, and there is spare industrial capacity. This is cost inflation. Cost inflation arises by migration causing, for example, an unrealistic real wage, either because the marginal product of labour is reduced by in-migration below that of the previous population from whom the in-migrants adopted the standard, or because in-migrants come from areas where the wage (and the marginal product of labour) is higher than in the area of in-migration. The first case is likely to arise when in-migration is into already congested areas, and the second case when a large influx of in-migration occurs into selected local areas of the north and west of Britain from the prosperous South East.

There is no necessary demand inflationary pressure induced by in-migration into a region, or by the capital formation that in-migration calls for, if the government, planners and policy makers hold to a policy of preventing excess demand developing. A 'cost inflation' can, however, develop, even under a strict monetary and fiscal policy, if 'unrealistic' real wage and income standards are strongly established. Cost inflation is also compatible with severe unemployment. It is important for planners to recognise whether inflation, induced by migration, is a cost inflation or a demand inflation, because policies that alleviate one kind of inflation may aggravate the other.

Inflation arises in some sectors as a result of migration, because migration affects demand as well as supply. Traditional labour mobility theory is orientated mainly to factor supply, since the labour mobility that occurs is generally taken to influence labour supplies in sending and receiving areas, while labour demand in each region is unaffected. Labour migrating from low- to high-wage regions increases labour supply in the high-wage area, placing a downward pressure on wage rates there, while decreased labour supply in the low-wage area results in upward pressure on its wage rates. This assumes labour demand functions are not infinitely elastic. Inter-area factor mobility thus tends to result in area wage equalisation. However, planners and decision makers are interested not only in distribution (equity) but also in efficiency. And there seems to be no strong *a priori* reason to suggest what effect migration has on income change for an area as a whole. This is because in- and out-migration associated with any area influences labour demand in that area as well as supply; and this occurs when the prices of locally-produced goods and services, or the marginal product of locally-supplied labour, is sensitive in a positive direction to in-migration, and sensitive in a negative direction to out-migration. The derived demand for labour will then tend to increase in the recipient region and decline in the sending region. Areas subject to increasing economies of scale are areas where this phenomenon is likely to occur. Moreover, the demand effect will be reinforced if, returning to our investment argument, in-migration induces increased investment in an area and out-migration induces a fall in investment in an area. If this occurs, then labour's marginal product may be expected to increase in the area of destination and decrease in the area of origin. These adjustments would result in an outward shift of the labour demand curve in the region of destination and an inward shift in the area of origin, causing upward pressure on wage and income levels in the former area and downward pressure in the latter area. In practice, there is no evidence in Britain of how migration affects saving and investment, and very little on the relation of migration to changes in marginal physical product between areas. This being so, there is no reason to suppose that the shift in labour demand associated with migration will dominate the labour supply shift, nor that the supply shift will dominate any demand shift, nor that the shifts will not offset one another. Nevertheless, planners must consider the effects of migration on an area's wage distribution, income and unemployment change. This can be achieved at present only by detailed empirical investigation in the area in question, to determine effects on wage and income levels. The effect of migration on employment is more certain, since this has been the subject of more investigation. In-migration into an area increases employment in that area, because it results in right shifts in both labour supply and demand curves; out-migration from any area has the effect of reducing employment in the area of origin, since it causes left shifts in demand and supply. Care must be taken here to define an area broad enough to encompass travel to work, for while many urban areas are experiencing employment growth due to in-migration into suburbs, their central areas are losing population. Migration also affects unemployment rates in areas. One of the chief causes of migration among skilled workers is unemployment and the related search for a job in which their existing skills can be used. The exact nature of the relationship between migration and unemployment can vary depending on the individual area under investigation and its characteristics. Again, the critical question for empirical evaluation is whether, for out-migration, the left shift in demand dominates the left shift in supply, creating more unemployment, or vice versa — in which case unemployment will be reduced. Much debate has centred on this issue in Britain, since its conclusion has implications for the lagging northern regions of Britain. If the left shift in demand does dominate the left shift in supply, any migration policy of encouraging people to move to the South and East of England is inappropriate, merely exacerbating the problem. In such a case, a policy of encouraging the establishment of industry in lagging regions would be more likely to achieve a target of reducing regional disparities in unemployment rates. This would be especially the case if, in the South and East, the right shift in demand associated with in-migration dominated the right shift in supply associated with in-migration, resulting in a fall in unemployment in the area of destination, at the given wage rate. However, it does seem more probable that the supply shift dominates the demand shift such that out-migration results in a fall in the unemployment rate. However, this relationship is not such, in Britain, that a policy of encouraging migration is the sole plan to pursue.

In-migration into various areas in Britain (non-congested areas and those not possessing outdated nineteenth-century industry structure) is likely to increase returns on various forms of capital, while out-migration reduces it. Net out-migration will increase the average rate of return on labour in the area of origin, unless the departure of out-migrants depresses long-run business expectations and the rate of investment sufficiently to offset the improvement initially occasioned in the ratio of productive wealth to the labour force.

The divergence between private costs and social costs associated with migration is largely a function of the externalities associated with fixed capital and services to residents. Migration affects the tax-price of public services, reducing it, in the area of in-migration, as the migrants' share in the cost of services, and raising it in the area of out-migration. On the other hand, migrants may create congestion of the public facilities in the area of in-migration, thus reducing public-service benefits received by previous residents. Where in-migration typically takes place in areas of population concentration and congestion, the negative benefit-side externalities are likely to be the predominating factor in the case of impure public goods. Since individuals do not usually consider, in their migration decision, the effects of their action on others, actual migration exceeds the social optimum level, which is clearly a case for government intervention. The divergence between private and social costs of migration can occur when charges for public services are based on the per capita cost, rather than the actual marginal cost, of providing these services to the migrant. Rating policies of local authorities, prices of public services, and most pricing policies of nationalised industries are based in Britain on average cost. When the charges for services collectively provided are based on the average cost, rather than the marginal cost, the social cost of migration can exceed the private cost.

Migration produces compositional changes and substitutive effects. In

Britain, migration between two areas probably increases the amount of employment in the two areas considered together. Chapter 2, on the economic problems in migration, has shown that migration would not have this effect if inter-occupational mobility of labour were great enough, and if the proportion in which labour might be combined with complementary agents of production were sufficiently variable. If these assumptions held, full employment would be attainable within all areas. Chapter 2 revealed that migration took place in preference to occupational change, because of the nature of economic rent accruing to occupations — whether this arose through supply and demand, historical accident or institutional perpetuation, or training costs. It is important, therefore, that some gross in- and out-migration takes place between areas, to encourage a reduction in unemployment by matching up demand for specific skills with supplies, encourage growth and equalise wage distributions. Government policy provides grants to encourage migrants to move, and these were outlined in Chapter 3. The implications of Chapter 2 for policy are great. The labour force is not homogenous, nor are the costs and benefits to migration to and from specific areas. At present, policies apply equally to all sections of the population and to all areas, and as such their effectiveness is questionable. Policies should be directed much more towards specific groups (occupations) and sub-groups (within occupations), and specific areas and types; that is, the economic rent accruing to individuals must be matched to influence movement significantly, and to take account of the costs and benefits associated with migration to and from specific areas.

There seem to be four main types of public policy instrument which the government could use: public expenditure (capital and current); public regulation; fiscal and monetary policies; and the form of government organisation. In different areas or regions, the proportion of expenditure that is public may vary considerably, and the fixing of this proportion is itself a policy instrument. Public regulation at present includes land-use control and company law, while fiscal and monetary policies range from taxes and regional government expenditure to manipulation of rates of interest in various markets. Finally, government organisation itself can have a major impact on the functional and spatial dimension of economic and social activity — from Public Transport Authorities to Regional Economic Planning Councils. It is recognised that these instruments are insufficient to exercise complete control on target goals, but, despite this, there has still been a general reluctance to experiment with the instruments that are available to influence migration. This reluctance has stemmed from a desire to apply all instruments with equal force in all areas: to set national rates. The instruments which have varied over space — the Regional Employment Premium, various capital grants and so on — have been too small or weak to achieve their targets or match the problems. This failure to allow instruments to vary significantly over space within Britain has meant that it has been difficult to influence migration in the interests of society's benefit; and secondly, it has been impossible to deal adequately with the effects of migration — for example, on local inflation, rate of return to local capital expenditure, regional differences in growth and employment opportunities. The result has been lagged *ad hoc* measures to deal with problems after they have arisen, instead of attempting to build into the system some flexible self-correcting mechanisms as problems arise. Thus, continued migration into congested areas could be stemmed by pricing services or taxing migrants according to size of population growth and congestion through migration. A general result of economic change in developed countries, including Britain, Western Europe and the United States, and of government policies, is that there appears to be insufficient migration of the right type in terms of economic opportunities available, and in the right direction in terms of costs borne by local authorities and local communities. Planners have exhibited a general reluctance to search for policy instruments and suggest new ones, yet as many policy instruments are required as there are different targets in a plan. There has also too frequently been too much public capital development as a solution to the problem of excess demand created by migrants in areas of destination, as well as in areas of origin, where the intention is to deter out-migration and attract in-migrants. Planners seldom think of pricing as a means of transferring capacity from one area to another, or attempting to bribe excess demanders or migrants to withhold their demands, or simply transferring capacity from one location or group of users to another by administrative fiat. It would seem sensible to check on the possibilities of achieving targets by rationalising existing economic capacity before seeking the lowest-cost way of spending public funds to achieve society's goals.

Migration may occur in response to non-economic factors, and at some juncture it can be viewed as an independent variable which sets some of the conditions for the movement of capital and other productive factors, and not merely as a dependent variable passively responding to economic differentials. In a first approximation and in Chapters 2 and 3, it was largely argued that internal migration can best be analysed in terms of its response to the changing economic opportunities which constitute potential economic growth. However, Chapters 6 and 8 argued that in planning and policy analysis migration should be viewed as part of a system. Migration is essentially a function of economic goals, and it can be used as a policy instrument in the achievement of those goals. As far as planners and planning are concerned, migration influences and creates changes in the factors which give rise to mobility; in income, employment, wage distribution and economic growth, which are the primary targets of plans. Any programme to influence migration as part of policy must consider the effects of this on targets and goals, but, equally important, the effect of the change in targets brought about by migration must be considered on subsequent migration volume and spatial direction. The interaction between cause and effect suggests that it is necessary, for planning and predictive purposes, in order to specify a model of migration which takes into account the interactions between the various 'independent' factors involved in the process. Chapter 8 also pointed to a number of previous studies that attempted to explain migration by means of a single equation multiple regression model, and found differing signs or insignificant coefficients on variables *a priori* thought to play a crucial role in the migrant's decision concerning his destination. Variables relating to income, unemployment and employment (labour demand) have been particularly prone to resulting errors. Ordinary least squares have been used to estimate single equation models. A possible explanation for the conflicting and surprising results obtained in these studies is that the parameter estimates possess simultaneous equation bias. Bias is likely to be particularly marked in studies employing some long-period measure of migration, since migration that has occurred over a long period of time is especially likely to have influenced the independent variables in the model. It is important, as a consquence, to adopt a simultaneous equations model of migration to improve model specification. Chapter 8 argued that such a model is much more useful to planners in adopting the 'system approach' to planning advocated by Chadwick (1971) and McLoughlin (1969).

Many of the existing migration models used in planning are naïve, and if migration is to be influenced in the interests of society, to maximise social benefits over social costs, and if the effects of migration on other variables in which planners are interested — income, labour demand, employment, consumption, labour supply — are to be ascertained, then more realistic models than gravity models are required (Chapter 6). A planning policy model of migration should accomplish four objectives to be of valuable practical use. It should show the time paths of accumulation and resource allocation of individual areas; demonstrate the interactions between resource allocation, factor payments and other determinants of migration; reactions of the system to changes in the data; and indicate the instrumental variables in the system that are amenable to influence by government policy. This requires careful *a priori* specification of the model and definition of the extent of the problem. Examples of badly specified *a priori* models were given in the chapter on regression models of migration. The definition of the extent of the problem is also important, and can determine the outcome of cost-benefit studies. It is important, therefore, in assessing conclusions, to bear in mind problem specification and techniques used. Studies of internal migration to date have also paid too little attention to time or an adequate spatial orientation. The great problem for the future development of migration research will be to build representative spatial dynamic migration systems. The use of stochastic models in this field is likely to become increasingly important, in providing both spatial analysis and depth in time, particularly in planning, by allowing the effects of a change in migration associated with one area on the composition of neighbouring areas to be determined. Migration can best be understood in terms of probabilities. Stochastic probability models seem to offer the greatest scope for development in migration research; for, although more is now known about migration and migration processes, of their characteristics, direction and effect, much cannot be said with certainty. It is worth remembering that Pearson's (1911) axiom 'No phenomena are causal; all phenomena are contingent' remains truer of migration than many other subjects.

Note

[1] Increasing population by natural increase is not favoured in Britain, but has played a large part in French population planning since the Second World War.

References

Adelman, I.G. (1958), 'A stochastic analysis of the size distribution of firms' *Journal of the American Statistical Association* 53, pp. 893–904.
Ahlberg, G. (1953), *Befolkningsutvecklingen och urbaniseringen i Sverige 1911–50,* Stockholm.
Allen, R.G.D. (1959), *Mathematical Economics,* 2nd. edition, London: Macmillan.
Anderson, T.R. (1955), 'Intermetropolitan migration : A comparison of the hypothesis of Zipf and Stouffer' *American Sociological Review* 20, pp. 287–91.
Anderson, T.W. (1958), *An Introduction to Multivariate Statistical Analysis,* New York: Wiley.
Anderson, T.W. and L.A. Goodman (1957), 'Statistical inference about Markov chain' *The Annals of Mathematical Statistics* 28, pp. 89–110.
van Arsdol, M.D. (1966), 'Metropolitan growth and environmental hazards: an illustrative case study' *Ekistics* 21, pp. 48–50.
van Arsdol, M.D., G. Sabagh and F. Alexander (1964), 'Reality and the perception of environmental hazards' *Journal of Health and Human Behaviour* 5, pp. 144–53.
Bachi R. (1958), 'Statistical analysis of geographical series' *Bulletin International Statistical Institute* 36 (2), pp. 229–40.
Bachi, R. (1961), 'Some methods for the study of geographical distributions of internal migrations'. *Paper presented to the International Population Conference,* New York.
Bachi R. (1965a), 'Analysis of geographical data on internal migration'. Paper presented at United Nations World Population Conference, Belgrade, Yugoslavia.
Bachi R. (1965b), *Population Distribution and Internal Migration in Israel*, report submitted to the Ford Foundation, Jerusalem: Hebrew University.
Bancroft, G., and S. Garfinkle (1963), 'Job mobility in 1961' *Monthly Labor Review* (US Dept. of Labor), August 1963.
Barclay, G.W. (1958), *Techniques of Population Analysis*, New York: Wiley.
Barkin, S. (1963), in *International Joint Seminar on Geographical and*

Occupational Mobility of Manpower. Final Report. 19th — 22nd November 1963, Paris: OECD.

Bartholomew, D.J. (1967), *Stochastic Models for social processes*, London: Wiley.

Bartlett, M.S. (1941), 'The statistical significance of canonical correlations' *Biometrika* 32, pp. 29–38.

Bartlett, M.S. (1947), 'Multivariate analysis' *Supplement to the Journal of the Royal Statistical Society* 9, pp. 176–97.

Beale, E.M.L., M.G. Kendall and D.W. Mann (1967), 'The discarding of variables in multivariate analysis' *Biometrika* 54, pp. 357–65.

Bell, W. (1958), 'Social choice, life styles, and suburban residence' in W.F. Dobriner (ed), *The Suburban Community*, New York: G.P. Putman's Sons.

Bellman, R. (1960), *Introduction to Matrix Analysis*, New York: McGraw-Hill.

Berry, B.J.L. (1966), 'Essays on commodity flows and the spatial structure of the Indian economy' *Research Paper no. 111*, Department of Geography, University of Chicago.

Beshers, J.M. (1967), 'Computer models of social processes: the case of migration' *Demography* 4, pp. 838–42.

Blau, P.M. (1965), 'The flow of occupational supply and recruitment' *American Sociological Review* 30, pp. 475–90.

Blumen, I., M. Kogan and P.J. McCarthy (1955), *The Industrial Mobility of Labour as a Probability Process*, Ithaca, New York: Cornell University Press.

Bogue, D.J. (1959), *The Use of Place of Birth and Duration of Residence Data for Studying Internal Migration*, United Nations: UNESCO E/CN.9/ CONF. 1/L.10.

Bogue, D.J., and M.J. Hagood (1953), 'Differential migration in corn and cotton belts' *Sub-regional Migration in the United States 1935–40* vol. 2, Scripps Foundation Studies in Population Distribution no. 6, Oxford, Ohio.

Bogue, D.J., Shryock H.S., and Hoermann S.A. (1957), *Sub-regional Migration in the United States, 1935–40* vol. 1, Scripps Foundation Studies in Population Distribution no. 5, Oxford, Ohio.

Borts, G.H. and J.L. Stein (1968), 'Regional growth and maturuty in the United States: a study of regional structural change' in L. Needleman (ed.), *Regional analysis*, Harmondsworth: Penguin.

Boudeville, J.R. (1966), *Problems of Regional Economic Planning*, Edinburgh: University Press.

Bowles, S. (1970), 'Migration as investment: empirical tests of the human investment approach to geographical mobility' *The Review of Economics and Statistics* 52, pp. 356–62.

van den Brink, T. (1954), 'Population registers and their significance for demographic statistics' *Proceeding of the World Population Conference 1954*, United Nations: sales no. 55.XIII. 8/vol. 4, pp. 917–18.

Brown, A.J. (1972), *The Framework of Regional Economics in the United Kingdom*, National Institute of Economic and Social Research, Cambridge University Press.

Brown, L.A. and D.B. Longbrake (1970), 'Migration flows in intra urban space, place utility considerations' *Annals of the Association of American Geographers* 60, pp. 368–84.

Brown, L.A., J. Odland and R.G. Golledge (1970), 'Migration, functional distance, and the urban hierarchy' *Economic Geography* 46, pp. 472–85.

Buckwell, A.E., and P.B.R. Hazell (1972), 'Implications of aggregation bias for the construction of static and dynamic linear programming supply models' *Journal of Agricultural Economics* 23, pp. 119–34.

Cartwright, A. (1963), 'Memory errors in a morbidity survey' *Milbank Memorial Fund Quarterly* 41, pp. 5–25.

Chadwick, G. (1971), *A Systems View of Planning*, Oxford: Pergamon Press.

Champernowne, D.B. (1953), 'A model of income distribution' *Economic Journal* 63, pp. 318–51.

Chiang, C.L. (1968) *Introduction to Stochastic Processes in Biostatistics*, New York: Wiley.

Christ, C.F. (1966), *Econometric Models and Methods*, New York: Wiley.

Cliff, A.D., and J.K. Ord (1970), 'The problem of spatial autocorrelation' in A.J. Scott (ed.), *Studies in Regional Science*, London: Pion.

Cooley, W.W., and P.R. Lohnes (1962), *Multivariate Procedures for the Behavioral Sciences*, New York: Wiley.

Cowie, W.G. and A.K. Giles (1957), *An Inquiry into Reasons for 'The Drift from the Land'*, Department of Economics, University of Bristol.

Cox, P.R. (1970), *Demography*, 4th edition, Cambridge University Press.

Cox, D.R., and H.D. Miller (1965), *The Theory of Stochastic Processes*, London: Methuen.

Craig, J. (1970), 'Estimating the age and sex structure of net migration for a sub-region. A case study: North and South Humberside 1951–1961' *Regional Studies* 4, pp. 333–47.

Cramond, R.D. (1965), 'Allocation of council houses' *University of Glasgow Social and Economic Studies, Occasional Paper no. 1*.

Davies, W.K.D. (1966), 'Latent migration potential and space preferences'

The Professional Geographer 18, pp.300—4.

Day, R.H. (1963), 'On aggregating linear programming models of production' *Journal of Farm Economics* 45, pp. 797—813.

Deming, W.E. (1950), *Some Theory of Sampling*, New York: Wiley.

Dent, W.T. (1967), 'The estimation of constant and non-constant transition probabilities from market shares'. Unpublished paper, University of Minnesota, quoted in W. Dent and R. Ballintine (1971), 'A review of the estimation of transition probabilities in Markov chains' *The Australian Journal of Agricultural Economics* 15, pp. 69—81.

Department of Economic Affairs (1969), *Progress Report no. 55*, HMSO, August 1969.

Department of Employment (1970), 'Approximate estimate of the flow of employees between industries' *Employment and Productivity Gazette*, April 1970, pp. 303—7.

Development Commission (1972), *Mid-Wales: an assessment of the impact of the Development Commission factory programme*, London: HMSO.

Donnison, D.V., C. Cockburn and T. Corlett (1961), *Housing Since the Rent Act*, Occasional Papers on Social Administration no. 3, Welwyn: Codicote Press.

Douglas, J.W.B., and J.M. Blomfield (1956), 'The reliability of longitudinal surveys' *Milbank Memorial Fund Quarterly* 34, pp. 227—52.

Draper, N.R., and H. Smith (1966), *Applied Regression Analysis*, New York: Wiley.

Dubin, R. (1958), *The World of Work*, New York, pp. 276—7.

Durham County Council (1966), 'Forecasting employment and population in South West Durham Sub Region'. Unpublished report by County Planning Officer, Planning Department, Durham County Council.

Durham County Council (1969). *Systems Manual on Population Forecasting*, Durham County Council.

Eisenstadt, S.N. (1955), *The Absorption of Immigrants*, Glencoe, Illinois: The Free Press.

Eldridge, H.T. (1965), 'Primary, secondary, and return migration in the USA 1955—60' *Demography* 2, pp. 444—55.

Fabricant, Ruth A. (1970), 'An expectational model of migration' *Journal of Regional Science* 10, pp. 13—24.

Ferriss, A.L. (1965), 'Predicting graduate student migration' *Social Forces* 43, pp. 310—19.

Fisher, L., and J.W. Van Ness (1971), 'Admissible clustering procedures' *Biometrika* 58, pp. 91—104.

Foote, N.N., J. Abu-Zughod, M.M. Foley and L. Winnick (1960), *Housing*

Choices and Constraints, New York: McGraw-Hill.
Friedlander D., and R.J. Roshier (1966), 'A study of international migration in England and Wales' *Population Studies* 19, pp. 239–79; *Population Studies* 20, pp. 45–59.
Funck, R. (1970), 'Welfare solutions and regional policy decisions' *Papers of the Regional Science Association* 24, pp. 157–62.
Galeotti, G. (1971), 'Les Migrations rurales et urbaines an Italie: synthèse statistique – explications programmes politiques' *International Population Conference (London)* vol. 4, International Union for the Scientific Study of Population, Liège 1971, pp. 2957–92.
Gallaway, L.E., R.R. Gilbert and P.E. Smith (1967), 'The economics of labor mobility and empirical analysis' *Western Economic Journal* 5, pp. 221–23.
Gerger, T. (1966), 'Vasterik – a migration study' *Geografiska Annaler* 48 (B), pp. 78–111.
Glass, D.V. (ed.); (1954), *Social Mobility in Britain*, London: Routledge and Kegan Paul.
Glick, P.C. (1957), *American Families*, New York: Wiley, p. 89.
Goddard, J.B. (1970), 'Functional regions within the city centre: a study by factor analysis of taxi flows in Central London' *Institute of British Geographers, Transactions* 49, pp. 161–82.
Goldberger, A.S. (1964), *Econometric Theory*, New York: Wiley.
Goldberger, A.S. (1968), *Topics in Regression Analysis* New York: The Macmillan Co.
Goldstein, S. (1954), 'Repeated migration as a factor in high mobility rates' *American Sociological Review* 19, pp. 536–41.
Goldstein, S. (1955), 'Migration and occupational mobility in Norristown, Pennsylvania' *American Sociological Review* 20, pp. 402–8.
Goldstein, S. (1958), *Patterns of Mobility 1910–1950. The Norristown Study*, Philadelphia: University of Pennsylvania Press.
Goldstein, S. (1964), 'The extent of repeated migration: an analysis based on the Danish Population Register' *American Statistical Association Journal* 59, pp. 1121–32.
Goldstein, S., and K.B. Mayer (1963), *Residential Mobility, Migration and Commuting in Rhode Island*, Providence: Rhode Island Development Council.
Goldstein, S., and K.B. Mayer (1965), 'Impact of migration on the socio-economic structure of cities and suburbs' *Sociology and Social Research* 50, pp. 5–23.
Goodman, L.A. (1961), 'Statistical methods for the "mover-stayer" model' *Journal of American Statistical Association* 56, pp. 841–68.

Goodman, L.A. (1963), 'Statistical methods for the preliminary analysis of transaction flows' *Econometrica* 31, pp. 197–208.

Goodrich, C. (1936), *Migration and Economic Opportunity*, University of Pennsylvania Press.

Goss, E. (1958), *Work and Society*, New York, p. 203.

Gould, P.R. (1967), 'On the geographical interpretation of eigenvalues' *Institute of British Geographers, Transactions* 43, pp. 53–86.

Goux, J.M., 'Structure de l'espace et migration' in J. Sutter (ed.) (1962), *Les Déplacements Humains: Aspects methodologiques de leur mesure*, Entretiens de Monace en Sciences Humaines, Monaco, 1962.

Gray, J.R. (1967), *Probability*, Edinburgh: Oliver and Boyd.

Gray, P., and F.A. Gee (1972), *A Quality Check on the 1966 Ten Per Cent Sample Census of England and Wales*, Office of Population Censuses and Surveys, London: HMSO.

Greenwood, M.J. (1970), 'Lagged response in the decision to migrate' *Journal of Regional Science* 10, pp. 375–84.

Greenwood, M.J. (1973), 'Urban growth and migration: their interaction' *Environment and Planning* 5, pp. 91–112.

Greenwood, N.J., and P.J. Gormely (1971), 'A comparison of the determinants of white and non-white interstate migration' *Demography* 8, pp. 141–55.

Grigson, S. (1968), *Population Projections, Problems and Requirements*, PATRC Seminar, London.

Guthrie, D., and M.N. Youssef (1970), 'Empirical evaluation of some chi-square tests for the order of a Markov chain' *Journal of the American Statistical Association* 65, pp. 631–4.

Hadjifotiou, N. (1971), 'The multivariate classification of local labour market areas' *Housing and Labour Mobility Study Working Paper no. 2.*, Department of Geography, University College, London.

Hadjifotiou, N. (1972), 'The analysis of migration between standard metropolitan labour market areas in England and Wales' *Housing and Labour Mobility Survey Working Paper no. 4*, Department of Geography, University College, London.

Hägerstrand, T. (1947), *En landsbygdsbefolknings flyttningsrörelser* (Svensk geografiska årsbok).

Hägerstrand, T. (1962), 'Geographic measurements of migration' in J. Sutter (ed.), *Les Déplacements Humains*, Entretiens de Monaco en Sciences Humaines.

Haggett, P., 'Leads and lags in inter-regional systems: a study of cyclic fluctuations in the South West economy' in M. Chisholm and G. Manners (eds) (1971) *Spatial Policy Problems of the British Economy*, Cam-

bridge University Press.
Hall, P. (1970), *Theory and Practice of Regional Planning*, Pemberton Books.
Hallberg, M.C. (1969), 'Projecting the size distribution of agricultural firms — an application of a Markov process with non-stationary transition probabilities' *Journal of Farm Economics* 51, pp. 289—302.
Hamilton, C.H. (1965), 'County net migration rates' *Rural Sociology* 30, pp. 13—17.
Hamilton, C.H. (1966), 'Effect of census errors on the measurement of net migration' *Demography* 3, pp. 393—415.
Hamilton, C.H. (1967), 'The vital statistics method of estimating net migration by age cohorts' *Demography* 4, pp. 464—78.
Hanna, F.A. (1959), *State income differentials, 1919—1954* Durham N.C: Duke University Press.
Harman, H. (1965), *Modern Factor Analysis*, 2nd edition, Chicago University Press.
Hart, P.E., and S.J. Prais (1956), 'The analysis of business concentration' *Journal of the Royal Statistical Society* A, 119, pp. 150—91.
Heath, C.E., and M.C. Whitby (1970), *The Changing Agricultural Labour Force*, Bulletin 10, Agricultural Adjustment Unit, University of Newcastle upon Tyne.
ter Heide, H. (1963), 'Migration models and their significance for population forecasts' *Milbank Memorial Fund Quarterly* 41, pp. 56—76.
Hillery, G.A. (1955), 'Definition of community, areas of agreement' *Rural Sociology* 20, pp. 111—23.
Hirschman, A.O. (1958), *The Stategy of Economic Development*, New Haven: Yale University Press.
Hocking, R.R. (1965), 'The distribution of a projected least squares estimator' *Annals of the Institute of Statistical Mathematics* 17, pp. 357—62.
House, J.W., and E.M. Knight (1965), 'Migrants of North East England 1951—61: character, age and sex' *Papers on Migration and Mobility no. 2*, Department of Geography, University of Newcastle upon Tyne.
House, J.W., and E.M. Knight (1966), 'People on the move: The South Tyne in the sixties' *Papers on Migration and Mobility no. 3*, Department of Geography, University of Newcastle upon Tyne.
House, J.W., and K.G. Willis (1967), 'Northern region and nation: a short migration atlas 1960—61' *Papers on Migration and Mobility in Northern England no. 4*, Department of Geography, University of Newcastle upon Tyne.
House, J.W., and E.M. Knight (1967), 'Pit closure and the community'

Papers on Migration and Mobility no 5, Department of Geography, University of Newcastle upon Tyne.

House, J.W., A.D. Thomas and K.G. Willis (1968), 'Where did the school leavers go?' *Papers on Migration and Mobility no. 7*, Department of Geography, University of Newcastle upon Tyne.

House, J.W., et al. (1968), 'Mobility of the Northern business manager' *Papers on Migration and Mobility no. 8*, Department of Geography, University of Newcastle upon Tyne.

House, J.W., and A.D. Thomas (1968), 'Northern graduates of '64: brain-drain or brain-bank?' *Papers on Migration and Mobility no. 9*, Department of Geography, University of Newcastle upon Tyne.

Huang, D.S. (1970), *Regression and Econometric Methods*, New York: Wiley.

Hubert, J. (1965), 'Kinship and geographical mobility in a sample from a London middle class area' *International Journal of Comparative Sociology* 6, pp. 61–80.

Inland Revenue (1972), *The Survey of Personal Incomes 1969–70*, London: HMSO.

Isard, W. (1960), *Methods of Regional Analysis: an Introduction to Regional Science*, Massachusetts Institute of Technology Press.

Jackson, V.J. (1968), *Population in the Countryside: Growth and Stagnation in the Cotswolds*, London: Frank Cass.

Jansen, C. (1968), *Social Aspects of Internal Migration*, Bath University Press.

Johnston, J. (1972), *Econometric Methods*, 2nd edition, New York: McGraw Hill.

Kahn, H.R. (1964), *Repercussions of Redundancy*, London: Allen and Unwin.

Kaiser, H.F. (1960), 'Comments on communalities and the number of factors', read at an informal conference 'The Communality Problem in Factor Analysis', St. Louis: Washington University.

Kalbach, W.E., G.C. Myers and J.R. Walker (1963–64), 'Metropolitan area mobility: a comparative analysis of familiy spatial mobility in a central city and selected suburbs' *Social Forces* 42, pp. 310–14.

Kaldor, N. (1970), 'The case for regional policies' *Scottish Journal of Political Economy* 17, pp. 337–48.

Karlin, S. (1966), *A First Course in Stochastic Processes*, London: Academic Press.

Katz, F.E. (1958), 'Occupational contact networks' *Social Forces* 37, pp. 52–5.

Keating, E., and C.H. Stone, *Validity of Work Histories Obtained by Inter-*

views, University of Minnesota: Industrial Relations Centre.

Kelley, A.C., and L.W. Weiss (1969), 'Markov processes and economic analysis' *Econometrica* 37, pp 280–97.

Kemeny, J.G., et al. (1959), *Finite Mathematical Structures*, New York: Prentice-Hall.

Kemeny, J.G., and J.L. Snell (1960), *Finite Markov Chains*, Princeton: Van Nostrand.

Kendall, M.G. (1957), *A Course in Multivariate Analysis*, London: Griffin.

Kerr, C., 'The balkinisation of labor markets' in E.W. Bakke et al. (1954), Labor Mobility and Economic Opportunity, New York: Wiley and MIT.

Klatzky, Sheila R., and R.W. Hodge (1971), 'A canonical correlation analysis of occupational mobility' *Journal of the American Statistical Association* 66, pp. 16–22.

Kono, S. (1971), 'Evaluation of the Japanese population register data on internal migration' *International Population Conference London (1969)*, vol. 4, International Union for the Scientific Study of Population, Liège, pp. 2766–75.

Kulldorf, G. (1955), *Migration Probabilities*, Lund Studies in Geography B, 14.

Laber, G. (1972), 'Lagged response in the decision to migrate: a comment' *Journal of Regional Science* 12, pp. 307–10.

Ladinsky, J. (1967a), 'Occupational determinants of geographic mobility among professional workers' *American Sociological Review* 32, pp. 253–64.

Ladinsky, J. (1967b), 'Sources of geographic mobility among professional workers: a multivariate analysis' *Demography* 4, pp. 293–310.

Lazarsfeld, P.E. (1955), 'Some general principles of questionnaire classification' in P.F. Lazarsfeld (ed.), *The Language of Social Research*, Glencoe, Illinois: The Free Press.

Lee, E.S. (1957), *Population Redistribution and Economic Growth*, United States 1870–1950, American Philosophical Society and University of Pennsylvania.

Lee, E.S. (1966), 'A theory of migration' *Demography* 3, pp. 47–57.

Lee, T.C., G.G. Judge and T. Takayama (1965), 'On estimating the transition probabilities of a Markov process' *Journal of Farm Economics* 47, pp. 742–62.

Lee, T.C., G.G. Judge and A. Zellner (1968), 'A maximum likelihood and Baynesian estimation of transition probabilities' *Journal of the American Statistical Association* 63, pp. 1162–79.

Lee, T.C., G.G. Judge and R.L. Cain (1969), 'A sampling study of the properties of estimators of transition probabilities' *Management*

Science 15 (A), pp. 374–98.

Lee, T.C., G.G. Judge and A. Zellner (1970), *Estimating the Parameters of the Markov Probability Model from Aggregate Time Series Data*, Amsterdam: North-Holland Publishing Co.

Lerner, A.P. (1958), 'Immigration, capital formation and inflationary pressure' in B. Thomas (ed.) (1958), *The Economics of International Migration*, London: Macmillan.

Leser, C.E.V. (1966), *Econometric Techniques and Problems,* Griffin's statistical monographs and courses no. 20, London: Griffin.

Leslie, G.R., and A.H. Richardson (1961), 'Life cycle, career pattern and decision to move' *American Sociological Review* 26, pp. 894–902.

Leven, C.L. (1970), 'A framework for the evaluation of secondary impacts of public investments' *American Journal of Agricultural Economics* 52, pp. 723–9.

Linder, F.E. (1959), 'World demographic data' in P.M. Hauser and O.D. Duncan (eds), *The Study of Population*, Chicago University Press.

Lipset, S., and R. Bendix (1952), 'Social mobility and occupational career paths' *American Journal of Sociology* 57, pp. 366–74.

Lipstein, B. (1965), 'A mathematical model of consumer behaviour' *Journal of Marketing Research* 2, pp. 259–65.

Litwak, E. (1960), 'Geographic mobility and extended family cohesion' *American Sociological Review* 25, pp. 385–94.

Lövgren, E. (1956), 'The geographical mobility of labour – a study of migrations.' *Geografiska Annalar* 38, pp. 344–94.

Lowry, I.S. (1966), *Migration and Metropolitan Growth: Two Analytical Models*, San Francisco: Chandler Publishing Co..

Luu-Mau-Thanh, 'Distribution théoriques des distances entre deux points répartis uniformement sur une surface' in J. Sutter (ed.) (1962) op. cit.

McColl, G.D., and C. D. Throsby (1972), 'Multiple objective benefit-cost analysis and regional development' *The Economic Record* 48, pp. 201–19.

McCrone, G. (1969), *Regional Policy in Britain*, London: Allen and Unwin.

McGuire, M.C., and H.A. Garn (1969), 'The integration of equity and efficiency criteria in public project selection' *The Economic Journal* 79, pp. 882–93.

MacIver (1932), *Society, Its Structure and Changes*, New York.

Mackintosh, J.P. (1968), *The Devolution of Power*, Harmondsworth: Penguin.

McLoughlin, J.B. (1969), *Urban and Regional Planning,* London: Faber.

Makower, H., J. Marschak and H.W. Robinson. (1938), 'Studies in the

mobility of labour' *Oxford Economic Papers* 1, pp. 83–123.
Mangalam, J.J., and H.K. Schwarzweller (1968), 'General theory in the study of migration: current needs and difficulties' *International Migration Review* 3, pp. 3–18.
Masser, I. (1970), 'A test of some models for predicting intermetropolitan movement of population in England and Wales' *CES-UP-9*, London: Centre for Environmental Studies.
Matras, J. (1960a), 'Comparison of intergenerational occupational mobility patterns: an application of the formal theory of social mobility' *Population Studies* 14, pp. 163–9.
Matras, J. (1960b), 'Differential fertility, intergenerational occupational mobility and change in the occupational distribution: some elementary inter-relationships' *Population Studies* 15, pp. 187–97.
Matras, J. (1966), 'Social mobility and social structure: some insights from the linear model.' Paper presented at the Sixth World Congress of Sociology, Evian, France.
Miller, A.R. (1965), 'Migration differentials among occupation groups: United States, 1960' *WPC/WP/179*, Belgrade: United Nations World Population Conference.
Miller, G.A. (1952), 'Finite Markov processes in Psychology' *Psychometrika* 17, pp. 137–44.
Miller, T.A. (1966), 'Sufficient conditions for exact aggregation in linear programming models' *Agricultural Economics Research* 18, pp. 52–7.
Mishan, E.J. (1971a), *Cost-Benefit Analysis. An Informal Introduction*, London: Allen and Unwin.
Mishan, E.J. (1971b), 'The ABC of cost-benefit.' *Lloyds Bank Review* 101, pp. 12–25.
Mishan, E.J. (1971c), *21 Popular Economic Fallacies*, Harmondsworth: Pelican.
Moody, H.T., and F.W. Puffer (1969), 'Some statistical problems in migration analysis' *The Annals of Regional Science* 3 pp. 192–201.
Moore, B., and J. Rhodes (1973), 'Evaluating the effects of British regional economic policy' *Economic Journal* 83, pp. 87–110.
Morrill, R.L. (1963), 'The distribution of migration distances' *Papers and Proceedings of the Regional Science Association* 11, pp. 75–84.
Morrill, R.L. (1965), *Migration and the Spread and Growth of Urban Settlement*, Lund Studies in Geography, Series B, No. 26.
Morrill, R.L., and F.R. Pitts (1967), 'Marriage, migration and the mean information field: a study in uniqueness and generality' Annals of the Association of American Geographers 57, pp. 401-22.
Morrison, P.A. (1967), 'Duration of residence and prospective migration.

The evaluation of a stochastic model' *Demography* 4, pp. 553–61.

Morrison, D.G., W.F. Massey and F.N. Silverman (1971), 'Effect of non-homogenous populations on Markov steady state probabilities.' *Journal of the American Statistical Association* 66, pp. 268–74.

Muhsam, H.V. (1961), 'Toward a formal theory of internal migration.' *International Population Conference, New York* vol. 1, International Union for the Scientific Study of the Population, Liège 1963, pp. 333–40.

Muhsam, H.V. (1962), 'Internal migration in open populations' in J. Sutter (ed.), op. cit.

Mydral, G. (1963), *Economic Theory in Underdeveloped Regions*, London: Methuen.

Myers, G.C., R. McGinnis, and G. Masnick (1967), 'The duration of residence approach to a dynamic stochastic model of internal migration: a test of the axiom of cumulative inertia' *Eugenics Quarterly* 14, pp. 121–6.

Nalson, J.S. (1968), *Mobility of Farm Families*, Manchester University Press.

Needleman L. (1965), 'What are we to do about the regional problem?' *Lloyds Bank Review*, (January), pp. 45–58.

Newton, M.P., and J.R. Jeffery (1951), *Internal Migration: Some Aspects of Population Movements within England and Wales*, General Register Office Studies on Medical and Population Subjects no. 5, London: HMSO.

Neymark, E. (1963), 'Migration differentials in education, intelligence and social background: analysis of a cohort of Swedish males' *International Statistical Institute Bulletin* 40, (vol. 1), pp. 350–79.

North Regional Planning Committee (1967), *Mobility and the North*, Newcastle: NRPC.

Northern Economic Planning Council (1966), *Challenge of the Changing North*, London: HMSO.

Northern Economic Planning Council (1969), *Outline Strategy for the North*, London: HMSO.

Nottingham and Derbyshire County Councils (1969), *Nottingham and Derbyshire Sub-regional Study*.

Office of Manpower Economics (1973), *Wage Drift: review of literature and research*, London: HMSO.

Oliver, P.R. (1964), 'Inter-regional migration and unemployment 1951–61' *Journal of the Royal Statistical Society* (A) 127, pp. 42–75.

Olsson, G. (1965), 'Distance and human interaction: a migration study' *Geografiska Annaler* B 47, pp. 3–43.

Oppenheim, A.N. (1966), *Questionnaire Design and Attitude Measure-*

ment, New York: Basic Books Inc.

Orcutt, G., et al. (1961), *Micro-analysis of Socio-economic Systems. A Simulation Study*, Harpers.

Organisation for Economic Co-operation and Development (1964), *International Management Seminar on Active Manpower Policy, Final Report*, Paris: OECD.

Organisation for Economic Co-operation and Development (1965), *Geographic and Occupational Mobility of Rural Manpower*, Paris: OECD.

Organisation for Economic Co-operation and Development (1967), *Government Financial Aids to Geographical Mobility in OECD Countries*, Paris: OECD.

Palmer, G.L. (1942), 'Reliability of response in labour market inquiries' *Technical Paper no. 22*, US Bureau of the Budget, Division of Statistical Standards.

Parnes, H.S. (1954), *Research on Labor Mobility*, New York: Social Science Research Council.

Pearson, Karl (1911), *The Grammar of Science*, 3rd edition, London, p. 174.

Perkins, B.B. (1964), *Labor Mobility between the Farm and Nonfarm Sector*, Michigan State University: Ph.D. dissertation.

Peston, M.H. (1972), 'The correlation between targets and instruments' *Economica* 39, pp. 427–31.

Pihlblad, C.T., and C.L. Gregory (1957), 'Occupation and patterns of migration' *Social Forces* 36, pp. 56–64.

Prais, S.J. (1955), 'Measuring social mobility' *Journal of the Royal Statistical Society* A, 118, pp. 56–66.

Preston, L.E., and E.J. Bell (1961), 'The statistical analysis of industrial structure' *Journal of the American Statistical Association* 56, pp. 925–32.

Price, D.O. (1948), 'Distance and direction as vectors of internal migration 1935–40' *Social Forces* 47, pp. 48–53.

Price, D.O. (1955), 'Examination of two sources of error in the estimation of net migration' *Journal of the American Statistical Association* 50, 689–700.

Price, D.O. (1959), 'A mathematical model of migration suitable for simulation on an electronic computer' *International Population Conference (Vienna)*, pp. 665–73.

Prothero, R.M. (1965), *Migrants and Malaria*, London: Longmans.

Randall, H.R., K.G. Willis et al. (1969), 'A library of computer programmes for use in geography. The case of migration' *Seminar Paper no. 9*, Department of Geography, University of Newcastle upon Tyne.

Ravenstein, E.G. (1885) and (1889), 'The laws of Migration' *Journal of Royal Statistical Society* 48, pp. 167–235; and 52, pp. 241–305.

Registrar General (1967), *Decennial Supplement, England and Wales (1961) Area Mortality Tables*, London: HMSO.

Registrar General (1970), *Statistical Review of England and Wales. Part 2. Population Tables*, London: HMSO.

Reynolds, L.G. (1951), *The Structure of Labor Markets,* New York: Harper.

Rhodes, J., and A. Kan (1971), *Office Dispersal and Regional Policy*, Cambridge University Press.

Richardson, H.W., and E.G. West (1964), 'Must we always take work to the workers?' *Lloyds Bank Review* 71, pp. 35–48.

Riddell, J.B. (1969), *A More Realistic Derivation of Regression Parameters*, Papers in Geography no. 2, Pennsylvania State University.

Rider, R.V., and G.F. Badger (1943), 'Family studies in the Eastern Health District (Baltimore). A consideration of issues involved in determining migration rates for families' *Human Biology* 15, pp. 101–26.

Riew, J. (1973), 'Migration and public policy' *Journal of Regional Science* 13, pp. 65–76.

Robinson, Hilary (1971), 'Survey method and questionnaire design' *Housing and Labour Mobility Study Working Paper 3*, Department of Geography, University College, London.

Rogers, A. (1966), 'A Markovian policy model of inter-regional migration' *Papers of the Regional Science Association* 17, pp. 205–24.

Rogers, A. (1967a), 'A regression analysis of inter-regional migration in California' *The Review of Economics and Statistics* 49, 262–71.

Rogers, A. (1967b), 'Estimating inter-regional population and migration operators from inter-regional population distributions' *Demography* 4, pp. 515–31.

Rogers, A. (1967c), 'The aggregation problem in demography' *American– Yugoslav Project in Regional and Urban Planning*, Urbanisticni Institut, Ljubljana, Yugoslavia.

Rogers, A. (1968), *Matrix Analysis of Inter-regional Population Growth and Distribution*, Los Angeles: University of California Press.

Rogoff, N. (1953), *Recent Trends in Occupational Mobility*, Glencoe, Illinois: The Free Press.

Rose, A.M. (1958), 'Distance of migration and socio-economic status of migrants' *American Sociological Review* 23, pp. 420–3.

Rossi, P.H. (1955), *Why Families Move*, Glencoe, Illinois: The Free Press.

Rossi, P.H. (1955), 'Why families move.' in P.F. Lazarsfeld (ed.) *The Language of Social Research*, New York: The Free Press.

Rowntree, J.A. (1957), *Internal Migration – a study of frequency of movement of migrants*, Studies on Medical and Population Subjects no. 11, London: HMSO.

Schneider, J.R.L. (1956), 'Local population projections in England and Wales' *Population Studies* 10, pp. 95–114.

Seal, H.L. (1964), *Multivariate Statistical Analysis for Biologists*, London: Methuen.

Sheps, M.C., and E.B. Perrin (1964), 'The distribution of birth intervals under a class of stochastic fertility models' *Population Studies* 27, pp. 321–31.

Shryock, H.S. (1964), *Population Mobility within the United States*, Community and Family Study Center, University of Chicago.

Shryock, H.S., and E.A. Larmon (1965), 'Some longitudinal data on internal migration' *Demography* 2, pp. 579–93.

Siegel, J.S., and C.H. Hamilton (1952), 'Some considerations in the use of the residual method of estimating net migration' *Journal of the American Statistical Association* 47, pp. 475–500.

Sjaastad, L.A. (1961), *Income and Migration in the United States*, Chicago University: Ph.D. dissertation.

Sjaastad, L.A. (1962), 'The costs and returns of human migration' *Journal of Political Economy* 70, pp. 80–93.

Smith, G.J.W. (1958), 'Stable and unstable factory workers in a Swedish city: a psychological investigation by means of a new type of questionnaire' *Lund Universitets Årsskrift NF* part 1, vol. 53, no. 3.

Smith, J.H. (1966), 'The analysis of labour mobility' in B.C. Roberts and J.H. Smith (eds), *Manpower Policy and Employment Trends,* London: Bell.

Solow, R. (1951), 'Some long-run aspects of the distribution of wage incomes' *Econometrica* 19, pp. 333–4.

Somermeijer, W.H. (1961), 'Een anlyse van de binnen landse migratie in Nederland eot 1947 en van 1948–1957' *Statische en Econometrische Onderzoekingen*, pp. 115–74.

Sonin, M., and E. Zhiltsov, (1967), 'Economic development and employment in the Soviet Union' in *International Labour Review* 96, Geneva: International Labour Office, p. 89.

Speare, A. (1971), 'A cost benefit model of rural to urban migration in Taiwan' *Population Studies* 25, pp. 117–30.

Stacey, M. (1960), *Tradition and Change: A study of Banbury*, Oxford University Press.

Standing Conference of Local Planning Authorities, Yorkshire and Humberside Region (1973), *A Study of Migration*, Wakefield: West Riding County Council.

Steele, D.B. (1972), 'A numbers game (or, the return of regional multipliers)' *Regional Studies* 6, pp. 115–30.

Stern, J., and D. Johnson (1964), 'Blue to white collar job mobility: a preliminary report' *American Statistical Association (Proceedings of the Social Statistics Section)*, pp. 166–86.

Stewart, J.Q. (1948), 'Demographic gravitation: evidence and applications' *Sociometry* 11, pp. 31–58.

Stidd, C.K. (1967), 'The use of eigenvectors for climatic estimates' *Journal of Applied Meteorology* 6, pp. 255–64.

Stouffer, S.A. (1940), 'Intervening opportunities: a theory relating mobility and distance' *American Sociological Review* 5, pp. 845–67.

Taeuber, K.E. (1961), 'Duration of residence analysis of internal migration in the United States' *Milbank Memorial Fund Quarterly* 39, pp. 116–31.

Taeuber, K.E. (1965), 'Cohort population redistribution and the urban hierarchy' *Milbank Memorial Fund Quarterly* 43, pp. 450–62.

Taeuber, K.E. (1966), 'Cohort migration' *Demography* 3, pp. 416–22.

Taeuber, K.E., W. Haenszel and M.G. Sirken (1961), 'Residence histories and exposure residences for the US population' *American Statistical Association Journal* 56, pp. 824–34.

Taeuber, K.E., and A. Taeuber (1964), 'White migration and socio-economic differences between cities and suburbs' *American Sociological Review* 29, pp. 718–29.

Taeuber, K.E., L. Chiazze and W. Haenszel (1968), *Migration in the United States: an analysis of residence histories*, Public Health Monograph no. 77, Washington DC: US Department of Health, Education and Welfare.

Tarver, J.D. (1961), 'Predicting migration' *Social Forces* 39, pp. 207–13.

Tarver, J.D. (1962), 'Evaluation of census survival rates in estimating intercensal state net migration' *Journal of the American Statistical Association* 57, pp. 841–62.

Tarver, J.D. (1964), 'Occupation migration differentials' *Social Forces* 43, pp. 231–41.

Tarver, J.D., and W.R. Gurley (1965a), 'A stochastic analysis of geographic mobility and population projections of the census divisions in the United States' *Demography* 2, pp. 134–9.

Tarver, J.D., and W.R. Gurley (1965b), 'Relationship of selected variables with county net migration rates in US, 1950 to 1960' *Rural Sociology* 30, pp. 3–22.

Tarver, J.D., W.R. Gurley and P.M. Skees (1967), 'Vector representation of migration streams among selected state Economic Areas during 1955 to 1960' *Demography* 4, pp. 1–19.

Tarver, J.D., and P.M. Skees (1967), 'Vector representation of interstate migration streams' *Rural Sociology* 32, pp. 178–93.

Taylor, P.J. (1968), 'A general spatial model of migration'. Paper presented in Salford to IBG Population Study Group 'Symposium on Migration'.

Taylor, R.C. (1969), 'Migration and motivation: a study of determinants and types' in J.A. Jackson (ed.), *Migration*, Cambridge University Press.

Telser, L.G. (1963), 'Least squares estimation of transition probabilities' in C.F. Christ (ed.), *Measurement of Economics*, Standford University Press.

Theil, H., and G. Ray (1966), 'A quadratic programming approach to the estimation of transition probabilities' *Management Science* 12(A), pp. 714–21.

Thirlwall, A.P. (1966), 'Migration and regional unemployment: some lessons for regional planning' *Westminster Bank Review*, November 1966, pp. 31–44.

Thomas, D.S. (1938), *Research Memorandum on Migration Differentials*, New York: Social Science Research Council.

Thomas, D.S. (1941), *Social and Economic Aspects of Swedish Population Movements 1750–1933*, New York: Macmillan.

Thomas, E.N., 'Maps of residuals from regression' in B.J.L. Berry and D.F. Marble (1968), *Spatial Analysis: a reader in statistical geography*, New Jersey: Prentice Hall.

Thomlinson, R. (1961), 'A model for migration analysis' *Journal of American Statistical Association* 56, pp. 675–89.

Thompson, W.S., and D.J. Bogue (1949), 'Subregional migration as an area of research' *Social Forces* 27, pp. 392–400.

Thornthwaite, C.W. (1934), *Internal Migration in the United States*, Philadelphia: University of Pennsylvania Press.

Tinbergen, J. (1955), *On the Theory of Economic Policy*, Amsterdam: North Holland Publishing Co.

Tinbergen, J. (1956), *Economic Policy, Principles and Design*, Amsterdam: North Holland Publishing Co.

Tintner, G. (1952), *Econometrics*, New York: Wiley.

Toothill Committee (1962), *Report of the Committee of Inquiry into the Scottish Economy*, Scottish Council Development and Industry.

Tyne–Wear Plan, *Urban Strategy* (1973), Voohees and Associates and Colin Buchanan and Partners.

UK Social Survey (1967), *Occupational Mobility in Great Britain*, London: HMSO.

United Nations Economic and Social Council (1962), *Methodology and evaluation of continuous population registers*, Document E/CN.3/293. See also United Nations Department of Economic and Social Affairs (1970), *Methods of Measuring Internal Migration*, Manuals on methods of estimating population, Manual VI, sales no. 70.XIII.3.

US Bureau of the Census (1951), *Handbook of Statistical Methods for Demographers*, Washington DC: US Government Printing Office.

US Water Resources Council Special Task Force (1970), *Summary Analyses of Nineteen Tests of Proposed Evaluation Procedures on Selected Water and Land Resource Projects*, Washington DC.

Vance, R.B. (1952), 'Is theory for demographers?' *Social Forces* 31, pp. 9–13.

Vimont, C., and J. Baudot (1965), 'Les Titulaires d'un diplôme d' enseignement technique ou professionnel dans la population active 1962' *Population* 20, pp. 763–84.

Walters, A.A. (1968), *An Introduction to Econometrics*, London: Macmillan.

Ward, J.H. (1963), 'Hierarchical grouping to optimise an objective function' *Journal of the American Statistical Association* 58, pp. 236–44.

Warford, J.J. (1969), *The South Atcham Scheme. An Economic Appraisal*, Ministry of Housing and Local Government, HMSO.

Wattenberg, W. (1948), 'Attitude toward community size as evidence in migration behaviour' *Social Forces* 26, pp. 437–42.

Waugh, F.V., and M.E. Abel (1967), 'On fractional powers of a matrix' *Journal of the American Statistical Association* 62, pp. 1018–19.

Welch, R.L. (1970), 'Migration research and migration in Britain' *Occasional Paper no. 14*, Centre for Urban and Regional Studies, University of Birmingham.

Whitby, M.C., D.L.J. Robins, A.W. Tansey and K.G. Willis (1974), *Rural Resource Development*, London: Methuen.

Wilber, G.L. (1965), 'A Baysian model for migration decisions in a population'. Paper presented at the annual meeting of the Population Association of America, Chicago, Illinois, April 1965.

Wilkinson, R.K. (1973), 'House prices and the measurement of externalities' *Economic Journal* 83, pp. 72–86.

Wilkinson, R.K., and D.M. Merry (1965), 'A statistical analysis of attitudes to moving (a survey of slum clearance areas in Leeds)' *Urban Studies* 2, pp. 1–14.

Williams, W.M. (1956), *The Sociology of an English Village: Gosforth*, London: Routledge and Kegan Paul.

Willis, J. (1968), 'Population growth and movement' *CES-WP-8*, Centre

for Environmental Studies, London.
Willis, K.G. (1968), 'Vector analysis and the representation of movement: the case of migration' *Seminar Paper no. 2*, Department of Geography, University of Newcastle upon Tyne.
Willis, K.G. (1970), *Differential Migration in Selected Areas of North-East England*, Ph.D. Thesis, University of Newcastle upon Tyne.
Willis, K.G. (1971), 'Models of population and income: economic planning in rural areas' *Research Monograph no. 1*, Department of Agricultural Economics, University of Newcastle upon Tyne.
Willis, K.G. (1972a), 'Geographical and labour mobility' *Papers on Migration and Mobility no. 11*, Department of Geography, University of Newcastle upon Tyne.
Willis, K.G. (1972b), 'Population studies in planning' *Planning Outlook* 12, pp. 51–7.
Willis, K.G. (1972c), 'The influence of spatial structure and socio-economic factors on migration rates' *Regional Studies* 6, pp. 69–82.
Winch, D.M. (1971), *Analytical Welfare Economics*, Harmondsworth: Penguin.
Wolpert, J. (1965), 'Behavioural aspects of the decision to migrate' *Papers and Proceeding of the Regional Science Association* 15, pp. 159–69.
Wolpert, J. (1966), 'Migration as an adjustment to an environmental stress' *Journal of Social Issues* 22, pp. 92–102.
Wolpert, J. (1967), 'Distance and direction bias in inter urban migration streams' *Annals of the Association of American Geographers* 57, pp. 605–16.
Wonnacott, R.J., and T.H. Wonnacott (1970), *Econometrics*, New York: Wiley.
Yorkshire and Humberside Economic Planning Council (1970), *Yorkshire and Humberside Regional Strategy*, HMSO.
Young, M., and P. Willmott, (1957), *Family and Kinship in East London*, London: Routledge and Kegan Paul.
Zellner, A. (1961), *Linear Regression with Inequality Constraints on the Coefficients*, Report 6109 of the International Centre for Management Science.
Zipf, G.K. (1946), 'The $P_1 P_2 /D$ hypothesis: on the intercity movement of persons' *American Sociological Review* 11, pp. 677–86.

Index

Indexer's note: Authors are referred to by surname and year of publication, e.g. Willis (1970); where there are two authors, both appear under the first author's name only e.g. House and Willis (1967) under House. Three or more authors are referred to by the first named, followed by *et al.* Second, third and fourth authors of the same paper are given by their surnames followed by a *see* reference to the first named author and the words *et al.* Thus, McCarthy appears as McCarthy, *see* Blumen *et al.*

Full titles of Papers appear in the Reference section on pages 219–37 under first author's name, or, occasionally, an organisation such as Durham County Council. Where a specific page reference in the text is required, this index should be used.

Abu-Zughod, *see* Foote *et al*
Adelman (1958) 146
Age as a migratory factor 19, 42–3, 67, 73–8, 125–6, 189–90
Agricultural labour market, simple model for 98–9
Agricultural workers 26–7
Ahlberg (1953) 5
Allen (1959) 122, 201
Amenities to be considered for modern living standards listed 51
Anderson (1958) 138
Anderson and Goodman (1957) 204
Annual net migration, table of 85
Art graduates 22

Bachi (1958) 168; (1961) 168; (1965a) 168–9; (1965b) 168–9, 173
Banbury, Oxford 64
Bancroft and Garfinkle (1963) 23
Barclay (1958) 3
Barkin (1963) 18
Barlow Report 55
Bartholomew (1967) 182
Bartlett (1941, 1947) 139
Baysian methods 136, 196
Beale *et al,* (1967) 125
Bell (1958) 62
Bellman (1960) 175
Berry (1966) 178
Beshers (1967) 93
Bethnal Green, London 64
Blau (1965) 24–5
Blumen *et al* (1955) (BKM) 146, 149–51
Bogue (1957) 6; (1959) 72
Bogue and Hagood (1953) 2
Bogue *et al* (1957) 123
Borts and Stein (1968) 210
Boudeville (1966) 36
Boundaries, administrative, as a basis to establish migration 5
Bowles (1970) 136
Bristol, City of 62–3, 69, 113

239

Brown A. (1972) 55, 57
Brown L., and Longbrake (1970) 160
Brown L., et al (1970) 160
Buckwell and Hazell (1972) 122, 178

Cain see Lee et al (1969)
Capital, rates of return on, 12
Cartwright (1963) 116
Census of Population 5, 20, 71–7, 83–4, 108, 117–18, 147, 183, 187–9
Chadwick (1971) 216
Champernowne (1953) 145–6
Chiang (1963) 146
Chiazze, see Taeuber et al (1968)
Choropleth maps 167
Christ (1966) 130, 132–3, 137, 175
Cliff and Ord (1970) 137
Closing occupations 20–1
Clustering, analysis of 176–8
Coalmining 21
Cockburn, see Donnison et al
Cohort migration 73–5
Collingham, Leeds 69
Conclusions of the Study 207–17
Cooly and Lohnes (1962) 125, 138, 178.
Corleth, see Donnison et al
Cost–benefit analysis of migration 47–54
Cost–inflation 209–11
Cowie and Giles (1957) 27
Cox (1970) 185, 188
Cox and Miller (1965) 144
Craig (1970) 189
Cramond (1965) 65
Cross–section models, variables in 97

Darras Hall, Ponteland 69
Data on migration 103–20: sources of 103–8; survey design 108–10; questionnaire problems 110–16; quality of 116–18; enumerative value of 118–20; analytic studies of 118–20
Davies (1966) 105
Day (1963) 122, 178
Decentralisation of London and other cities 39–40
Decisions to migrate, what motivates 66–9, 144
Deming (1950) 117, 119
Dent (1967) 198
Development Commission (1972) 48
Disamenities, effect of, on migration 61–2
Distance analysis 167–74
Donnison et al (1961) 65
Douglas and Blomfield (1956) 116
Draper and Smith (1966) 136–7
Dubin (1958) 23
Duration of residence 71–80, 152–5
Durham County Council (1966) 199; (1969) 84–5, 186, 188

Earning power as a migratory factor 13
Earnings Related Supplements 44
Ecological aspects 59
Economic problems in migration 11–31
Economic rent 23
Eigenvalues and eigenvectors 174–6
Eisenstadt (1955) 69
Eldridge (1965) 72
Electoral rolls 104

Electricians 23–4, 28–9, 65, 75, 79
Employment exchanges, improved services at 44
Employment Transfer Scheme 41–3
Engineering workers 23–4, 28–9, 65, 75
Environment, effect of, on migration 60–2
Equilibrium distribution 155–9

Fabricant (1970) 19, 130, 136
Family, effect of, on migration 60
Farm workers 26–7
Fisher and Van Ness (1971) 177
Flax Bourton (Bristol) 69
Foley, see Foote et al
Foote et al (1960) 60
Forecasting migration, attempts at 85
French Fifth Plan (1966–70) 36
Frequency of moving house 71–80
Friedlander and Roshier (1966) 108
Friends, need for and effect of, on migration 63–4
Funck (1970) 57

Galeotti (1971) 56
Gallaway et al (1967) 126
Generalised least squares 96
Gerger (1966) 111, 113, 115, 118
Gilbert see Gallaway et al
Glass (1954) 148
Glick (1957) 60
Goddard (1970) 178
Goldberger (1964) 134; (1968) 125
Goldstein (1954) 78, 148; (1955) 25; (1958) 63, 78–9, 148; (1964) 73, 78

Goldstein and Mayer (1963) 4; (1965), 60
Golledge, see Brown et al
Goodman (1961) 154; (1963) 174
Goodrich (1936) 2
Goss (1958) 23
Gould (1967) 175–6
Goux (1962) 5, 126
Government: objectives of 33–7; policies 33–58; policies in regions 45–7
Grants 38–9, 42
Gray (1967) 144
Gray and Gee (1972) 117–18
Greenwood (1970) 128–9; (1973) 91, 94–7
Greenwood and Gormely (1971) 19, 129
Grigson (1968) 85
Gurley, see Tarver et al (1967)
Guthrie and Youssef (1970) 159
Guttman 115

Hadjifotiou (1971) 177; (1972) 179
Haenszel, see Taeuber et al (1961), Taeuber et al (1968)
Hägerstrand (1947) 5; (1962) 87, 167
Haggett (1971) 128
Hale, Liverpool 69
Hall (1970) 90
Hallberg (1969) 198, 204
Hamilton (1965) 124–5; (1966, 1967) 189
Hanna (1959) 19
Harman (1960) 178
Hart and Prais (1956) 146
Health hazard areas 61
Heath and Whitby (1970) 99
Hebburn see Jarrow–Hebburn

Employment Exchange Scheme Heide, ter (1963) 87–90
Hirschman (1958) 17
Hocking (1965) 196
Hoermann, *see* Bogue *et al*
Homogeneity in time and space 147–52
House and Knight (1965) 186, 188, 190; (1966) 63, 104, 143–4, 167; (1967) 21, 110
House and Thomas (1968) 22, 115
House and Willis (1967) 20, 77, 167
House *et al* (1968) 21, 112–15, 118
House, Thomas and Willis (1968) 22
House–moving, frequency of 71–80
Housing, effects of, on migration 65
Huang (1970) 132
Hubert (1965–66) 63–4

Industrial Development Certificates 39
Industrial Training Boards 44
Industrial Transference Board, report of, (1928) 35
Industry Act (1972) 38
Inflation 209–11
Institutional factors 30–1
Investment 209–12
Isard (1960) 185, 199

Jackson (1968) 186, 190
Jansen (1968) 62, 112–13, 118
Jarrow–Hebburn Employment Exchange Scheme 42–3
Jarrow and Whickham 61, 75, 80; *see also* Tyneside
Johnston (1972) 134

Judge, *see* Lee *et al* (1965 and 1970); Lee *et al* (1968); Lee *et al* (1969)

Kahn (1964) 28
Kaiser (1960) 179
Kalbach *et al* (1963–64) 60
Kaldor (1970) 38
Karlin (1966) 144
Katz (1958) 21
Keating and Stone 116
Kelley and Weiss (1969) 146
Kemeny (1959) 161
Kemeny and Snell (1960) 144, 147, 160
Kemeny *et al* (1959) 144
Kendall (1957) 125; *see also* Beale *et al*
Kerr (1954) 30
Keynesian theory 17
Key–Workers' Scheme 41
Klatzky and Hodge (1971) 139
Kogan, *see* Blumen *et al*
Kono (1971) 106–7
Kulldorf (1955) 5, 88, 126

Laber (1972) 129
Labour, supply and demand of 11–12
Ladinsky (1967a, 1967b) 21
Lazarsfeld (1955) 112
Lee (1957) 5; (1966) 6, 8
Lee *et al* (1965) 194–5; (1968) 196; (1969) 196; (1970) 156, 159, 194, 196
Lerner (1958) 210
Leser (1966) 133
Leslie and Richardson (1961) 20, 62
Leven (1970) 56

Life cycle, effects of, on migration 60
Likert 115
Linder (1959) 107
Lipset and Bendix (1952) 23, 25
Lipstein (1965) 198
Litwak (1960) 63
Local Employment Act (1960) 35, 38, 48; (1970) 38
Locality participation 63–4
Location of Offices Bureau 39
Lövgren (1956) 5, 87
Lowry (1966) 89–90, 127, 199–200
Luu–Mau–Thanh (1962) 5, 126

McCarthy, see Blumen et al
McColl and Throsby (1972) 49
McCrone (1969) 35
McGinnis model, see Myers et al
McGuire and Garn (1969) 49
MacIver (1932) 4
McLoughlin (1969) 216
Makower et al (1938) 128
Mangalam and Schwarzweller (1968) 69
Mann, see Beale et al
Manpower Economics, Office of (1973) 36
Marginal Physical Product (MPP) 17
Marginal Revenue Product (MRP) 17
Marital status, effects of, on migration 42–3, 73–4
Markov chains 144–64, 177, 196, 204–5
Marschak, see Makower et al
Masnick, see Myers et al
Masser (1970) 89, 200
Massey, see Morrison et al
Matras (1960a, 1960b, 1966) 146

Matrix estimation 192–8
Mean migration times 160–4
Micro–data 198
Migration: and motivation 59–70; and occupation 19–28; cost–benefit analysis of 47–54; data, see data on migration; definition 3–7; economic problems in 11–31; effects of redundancy on 7–8, 28, 44; estimating of 185–206 (methods 185–190, interregional cohort methods 190–1, matrixes 192–8); industrial changes, a cause of 28–30; mean times of 160–4; nature and importance of 1–3; personal and family reasons for 28; policies, implementation of Government 37–40; projection of 199–206 (cross-section models 204–6); random (stochastic) processes in 143–64; Ravenstein's 'laws' of 8; revenue from and costs of 13–16; sequences of 76–7; should it be controlled by taxation? 215; study of pattern of 7–9
Migrants, Government assistance to 40–5; primary and secondary defined 81
Miller, A., (1965) 19
Miller G., (1952) 198
Miller T., (1966) 177
Minimum Absolute Deviation Procedure (MAD) 196
Mirkil, see Kemeny et al
Mishan (1971a) 48; (1971c) 18
Mobility, measurement of 180–3
Models in migration 83–101: current 83–6; gravity 86–90; policy 90–100; stochastic 143–64 (and

duration of residence 152–5, Markov chains 145–55)
Moody and Puffer (1969) 127
Moore and Rhodes (1973) 40
Morrill (1963) 88; (1965) 203
Morrill and Pitts (1967) 88
Morrison D., et al (1971) 147
Morrison P., (1967) 153
Motivation in migration 59–70
Moving house, costs of, as a factor in migration 13–16; frequency of 71–80
Muhsam (1961) 146, 159, 180–1; (1962) 146
Multivariate techniques 167–83: distance and vector analysis 167–74; eigenvalues and eigenvectors 174–6; clustering 176–8; factor analysis 178–80; mobility, measurement of 180–3
Mydral (1963) 17
Myers et al (1967) 152–3
Myers, see Kalbach et al

Nalson (1968) 26
National Health Service Executive Council's Register 104
National Insurance Act (1966) 44
National Plan (1965) 55
National Register 78, 103
Natural hazards, effects of, on migration 61
Needleman (1965) 48
Neighbourhood, changes in character of, and migration 61
Newton and Jeffery (1951) 104
New Town Policies 47, 55, 83
Neymark (1963) 126
Noise, effect of, on migration 61
Non–money costs in migration 14
Norristown (Pa, USA) 78

Northern Economic Planning Council (1966 and 1969) 45, 84
North Regional Planning Committee (1967) 104–5, 111–13, 118
Nucleus Labour Force Scheme 41

Occupation and migration 19–28, 75–6
Occupations most and least likely to migrate, list of 19–20
Odland, see Brown et al
OECD (1964) 65; (1965) 26
Oliver (1964) 17, 105
Olsson (1965) 124, 126
OPCS (Office of Population Censuses and Surveys), see Census of Population
Oppenheim (1966) 111, 115
Orcut et al (1961) 203
Ordinary Least Squares (OLS) 95, 121–3, 130–4
Outline Strategy for the North (1969) 45

Palmer (1942) 116
Pareto optimality 34, 36, 57, 87–8
Parish Registers 103
Parnes (1954) 22–3, 29
Pearson (1911) 217
Perkins (1964) 26
Permits for office development 39
Peston (1972) 101
Pihlblad and Gregory (1957–58) 20
Poisson model 150–1, 154
Pollution, effects of, on migration 61–2
Population Census see Census of Population
Prais (1955) 146–8, 182; see also Hart and Prais

Preston and Bell (1961) 146
Price (1948) 168; (1955) 189; (1959) 91–3
Professions most and least likely to migrate, list of 19–20
Prothero (1965) 3
Purchase Tax 51–2
Push–pull scheme 113, 138

Questionnaire and response problems 111–16
Quinquennial reviews 83, 85
Quinquennial surveys of income 97

Randall and Willis, K., (1969) 168, 172
Ravenstein (1885) 8, 87
Redundancy, effects of, on migration 7–8, 28, 44
Redundancy Payments Act (1965) 44
Regional Economic Planning Boards 84, 214
Regional Employment Premium (1967) 38, 215
Regional Policies of Government 45–7
Registrar General (England and Wales) 83, 103, 189–90)
Regression techniques 121–41: general model 121–2; assumptions 122–5; joint influences 125–6; *a priori* 126–7; lagged responses 127–9; simultaneous equation 129–32; identification problem 132–4; interpretation 134–6; residuals 136–7; canonical co–relation 137–40; conclusions of study on 140–1
Removal grants 38–9, 42
Resettlement Transfer Scheme, *see* Employment Transfer Scheme
Residence, duration of 71–80, 152–5
Reynolds (1951) 29–30
Rhodes and Kan (1971) 39
Richardson and West (1964) 36, 65
Riddell (1969) 125, 129, 136
Rider and Badger (1943) 72–3, 148
Riew (1973) 53
Robins, *see* Whitby *et al*
Robinson, Hilary (1971) 111
Robinson, H.W., *see* Makower *et al*
Rogers (1965) 146; (1967a) 19, 89, 127; (1967b) 195–6; (1967c) 148; (1968) 136, 160, 190, 196
Rogoff (1953) 148
Rose (1958) 20, 105
Rossi (1954) 113–14; (1955) 60, 63–4
Rowntree (1957) 78, 104

Salaries, increase in, as a migratory factor 20–2
Saving and investment 209–12
Schneider (1956) 83
School leavers 22
Seal (1964) 175
Second homes 209
Selective Employment Tax 36
Self–employment, a disincentive to migrate 21
Sheps and Perrin (1964) 146
Shryock (1964) 6, 117; *see also* Bogue *et al*
Shryock and Larmon (1965) 72
Siegel and Hamilton (1952) 186
Silverman, *see* Morrison *et al*
Sirken, *see* Taeuber *et al* (1961)
Sjaastad (1961) 13, 47; (1962) 13–14, 47

Skees, *see* Tarver *et al* (1967)
Skilled and semi–skilled workers 24–5, 28–9
Smith (1958) 66
Smith J.H., (1966) 20
Smith P.E., *see* Gallaway *et al*
Snell, *see* Kemeny *et al*, Kemeny and Snell
Social mobility, effects of, on migration 62–3
Social participation 63–4
Social security benefits 44
Solow (1951) 145–6
Somermeijer (1961) 88, 90
Sonin and Zhiltsov (1967) 56
South Atcham Water Supply Scheme 50–1
Space, homogeneity in 147–52
Space, techniques involving 167–83: distance and vector analysis 167–74; clustering 176–8, factor analysis 178–80; mobility, measurement of 180–3
Speare (1971) 15–16, 47
Stacey (1960) 64
Standing Conference of Local Planning Authorities (Yorkshire and Humberside Region), (1973) 105, 111–12, 115; *see also* Yorkshire and Humberside Planning Council (1970)
Steele (1972) 18
Steelworkers 24–5, 75, 79
Stern and Johnson (1964) 25
Stewart (1948) 87
Stidd (1967) 175
Stouffer (1940) 64, 88–9
Study, Conclusions of this 207–17
Swedish methods of gathering statistical data 106

Taeuber (1961) 74; (1965) 76; (1966) 73
Taeuber and Taeuber (1964) 60
Taeuber *et al* (1961) 77; (1968) 71, 76–7, 109
Takayama, *see* Lee *et al* (1965)
Tansey, *see* Whitby *et al*
Tarver (1961) 123–4, 136; (1962) 189; (1964) 19
Tarver and Gurley (1965a) 148; (1965b) 124
Tarver and Skees (1967) 169, 171
Tarver *et al* (1967) 169–70, 173
Tax rebates 44
Taylor (1968) 173; (1969) 21, 59
Telser (1963) 195
Theil and Ray (1966) 195
Thirwall (1966) 2, 17
Thomas D., (1938) 3–4, 23, 73, 106; (1941) 5, 106
Thomas E.N., (1968) 136
Thomlinson (1961) 5, 126
Thompson, *see* Kemeny *et al*
Thompson and Bogue (1949) 60
Thornthwaite (1934) 167
Three–stage least squares (3SLS) 95–6
Time, homogeneity in 147–52
Time models, variables in 97
Tinbergen (1955, 1956) 91
Tintner (1952) 138
Toothill Commission (1962) 65
Trade Unions, records of 105
Training period for occupation, long, a disincentive to migration 30
Two–stage least squares (2SLS) 95–6
Tyneside 137–40, 157, 161–3, 172–3, 176, 179; *see also* Jar-

row—Hebburn, Jarrow and Whickham
UK Social Survey (1967) 29
Unemployment benefits 44
Unemployment, ways to reduce 35–7
United Nations Economic and Social Council (1962) 106
United States Water Resources Council Special TaskForce (1970) 49 (For United States *see also* under US)
University College, London, Housing and Mobility Survey 111
Urban residence, tendency towards 62–3
US Bureau of Census (1951) 187
US Current Population Survey (1958) 71

Value Added Tax 51–2
Van Arsdol (1966) 61
Van Arsdol *et al* (1964) 61
Vance (1952) 9
Van den Brink (1954) 106
Vastervik, Sweden 113–15
Vector analysis 167–74
Vimont and Baudot (1965) 21

Walker, *see* Kalbach *et al*
Walters (1968) 132
Ward (1963) 177
Warford (1969) 50–1
Wattenburg (1948) 60
Waugh and Abel (1967) 181
Welch (1970) 7

Whickham (Jarrow) 61, 73, 80
Whitby *et al* (1974) 27, 208
Wilber (1968) 67
Wilkinson (1973) 178
Wilkinson and Merry (1965) 115, 118
Williams (1956) 26
Willis J., (1968) 155, 171–2
Willis K., (1967) 134; (1968) 172; (1969) 172; (1970) 61, 112, 116, 136–7, 147, 157, 161, 172–3, 176, 179; (1971) 177, 189–90; (1972a) 19, 23, 42, 74, 79, 105, 118, 148; (1972b) 94, 134; (1972c) 5, 124, 126, 139; *see also* Whitby *et al*
Winch (1971) 58
Winnick, *see* Foote *et al*
Wolpert (1965) 67–8; (1966) 61; (1967) 168
Wonnacott and Wonnacott (1970) 96
Woodworkers 23–4, 28–9, 65, 75, 79
Work to the workers, policy of bringing 35–7

Yorkshire and Humberside Economic Planning Council (1970) and Region (1973) 46, 84, 105, 111
Young and Willmont (1957) 64

Zellner (1961) 196; *see also* Lee *et al* (1968) *and* Lee *et al* (1970)
Zipf (1946) 87